Guerrilla Theory

Guerrilla Theory

Political Concepts, Critical Digital Humanities

✦

Matthew Applegate

NORTHWESTERN UNIVERSITY PRESS
EVANSTON, ILLINOIS

Northwestern University Press
www.nupress.northwestern.edu

Printed in the United States of America

10 9 8 7 6 5 4 3 2 1

Library of Congress Cataloging-in-Publication Data

Names: Applegate, Matthew, author.
Title: Guerrilla theory : political concepts, critical digital humanities / Matthew
   Applegate.
Description: Evanston, Illinois : Northwestern University Press, 2020. | Includes
   bibliographical references and index.
Identifiers: LCCN 2019018291 | ISBN 9780810140844 (paper text : alk. paper) |
   ISBN 9780810140851 (cloth text : alk. paper) | ISBN 9780810140868 (e-book)
Subjects: LCSH: Digital humanities—Political aspects. | Politics and literature. |
   Critical theory. | Guerrillas in literature.
Classification: LCC AZ105 .A68 2019 | DDC 001.30285—dc23
LC record available at https://lccn.loc.gov/2019018291

CONTENTS

ACKNOWLEDGMENTS

I would like to begin by thanking the mentors and teachers who have supported me: William Haver, Ingeborg Majer-O'Sickey, Scott Henkel, and Brett Levinson. Thank you for teaching me to think critically and embracing critical theory's diverse traditions. I would like to thank William Haver in particular for challenging me to maintain ideological commitments in academic work, especially when it is difficult to do so.

I remain indebted to the friends and peers who have supported me and read my work at various stages of its development: Mark James, Izzy To, Jamie Cohen, Gabriel Piser, Graham Higgins, and James K. Stanescu. I would like to thank Northwestern University Press and Gianna Mosser for believing in this project and guiding me through each stage of the publication process. I am not sure this book would have been possible without her support. I would also like to thank my anonymous reviewers for pushing me to clarify my argument and justify its theoretical maneuvers.

Finally, I would like to thank my family for introducing me to literature early in life and making learning a priority. I would like to thank my parents for modeling the diligence and tenacity necessary to succeed in adverse circumstances. I would also like to thank my partner, Rochelle DuFord, for supporting me in every aspect of the book-writing process. She is the editor, critic, and friend I needed to believe this project was worth pursuing.

Everywhere there are allies, closeness, and an infinite gradation
of possible friendships.
—The Invisible Committee, *Now*

Even when you have conquered him, do not adopt his vices.
—Old Major, *Animal Farm*

Around the time my mother went back to school to get a college degree, my father, a warehouseman at a regional grocery store chain, decided that my family should read together. We would sit around our dinner table and take turns reading aloud. This was, for the most part, a bonding experience. My father worked nights. My mother worked days and went to school at night. Reading and discussing books was an opportunity to make up for lost time. Of the books we read together, one stands out in my memory: George Orwell's *Animal Farm*. I was captivated by the allegory. It was the first narrative focused on class struggle that I can remember reading—one in which the plot is driven explicitly by the transformation of political concepts—and it was one of the first stories I encountered as a child that averted a happy ending.

Narratives like *Animal Farm*, written with political and artistic purpose, are, fundamentally, narratives of failure. They ward off contemporary recuperations of failure that position it as necessary to success. Some traditions die even as political struggle anticipates an egalitarian horizon and pivots in its direction. The imaginative optimism of the text seems unwarranted. It seems especially unwarranted under whatever stage of capitalism we currently inhabit. What captivates me now (a Ph.D. with a tenure-track job reading and talking about books for a living) are political concepts that emerge from situations in which success is foreclosed, when failure is certain, and how those concepts contour the perception and need for political struggle.

This type of political work, articulated and revealed through aesthetic practice, is now a professional preoccupation. I mean this sincerely. I work at a small commuter college, teach primarily introductory material on a 4/4 load (when overloads can be avoided), recruit, hold significant service responsibilities, and try to accomplish as much research as I can. Thinking about politics and aesthetics often precedes and exceeds the duties I complete from day to day. I am preoccupied by this thinking; I have to channel it toward the few opportunities I have to present and publish research in order to make it "count." This preoccupation extends to my work in digital humanities (DH), and it is what led me to a career in academia in the first place. My brief experience as an academic thus far has also been shaped by it.

In 2008, I was accepted to a now-defunct interdisciplinary Ph.D. program, Philosophy, Interpretation, and Culture (PIC), at Binghamton University (SUNY). It was a program where faculty and students alike wore their politics openly. Marxism, anarchism, and decolonial feminism motivated the research trajectories of the program. I had the latitude to take classes on Deleuze, structural inequality, and Chicana art simultaneously, challenging me politically and intellectually on an equal footing. Interdisciplinarity was an open and constant question in this space, but it was, for me, short-lived. In the wake of the financial collapse of 2008–09, PIC was shuttered—first in 2010, and finally in 2012 when it was compelled to end admission. I served as the president of PIC's graduate student association during the administration's first attempt to end the program; I had escaped to the Comparative Literature program at Binghamton by the time of the second attempt. The motivations for closing the program were both financial and political. PIC was the only humanities program the university shuttered at that time, despite being ranked as the most diverse Ph.D. program in philosophy in the country by the National Research Council (it was tied with the University of Memphis in 2010).[1] Its closure underscored the fact that austerity is neither indifferently nor neutrally imposed.

This experience, perhaps more than any other I have had as an academic, was the most informative, but also the most difficult one. I learned to better organize in and as a diverse coalition during this time, but the interdisciplinary principles that the program forwarded could only be approximated elsewhere. I learned how a university administration, faculty, and graduate students bond when faculty and students are under direct threat, but the unities of the moment have been difficult for me to sustain. The antinomies, however, are still very much present in my mind and in my experience of the university as an institution. The austerity measures that led institutions of all kinds to shutter humanities programs in that time and afterward are now considered "sensible bottom-line thinking"; the violences undergirding this type of thinking are not always detectable. Few of us made expendable by the university are able to finish our degrees and secure permanent academic work, and our absence often makes the collective experience of austerity seem like a shallow debate over relative luxuries.

During this time, digital humanities' star was rising. Like many contemporary DHers, I was introduced to the discipline via its massive online presence. In 2012 and 2013, I read #transformDH blog posts and Tumblr pages as I progressed toward a new degree in Comparative Literature. I was excited by the discipline's proclamations of insurgency and its horizontal modes of organization. I started attending DH panels during my first Modern Language Association conference in 2014, and I created a Twitter account to follow all of the academics I read and saw speak. In that brief time, DH work inspired me to rebuild explicitly political, interdisciplinary intellectual relationships where I was and with the few resources I had. Some of these relationships had nothing to do with DH. Some failed. Others operate on the terms the collective establishes, rather than on any that the discipline dictates. My DH work is often slow, and much of it does not count in any substantive sense toward tenure. Furthermore, my work in DH is, given my current resources and needs, universally minimal. It is often politically driven. I am interested in thinking about political concepts that undergird DH work and subsequently adopting small-scale, agile technologies to meet political needs. I am interested in thinking about the aesthetic character of DH work in an often theory-focused (as opposed to technologically focused) style. The transformations I experience as a maker and DHer are in many ways more important than what is produced.

My approach to digital humanities is not always a popular one. It is broadly intersectional, but concepts of class, animated by their polemical histories, take center stage. This means empowering underserved, first-generation college students with technological knowledge and skill, as I have been able to do in a handful of DH-related classes. It also means channeling various technologies to home in on political antagonisms where they might otherwise be glossed over, both inside and outside of the university. In the case of this book, my approach to DH is not technological by any formal DH standard of measure. It is a theory-driven look at DH's political rhetoric, aesthetic undercurrents, and infrastructure. It is, beyond the limitations of declaring various methods and objects of intellectual inquiry "not neutral," an explicit attempt to imagine what non-neutral concepts of DH might be mobilized toward.

My experience of the university certainly informs much of what follows in this text, but its political character is not reducible to a biographical footnote. It is rather a meditation on making space, building collective bonds, and thinking through difficult problems that are inherent to DH's recent institutional advancement. I do so from the periphery of the discipline and with the will to ward off internalizing the austere logics under which we work and live. This is the basis of what I call "guerrilla theory" in the pages that follow. It is a constant exercise; perhaps frustrating without its end in sight, but one I approach with optimism and trepidation alike. Over and over again, I pair various iterations of guerrilla organization and tactics with politicized modes of DH praxis in order to think through DH's democratic proclamations. This is a means of extending unwarranted optimisms. DH has already proven to be a conduit for centering marginalized voices, creating space for many who are excluded from academic advancement, and rethinking how humanistic inquiry is practiced. *Guerrilla Theory* participates in this tradition of DH work, but from a position in which the experience of precarity and contingency is articulated as an experience both in and of conflict. The optimism this text forwards may, at times, seem cruel. There is much to critique in the guerrilla lineages I invoke. Yet, they are motivated by a desire to produce something radically different from our present political economies. *Guerrilla Theory* is thus theoretical with a purpose—the work of this text speculates on political iterations of DH praxis as it also shares in the desire to chart an alternative to our present academic-corporate situation.

Guerrilla Theory

Introduction

[The university] is that contradictory place where knowledges are colonized but also contested—a place that engenders mobilizations and progressive movements of various kinds. It is one of the few remaining spaces in a rapidly privatized world that offers some semblance of a public arena for dialogue, engagement, and visioning of democracy and justice.

—Chandra Talpade Mohanty, *Feminism without Borders: Decolonizing Theory, Practicing Solidarity*

The digital humanities' insistence on difference, difference in approach to scholarship, in types of methodologies, in the way that we do scholarship, is an active form of resistance to traditional academic hierarchies.

—Amy Earhart, *Traces of the Old, Uses of the New*

In this book I have tried to conceptualize and pair an agonistic political current in digital humanities (DH) with guerrilla lineages that precede its discourse. This political focus in DH praxis manifests, over and again, as a play between liberal democratic strategies for representation and inclusion and more radical political tactics for rethinking subjectivity, political formation, and infrastructure. It can be identified by many names: #transformDH, #guerrillaDH, postcolonialDH, #DHpoco, GO::DH, #femDH, and #activistDH, to name a few, and it extends across a broad range of critical analysis. The anterior political lineage I trace is a guerrilla lineage, one that is adversarial, illiberal, and situational. It is certainly contentious from a methodological standpoint, but it is not wholly foreign to DH praxis. The guerrilla is centralized in this text with historical and theoretical justification.

Where political concepts are debated in digital humanities, they are often characterized by precarity and axiomatic contradiction, even if we do not always recognize them as such. As DH scholar-practitioners, we find ourselves vying for institutional recognition, often bestowed in the form of project fund-ing and tenure, while also fighting to be disruptive and insurgent. We desire to produce transformative work across disciplinary divides, but disciplinary power often acts as a blockade. We prepare our students to be critical of the socioeconomic climate they will eventually graduate into, while also forming them into subjects ready for work. We seek to be radically inclusive while also working within neoliberal institutions that subsume radical difference. Indeed, if "DH takes the first steps toward a genuinely materialist and radical critique of scholarship in the 21st century," it does so from a contested posi-tion, defined by the play of its internal and external conflicts.[1] The political current I explore is characterized similarly: radical political concepts inherent to DH work are simultaneously clandestine and public, underdeveloped and commonplace, conflict-driven and cooperative. The guerrilla does not remedy the contradictions of politically oriented DH praxis, or its riskiness. In fact, it magnifies them.

The conceptual work of this book is best summarized as a guerrilla theory of DH praxis: a controverted political economy that prioritizes partisan rela-tions and collective becoming above all else. It is positioned to comment on the political dynamics of critical DH work, their agonistic *and* antagonistic modalities, while it also explores parallel radicalisms. This book intervenes well after the guerrilla's invocation in DH praxis. The book is an exercise in thinking in its wake. It formalizes tactics attributed to the guerrilla for the discipline's present. As a result, I deviate from common DH research interests. I do not focus on individual digital platforms or tools, provide a history of humanities computing up to DH, or dictate a future for DH as a discipline. Rather, I embark on an insurgent reading of DH praxis that is situated at the level of its current rhetoric and infrastructure.

Guerrilla Theory provides a paleonymy of guerrilla organization and tactics within DH praxis. Following the conceptual work of figures like Stefano Har-ney and Fred Moten, addressed in chapters 1 and 4, this paleonymic maneuver is a Derridean invention in need of political focus. Conceptually speaking, the paleonymic act is a kind of linguistic archaeology and mode of repur-posing. It is, in Derrida's account, "caught—both seized and entangled—in a binary opposition, one of the terms retains its old name so as to destroy the opposition to which it no longer quite belongs, to which in *any* event it has *never* quite yielded, the history of this opposition being one of incessant struggles generative of hierarchical configurations."[2] In this sense, the project of developing and mobilizing guerrilla theory is more than resurrecting a name, "guerrilla." It is the project of situating guerrilla organization and tac-tics in a circumstance outside of their own histories (and inside DH praxis) in order to speak to the politics of the present in a new way. It is a struggle, necessarily and incessantly, and one that never fully resolves. This is a gesture appropriate to the guerrilla concept, but one that is generative on both sides. If the guerrilla concept comes to be transformed by its inclusion in DH praxis,

DH praxis will also be transformed as it more fully considers the figure it has already invited into its theoretical lexicon.

The guerrilla is an untimely political form. It emerges at the declared end of capital and state power's reign, but prior to the formation of alternative forms of life. The guerrilla mobilizes absolute political opposition and collective self-making in tandem against its enemy. The guerrilla is a mode of decolonization. It is a protocological power. It is a means of producing collectivity. It is the public face of a populist milieu. As it develops out of concrete sites of political struggle, the guerrilla mobilizes antonymic modes of resistance, some long-term and some short-term, but always in its favor. The guerrilla unapologetically preserves life through power. Yet, its governing power does not function in a statist sense, as a stalwart territorializing enterprise. It exists as a process of manifesting corporeal fluidity, polycentricity, and speed. The guerrilla organizes disparate political forces over a heterogeneous milieu, relying on extended networks of social cooperation that flow beyond its collective body. Guerrilla organization and tactics elicit a more primary area of interest here, though, one that is both innovative and technologically oriented. The guerrilla holds a privileged position in contemporary discourse on partisan conflict precisely for its inherent techno-tactical abilities. Motorized and mobile, the guerrilla outmaneuvers its enemy as it adopts and models itself after new technological schemes.

My project relies on the qualities inherent to the guerrilla's political articulation as much as it relies on the rhetorics that uphold the guerrilla in DH praxis. Many have opened the door to such a concept. Perhaps most visibly articulated by the #transformDH movement, the guerrilla's invocation in this discourse is defined as both a threat and an act of hospitality: "#transformDH is an academic guerrilla movement seeking to (re)define capital-letter Digital Humanities as a force for transformative scholarship by collecting, sharing, and highlighting projects that push at its boundaries and work for social justice, accessibility, and inclusion."[3] Here, the guerrilla stands in for a grass-roots movement meant to radically upset the present conditions of academic scholarship. It stands in for what is already manifest, but also for what is yet to appear. At the same time, #transformDH invokes the guerrilla in order to invite what is outside in. It embraces a potential enemy, one that relies on a contentious political logic, but one that is not necessarily bound to its reproduction. The situatedness and particularity of what #transformDH proposes is informative of my conceptual offering. I refer to it and its architects' work throughout this text.

Prior to and beyond #transformDH, the guerrilla and its tactics are casually invoked in DH circles. For instance, Matthew K. Gold presented on what he termed "guerrilla pedagogy" in relation to DH tools as part of the Information 2.0 lecture series at LaGuardia Community College, valorizing teaching styles that are founded on openness, sharing, and transparency.[4] His pedagogical approach is now common, but this mode of teaching and learning persists in DH without the guerrilla moniker. Simon Rowberry calls for "a guerrilla digital humanities" in reference to illegal file-sharing, pondering this after the appearance of DH's "Napster moment."[5] Rowberry relies on a clandestine connotation of the word "guerrilla," perhaps a kind of cryptographic guerrilla tactics, but he does little to explain how or from what sites of production such a tactics would manifest outside of a discussion of copyright. "The Digital Humanities Manifesto 2.0" outlines three "(guerrilla) action items" in the same vein, all pertaining to questions of fair use and copyright. Its strongest claim provokes a tactics to address these issues where Rowberry does not, encouraging DH practitioners to "practice digital anarchy by creatively undermining copyright, mashing up media, recutting images, tracks, and texts."[6] Alex Gil is the most direct DH scholar-practitioner of the guerrilla concept to date, authoring a piece titled "#guerrilladh." There, like Rowberry and the authors of "The Digital Humanities Manifesto 2.0," Gil argues for the production of digital archives at the margin of the law. Paralleling themes previously articulated in "The Guerrilla Open Access Manifesto," the guerrilla spirit is manifest in Gil's argument, but the political concept is nascent. The texts listed here are almost exclusively focused on the guerrilla's assumed ability to operate "underground," but what goes untheorized in them is the guerrila's ontological status, as well as the breadth of its politics. The material conditions formative of the guerrilla's invocation given its political situation might require clandestine activity, but this occasional feature of its being is not tantamount to the whole of its political life.

As it is wherever it might be invoked, the guerrilla is a foreigner to DH praxis. The figure "shakes up the threatening dogmatism of the paternal *logos*" by acting as a threat to any preexisting order.[7] But it does more than this. The guerrilla reminds us that internality and externality are enmeshed, threat and comfort are dialectically linked, and that subjects who bear its status are simultaneously "other" and "same," identical and non-identical. A metaphor from Elizabeth Grosz's thoughts on Sputniko!'s "Menstruation Machine" is appropriate here. "Life is chemistry infected with a temporary coherence and cohesion," Grosz writes, a condition "which nevertheless leaks, sheds its insides and its surface now and then, and renews itself by exchanges sometimes (often) violent between what is inside (whether it is a cell's inner structure or a complex being's organs) and what is outside (a milieu or environment in which life and nonlife participate without reciprocity)."[8] The gendered politics of Grosz's argument are a challenge to the guerrilla's often hetero-masculinist articulations. Nevertheless, the guerrilla embodies violent irruption knowingly and without apology. This is the logic that the figure of the guerrilla relies on, develops, and deploys to its advantage. What are the methodological imperatives of embracing such political characteristics?

Providing a response to this question is my first step toward articulating a political concept that is endemic to guerrilla organization and tactics, and one that also describes its ontological particularities. Roger Whitson, for one, argued, and later retracted the claim, that applying military meta-phors to DH praxis is an appropriative move on behalf of "cool kid" theory nerds that destroys DH's collaborative good.[9] As Whitson notes, his com-ment echoes William Pannapacker's description of DH as a "cool-kids' table," "more exclusive, more cliquish" than ever before.[10] From this vantage point, the guerrilla operates as an imperial war machine. It destroys as it excludes. The answer? Exclude the guerrilla before it can destroy DH.[11] Characteristic of guerrilla organization and tactics, we already find ourselves situated within a contentious political logic. We have friends and we have enemies. The guer-rilla often elicits such responses because it also operates by the same logic. This is articulated quite clearly in "The Digital Humanities Manifesto 2.0": "*The digital is the realm of the : open source, open resources*, . [*sic*]. Any-thing that attempts to close this space should be recognized for what it is: the enemy."[12]

The digital humanities' partisan character is made manifest by the guer-rilla's invocation, and pertinent questions follow. Do we offer hospitality to such a figure, as others have done? Is it already within our hospices? Or, more fundamentally, is hospitality as such foreclosed when the guerrilla is excluded? In opposition to Whitson, Natalia Cecire rightly claims that "the valuation of the guerrilla, the oppositional, the maroon, and the fugitive that characterizes #transformDH is, as [she sees] it, clearly indebted to the legacies of queer theory and critical race studies."[13] These legacies are now more common to DH praxis, but they are legacies that have been excluded from its discourse historically. Though they do not reference the guerrilla or a #guerrillaDH in particular, the political tenor of Cecire's argument here is more fully realized in Roopika Risam's work on a South Asian digital humanities and postcolo-nial digital humanities, as it is in Tara McPherson's work when she asks, "Why are the digital humanities so white?"[14]

If the guerrilla, its modes of organization, and its tactics are invoked con-tradictorily (as both open and cryptographic, inclusive and exclusive), per-haps it is admissible to claim that this figure lurks behind some of DH's most central methodological debates. But in a much broader sense, the inclusive vision that DH has proclaimed for itself cannot exist apart from the inherent antagonism that is endemic to disciplinary power, neoliberal interest, and those that resist the coalescence of both. My project situates this conflicting interplay at the core of its disciplinary intervention by acknowledging that DH praxis is politically contested *all the way down*. This is perhaps the most primary but also the most controversial suggestion posed by this text: oppo-sition and conflict are both inherent to and symptomatic of any past, present, or future articulation of DH praxis. This does not limit its method or elimi-nate its inclusive and collaborative character. Rather, this kind of contestation preserves its democratic aspirations by related means.

In what follows, I further the content and argumentation of this book by reimagining three of DH's central concepts—generative thinking, inclusion, and collaboration—from a politically contested position. While there are certainly many concepts that form and guide DH praxis, I focus on these three in particular for both their profusion and depth. They appear often in DH scholarship, sometimes by a different name, but they also stand at the political core of the discipline's evolution. I refer to them consistently in the pages that follow, and specifically to the ways in which they have been formative of DH praxis. Reimagining these concepts is an example of what guerrilla theory might accomplish beyond the confines of this text, as well as a preview of what is to come.

I also explore a fourth concept, particular to some iterations of DH praxis, but specific to guerrilla organization and tactics: radical collectivity. I theorize the guerrilla as a conduit for the production of collective political subjects as a means to this end. While politicized concepts of collectivity are as diverse as the histories in which they are thought, the guerrilla is theorized most forcefully as a mode of collective self-making from a partisan divide. Articulating guerrilla organization and tactics in this manner allows me to comment on the concepts mentioned above as I extend beyond them. I attend to the ontological conditions that are formative of the guerrilla concept, while also offering an alternative political vantage point with which to intervene in DH's present critical discourse.

Generativity as Radical Act

One of my primary tasks in this book is to theorize the productive power of political conflict and identify it as an act of generative thinking. I follow a line of thought detailed in "The Digital Humanities Manifesto 2.0" that argues: "Digital Humanities have a utopian core shaped by its genealogical descent from the counterculture-cyberculture intertwinglings of the 60s and 70s. This is why it affirms the value of the open, the infinite, the expansive, the university/museum/archive/library *without walls*, the democratization of culture and scholarship."[15] If the revolutionary countercultures have taught us anything, it is that walls do not fall on their own, nor do they fall in a way that pleases everyone. Mark Sample is quoted with reason in the now infamous article by Stanley Fish, "Digital Humanities and the Transcending of Morality," where he states that "the digital humanities is really an insurgent humanities."[16] Rhetorics of counterculture and insurgency remind DH that the radicalisms of the 1960s and '70s were also productive of the guerrilla ethos reimagined by this text.

If DH is both countercultural and insurgent, its modes of articulation are fundamentally that of thinking and making. Generative thinking is predicated on acts of making—it is a theoretical standpoint that is realized *in production*. I follow the authors of the "Digital Humanities Manifesto 2.0" even further by recognizing that generative thinking is a practice of building *"bigger pic-*

tures out of the tesserae *of expert knowledge.* It is not about the emergence of a new general culture, Renaissance humanism/Humanities, or universal literacy. On the contrary, it promotes collaboration and creation across domains of expertise."[17] Like the authors of *Digital_Humanities* argue, one could say that generative thinking is our collective-singular occupation.[18] It prefigures our work even as it guides it, and, even though some #transformDH thinkers have distanced themselves from this theoretical lineage, it can be likened to concepts I explore in chapter 1: what Foucault called a philosophical relation to the present, or even perhaps what Michael Hardt theorizes as a militancy of theory.[19] When we think generatively, we exceed cults of individualism in order to fashion ourselves in and of a collective milieu.

I aim to push this concept further in order to draw out its alternative political potential. My argument follows two axioms: (1) generative thinking is transformative if and when it operates as a transformational politic, and (2) DH stifles its own collaborative good when "all that is solid melts into air."[20] The first axiom grounds my conceptual engagement with DH's transformative power in bell hooks's work, specifically where she argues that transformational politics require "us to alter our person, our personal engagement (either as victims or perpetrators or both) in a system of domination."[21] It is a feminist imperative, one which recognizes that "we all have the capacity to act in ways that oppress, dominate, [and] wound."[22] Such capacities are inevitable within any collaborative effort, especially among friends, and must be forefronted. By following hooks, I also follow imperatives that are endemic to a #femDH and postcolonial DH, demanding that DH center its methodological ground on the difficult negotiation between personal and systemic modes of domination. The second axiom forefronts my conceptual engagement with DH's transformative power in an aphorism from *The Communist Manifesto*, describing the transformative power of capital. Capital reshapes entire forms of life into repositories for its reproduction, both intimate and foreign. When all that is solid melts into air, capital has co-opted its object. Grounding a concept of generative thinking in an explicit refutation of capital's co-optive power is out of step with some modes of DH praxis, but this is an attempt to work in parallel with those who refuse neoliberalism's grip on higher education. Moreover, if our modes of production mimic the capitalist mode of production in DH praxis, we become, perhaps inadvertently so, perpetrators of brutality along lines of race, class, and gender *because* subjective formation itself is made to be productive for capital.

My approach underscores the inherent antagonism and irreconcilable difference that are situated at DH's core. The specter of neoliberalism looms large in DH praxis. It has already created lines of division and sites of opposition for DH praxis in particular. In 2011, for instance, Alan Liu presented a paper at the Modern Language Association titled "Where Is Cultural Criticism in the Digital Humanities?" Now an infamous intervention, Liu states, "How the digital humanities advance, channel, or resist the great postindustrial, neoliberal, corporatist, and globalist flows of information-cum-capital . . . is a question rarely heard in the digital humanities associations, conferences, journals, and projects with which I am familiar."[23] The clarity of Liu's argument cannot be ignored. If DH functions transformatively within institutional settings, what is our socioeconomic responsibility to and for what gets transformed? Rita Raley doubles down on Liu's comment, arguing that "in our current mercantile knowledge regime, with its rational calculus of academic value—seats occupied, publications counted, funds procured—the digital humanities are particularly well positioned to answer administrative and public demands to make knowledge useful."[24] Todd Presner adds to this powerful chorus, arguing that without critical theory, "the digital humanities will largely ape and extend the technological imaginary as defined by corporate needs and the bottom line through instrumentalized approaches to technology that are insufficiently aware of their cultural and social conditions of possibility."[25] It is Adeline Koh, however, who formulates this set of issues most forcefully: "How much does digital humanities work, through the way it is processed and organized through computational models, actually follow the Fordist logic of modularity?"[26]

While not wholly focused on counter-cybercultures, my approach to generative thinking is plain: disciplinary conflict is a necessary condition for a concept of DH to take place. This approach does not preclude inclusion, collaboration, or collectivity; it preserves its democratic core. However, the status of the guerrilla's friend-enemy logic—how far it contours our political thought—is a point of debate. Again, one can see echoes of this in DH scholarship and new media. Amy Earhart, critiquing Whitson's statement cited above, argues that "current critiques couched as a battle between insiders and outsiders are unnuanced and potentially destructive forms of resistance to what could be productive dissention."[27] McKenzie Wark offers a similar warning via Twitter: "to only see friends versus enemies is to misunderstand the whole art of politics."[28] Wark's argument is one of political reduction. If we conflate politics with the friend-enemy concept, we misunderstand politics altogether. Earhart's argument is one predicated on a method of particularity toward DH praxis. To think solely in terms of insiders and outsiders is not only unnuanced, it is to generalize friend-enemy logic in a disadvantageous way.

If these comments tell us something about the process of generative thinking, it is that such acts are not free-flowing. At the same time, if generative thinking in a DH setting is to be transformative, if it is to be insurgent, it cannot dismiss its partisan situation. The guerrilla therefore offers DH scholar-practitioners a means of thinking disciplinary politics from a different vantage point. The friend-enemy relation is not one that can be dismissed. It precedes and shapes our particular standpoint to our work. And yet it is not a necessary governing principle. The debate between insiders and outsiders is rather representative of a complex of forces that are generative of our disciplinary situation and the baseline of our political formation. Radical strains of DH praxis emerge from adversarial environments. This is what insurgents do. The generative task is therefore to think from this position, attending to the conflicts that such a political condition manifests as we proceed beyond its scope.

Inclusion Isn't Enough

What do we mean when we call for a more inclusive digital humanities? The problem of inclusion rests, as it always does, on the politics of difference. However, it also rests on the status of conflict. This is both a feminist and a postcolonial imperative. For instance, in their coauthored essay "Putting the Human Back into the Digital Humanities: Feminism, Generosity, and Mess," Elizabeth Losh, Jacqueline Wernimont, Laura Wexler, and Hong-An Wu argue that "asserting an absence of conflict around power relations can undermine claims for diversity, equity, and inclusion."[29] Following Cecire's comments above, this is precisely where the guerrilla stands in for queer theory and critical race studies. The oppositional, the maroon, and the fugitive signify the ontological fact of inclusive and exclusionary acts that are endemic to DH praxis. However, it is Risam's work that deftly articulates the gendered and racial politics of the discipline from a position of radical difference in long form: "Groups like #transformDH, Postcolonial Digital Humanities, and GO::DH situate their missions at the intersections of multiple axes of difference," she writes, "recognizing the need for attention to the complex power relations that serve as barriers to achieving inclusivity within the digital humanities."[30]

Following thinkers like Jamie "Skye" Bianco, Lisa Nakamura, and Amy Earhart, Risam goes on to articulate an intersectional approach to DH's axes of difference "that suggests practitioners begin their work with an understanding of the particularities necessary to design projects that account for influences of difference on knowledge-production."[31] This concern manifests in problems related to epistemological access, resource allocation, and cooperative labor, but it also signifies as a potentially irreconcilable approach to the problem of inclusion. If the trend among more dominant articulations of DH praxis has been to valorize a mode of inclusion without borders, then an intersectional approach to DH praxis challenges this political notion. Stated directly, the refusal of an additive model for political articulation complicates any claim to a "big tent" politics. In the same way that one cannot presuppose a universal material basis for political action, one cannot assume a universal category that creates and constrains the production of subjectivity. An intersectional approach to DH praxis is not simply a question of ensuring that everyone's voice is heard or that every form of subjectivity is represented at the DH table. Thinking from a position of radical difference is a tendentious and contested process. It is one of thinking *at* the border—a territorial condition that exceeds geopolitical lines of division—and from a position of liminality.[32] An intersectional approach to the problem of radical difference remains "in process" because difference is never something to be resolved and inclusion is never complete.

For the purposes of my argument, intersectional approaches to DH praxis demand that DH scholar-practitioners conceptualize radical difference in subjective terms. Identity and difference are never complete, either. When we conceptualize an intersectional approach to DH praxis at the level of subjectivity, it certainly is a process of *thinking from* positions of difference if and when they are accessible. It also demands that we recognize the function of ontological foreclosure and epistemological (in)access when it remains opaque to us. But an intersectional approach to DH praxis also allows for a collective concept of subjectivity that departs from political liberalism at the same time that it augments the argument for radical difference. Think of Maria Lugones's decolonial feminism here: "modernity organizes the world ontologically in terms of atomic, homogeneous, separable categories. Contemporary women of color and third-world women's critique of feminist universalism centers the claim that the intersection of race, class, sexuality, and gender exceeds the categories of modernity."[33] As race, class, and gender are thought co-constitutively, an intersectional approach to DH praxis is invoked in this text where it might *exceed* the ontological limits of our present political order. As a result, the bridge between DH work like Risam's and those she cites runs parallel to those I rely on in order to provide a conceptual history of neoliberalism's incursion into subjective formation.

Michel Foucault's 1978–79 lectures at the Collège de France, *The Birth of Biopolitics*, and the figure he develops therein, *homo oeconomicus*, is by now the universally recognized foundation for these twin concerns in contemporary radical thought. Focused heavily on the means by which subjectivity is determined economically, Foucault's figure is a variation on Louis Althusser's characterization of the "Absolute Subject," or the situation in which "the individual is interpellated as a (free) subject in order that he shall submit freely to the commandments of the subject."[34] By way of summary, Steven Shaviro characterizes this position well:

> The objective function of the market is that it "forces us to be free," forces us to behave "rationally" and "efficiently," forces us to act concertedly in our own individual interests—any broader considerations be damned . . . The "price system" continually forces us into debt. And thereby it confines, restricts, and channels our behavior far more rigidly, and effectively, than any compulsion based upon mere brute force would be able to do.[35]

Neoliberalism's force manifests here as a modality of biopolitical control, redefining the conditions under which subjects fashion themselves in relation to their surroundings. What it means "to be free" in this discourse is quite clear: "free" to accumulate debt, "free" to participate in a "free market economy," and therefore "free" to limit one's sociopolitical horizons to the variances of the market.

Jason Read parallels Shaviro's argument. In marking a substantive difference between Marx's concepts of formal subsumption and real subsumption Read argues that "*in formal subsumption the production of subjectivity is linked primarily to reproduction, while in real subsumption the production of subjectivity itself becomes productive for capital.*"[36] The historical transition is key. From the situation in which precapitalist modes of production are incorporated into the circuits of capital, subjectivity is linked to the reproduction of the capitalist mode of production. In our contemporary situation, where processes of production refer to and are transformed by capital itself, capital is the ground from which subjectivity emerges and an end to which it is made to refer. Here, the capitalist mode of production expands beyond the production of things to the production of capitalist forms of life. This is precisely where an intersectional approach to DH holds some of its most radical potential for my project.

If our current socioeconomic condition is characterized by individualizing forces fully infused with the capitalist mode of production, then relying on intersectional approaches to DH that stem from post- and decolonial traditions allows a multiplicity of subjective markers to be conceptualized as constitutive of one's existence along multiple axes of privilege. Not all capitalist forms of life (here we could simply say forms of life) are equal, and an intersectional approach better connects the confluence of structural inequality with and against inclusive approaches to DH. In fact, it is quite easy to see how Risam's work allows DH to centralize interventions made by women of color feminists when such antagonisms are named and parsed out. In the same way that real subsumption's effects are diffuse and uneven, so too are its resistances.

Although not typically aligned with DH or its praxis, Chela Sandoval's work in her book *Methodology of the Oppressed* (2000) is informative here. Like Shaviro, Sandoval enters into this discourse via Althusser, arguing that his theory of ideology assists in conceptualizing "U.S. third world feminism as a model for oppositional political activity and consciousness in the postmodern world."[37] Where Sandoval centers her work on the contemporary development of feminist thought in the United States, her focus on subjectivity is ideologically driven. Again, her work is not formative of a "big tent" politics, but is rather a conflictual mode of relation that develops from preexisting lines of division—territorial, economic, and political. Conflict is formative of political consciousness for Sandoval. It preexists any form of coalitional or collective political potential, and it can be traced even after such alliances are made. Sandoval's dialogue with Althusser therefore positions her to theorize a coalitional standard predicated on the fact of political conflict, "one that apprehends an effective oppositional consciousness igniting in dialectical engagement between varying ideological formations," but one that is also "cinematographic," a mode of political engagement that is like "a kinetic motion that maneuvers, poetically transfigures, and orchestrates while demanding alienation, perversion, and reformation, in both spectators and practitioners."[38]

Sandoval's model is already indicative of my approach to DH praxis and is rhetorically similar to Risam's argument above. Sandoval's claim to political opposition is a method and approach to generative thinking by another name (thinking as a form of making), underscoring the political relations that precede it. On the one hand, her cinematographic mode of political engagement operates on the basis of affinity—it connects political subjects through the movement of politics—forming makers out of spectators. On the other hand, forces of alienation and perversion guide this kinetic motion. While it might seem counterintuitive from a liberal standpoint, the liberatory aspects of Sandoval's politics rest on a concept of productive but intentional othering—one which, as I will explore in more detail in chapter 2, parallels feminist women of color's invocations of a guerrilla politics. These constellations address DH's concerns for conflict and power, but extend beyond its discourse.

Collaboration Demands Difference

It almost goes without saying that much of the DH literature focused on collaboration provides us with various *models for* collaboration. Large-scale collaboration, small-scale collaboration, long form and short form, micro-collaboration, ground-floor concepts—all of these are discussed enthusiastically in DH circles. When we talk about what models our collaborative efforts might take, we often also assume their politics. DH models for collaboration are typically based on imperatives for inclusion by addition and knowledge-sharing that presuppose either an affinity or an aptitude for DH praxis. Some assume the preexistence of a collective goodwill where DH projects are undertaken. Others assume a certain amount of fluidity in the way that collaborations form and persist as we make things together. Most certainly assume that collaboration will improve their work, and that the communities one forms as a result will continue to better the discipline as a whole. The number of DH labs where collaborative work is produced is almost too great to count. The number of tools created in a collaborative context follows suit.

The concern for individual achievement in the instance of collaborative work is manifest, hence our obsession with models. How can we know who contributed? How will we be assessed for our contribution? The question of what collaboration is for, but also why we want it, speaks to a larger political concern almost immediately. Are we individuals who collaborate in order to better our institutional standing, or are we building an active and collective mode of relation *in the first instance*, prior to our individual achievement and motivation? Dorothy Kim and Jesse Stommel's introduction to their *Disrupting the Digital Humanities* anthology offers an excellent articulation of the latter, favoring a communal concept:

> Building a truly communal space for the digital humanities requires that we all approach that space with a commitment to: 1) creating open and non-hierarchical dialogues; 2) championing non-traditional work that might not otherwise be recognized through conventional scholarly channels; 3) amplifying marginalized voices; 4) advocating for students and learners; and 5) sharing generously to support the work of our peers.[39]

I pose the questions above because collaboration is perhaps the most widely recognized methodological imperative endemic to DH praxis that is meant to upset academic siloism. As Kim and Stommel make plain, collaboration is an ethic of relation—a practice of "working with" as opposed to "working for." But where collaboration might transform institutional hierarchies and disciplinary imperatives over our work, it has not remedied its neoliberal contours. It would be naive to think that an open and collaborative DH would do this inherently or holistically.

My intervention is not one of organizing a lab or parsing out individual claims to intellectual property. I am not specifically concerned with the problematics of individual achievement within higher education or beyond. Taking the guerrilla as my lead, my approach deepens the contrast between political affinity-making and neoliberalism's grip on the production of subjectivity. The scope of opposition is therefore best articulated as a landscape in which our affinities and conflicts are made manifest and from which we move to act. This landscape is perhaps centered within the university, but is not limited to it. The guerrilla is a territorial figure, but one that is not bound to territorial fixity. With and beyond its institutional function, DH is an open and inclusive space, but preserving the future of this space elicits political conflict.

Our methods for preserving DH as an open space with open resources are therefore partisan acts. *Guerrilla Theory* positions collaboration as the partisan force of articulation that maintains a productive conflict between territorializing and deterritorializing disciplinary powers. The friend-enemy relation—manifest where the guerrilla is invoked—contours my approach to collaborative work, but it is not its telos. My attempt here is not to reduce the political situation expressed by DH praxis to a simple binary opposition. The friend-enemy relation endemic to the guerrilla's invocation is rather mobilized as a proleptic political tactic that foments a host of possible futures. It draws out the inherent antagonism between DH's disciplinary power and its responsibility to be critical. The friend-enemy relation is a reminder of a simple fact: collaboration is neither a neutral concept nor a neutral act. But what does an explicitly non-neutral practice of collaboration look like? The problematic inherent to these concerns is precisely how we are to distinguish those modes of DH praxis with which we can align. How are we to distinguish those modes of DH praxis that we must oppose in order to resist the reduction of our work to corporate need?

The scope of what DH praxis can accomplish with and against institutional power is already a central point of debate. Led by figures like Alan Liu and Rita Raley, there is a growing chorus of academics who address these problems head-on. Raley, for example, argues that "the digital humanities should not, and cannot, bear the burden of transforming technocracy, the academic-corporate situation in which we are all mired."[40] But it does, as she notes, have "the capacity to tinker with the symbolic order of computing, such that it is not ultimately constrained by an agenda of efficiency, rationality, and optimization."[41] Liu refines this argument, claiming that DH's critical function is to "help adjudicate how academic infrastructure connects higher education to, but also differentiates it from, the workings of other institutions in advanced technological societies."[42] While I explore many guerrilla concepts that intervene at this juncture, Cathy N. Davidson's concept of "collaboration by difference" is a strong point of departure for eliciting these political qualities.

In her blog post "Collaboration by Difference, Yet Again," Davidson argues that "in collaboration by difference, you start with people who do not share assumptions, who do not share backgrounds, who do not share institutions, who do not share ideas, and who may not even share the same goals. And you see what happens."[43] Collaboration by difference is experimental and fluid. It is a risk if and when it is practiced, but it's a risk worth taking. The riskiness and force of her concept is also reminiscent of radical approaches to popular education, perhaps best articulated by Jesse Stommel through critical digital pedagogy: "Knowledge emerges in the interplay between multiple people in conversation," he writes, "brushing against one another in a mutual and charged exchange or *dialogue*. Freire writes, 'Authentic education is not carried on by 'A' *for* 'B' or by 'A' *about* 'B,' but rather by 'A' *with* 'B.' It is through this impatient dialogue, and the implicit collaboration within it, that Critical Pedagogy finds its impetus toward change."[44] Where radical difference structures our acts of collaboration, it leads to alternative modes of relation that transform how we understand our work, as well as its political function.

Risam's work on theorizing love as a motivating factor for collaborative work in DH perhaps also clarifies Davidson's argument here. To paraphrase a portion of her keynote address at the 2016 Keystone DH conference at the University of Pittsburgh, Risam argued for a concept of love as a hermeneutics of social change. It is a binding force, an extension of feminist care ethics, and one that identifies the injustices at stake in knowledge production. If collaboration by difference is paired with the kind of love that Risam endorses, perhaps we can begin to form an alternative relationship to our work and our collaborators. At the same time, Davidson's and Risam's work forms a productive dialogue with concepts of love articulated in a guerrilla context, a conversation that Risam has already begun on Twitter, writing: "As Che says. . . . 'At the risk of sounding ridiculous, the true revolutionary is guided by a feeling of great love.' #guerrilladh #keydh."[45]

Collectivity as Decentralized Power

In a 2014 article titled "Digital Humanities for the Next Five Minutes," Rita Raley promotes a nimble and politically focused DH methodology that forefronts situational intervention. She argues that DH scholars should embark on "a structural shift away from the question of what is or is not properly DH" and impose "a corresponding abandonment of attempts to fix the digital humanities as a monolithic entity with an ontological core."[46] Raley's work relies on a tactical DH method, one wary of top-down administrative directives, "bureaucratic stasis, and fantasies of institutional permanence," and one that also prioritizes "seeking alliances" to reinforce its transformative potential.[47] Let's recall Matthew Kirschenbaum's concept of DH as a tactical term: DH manifested, "some might even say radicalized," he argues, "as precisely that space where traditional academic and institutional practices are vulnerable to intervention, with individual scholars or self-organizing affinity groups utilizing the tools and channels of online communication to effect real institutional change."[48] DH is a contingent enterprise. Its tactical valuation of affinity-making, institutional suspicion, and self-organized political intervention situates its praxis along a spectrum of insurgent modes and acts.

I follow this line of thought. I want to identify critical DH work alongside partisan logics, looking to make participation in DH a tactical expression of our collective desires. This concern is reflected in Moya Bailey, Anne Cong-Huyen, Alexis Lothian, and Amanda Phillips's coauthored piece, "Reflections on a Movement: #transformDH, Growing Up." There, the collective describes their own tactics formative of DH praxis that eschews institutional affiliation and grant funding. Rather, they articulate the political work of #transformDH as one of inherent collectivity, writing, "Our desire is to deflect the academy's imperative to take personal credit for work that is always collective."[49] Bailey et al.'s short essay converses with Raley's tactical DH in several interesting ways. Bailey et al. also reject top-down directives and DH's obsession with methodological certainty. They also describe their processes of non-institutional labor (Tumblr curation, hashtag development, DOCC development, etc.) as potential desire lines for those interested in #transformDH. Raley, however, offers a formal response to the question of collectivity that exceeds the work articulated in Bailey et al.'s short essay, as well as Kisrchenbaum's. Citing Geert Lovink, Raley calls for the formation of "temporary consensus zones" (TCZs) in DH praxis—zones that are by definition ephemeral, but which are also radically diverse at the moment of their inception and implementation. Lovink imagines the formation and implementation of TCZs in particular, comprised of "hackers, artists, critics, journalists and activists" who maintain the right to disconnect at will.[50]

Importantly, TCZs stand within a broader political lineage. They stem from an anarcho-communist ethos—what Hakim Bey would call "Temporary Autonomous Zones," or what groups like the Invisible Committee and Tiqqun would call the commune: a "mutual oath" sworn by those who inhabit a given situation *"to stand together as a body."*[51] The ephemeral quality of such bonds is principal. Their partisan character is constitutive. A TCZ, TAZ, or any similar ephemeral model for collectivization does not operate through a charter, constitution, or force of law. It is rather a comportment or attitude, singularly attributable to political subjects who are collectively constituted at a partisan divide. This is perhaps what is so alluring about the guerrilla to thinkers of a #guerrillaDH. The individuals who participate in such a political formation do not conceive of themselves as partners embarking on their latest venture. They are rather precariously linked, sometimes indiscernibly so, and are opposed to any political intervention that would compel rigid unification.

Raley's approach heavily influences what I call "collective becoming" and "collective self-making" in this text. The primary and perhaps the most dominant concept of collectivity that I rely on stems from network organization and power. It is undeniable that the network, conceptually, organizationally, and historically, has eclipsed the guerrilla as an organizational form and ontological novelty. But again, the guerrilla does not disappear with the appearance of the network, it can be found at its roots. In a letter detailing the form and tactics of the Italian urban guerrillas, the Red Brigades, Paolo Virno offers a definition of guerrilla organization and tactics that prefigures autonomist Marxist iterations of network power. On an organizational level, Virno describes the guerrilla as a "model [which] involves a high level of social cooperation, a freedom of movement in enemy territory, [and] a capacity to cope with a multiplicity of variables in the course of action."[52] On a tactical level, he argues that the guerrilla model is characterized as a constellation of autonomous units—a polycentric political mode allowing for total opposition to state power and transnational capital.

While the guerrilla is organized out of an overall position of weakness—in terms of numbers and resources, any guerrilla is dwarfed by comparison to the state—it emphasizes variability and continued tactical experimentation. For Virno, the absence of a centralized command structure is its strength: not only can individual guerrilla units organize and execute actions on their own, but resistance is maintained even if one or several units withdraw. In fact, he goes on to claim that "guerrilla action . . . exercises direct power, a decentralized and diffused power, as pluralistic as the enemy's power."[53]

The pluralism and autonomy that Virno refers to here are key to understanding the collective character of guerrilla organization and tactics. They are also formative of its technological character. As I show in chapter 1, as the partisan advances technologically or "speeds up," an absolute degree of opposition is fomented between it and its enemy. At the same time, the guerrilla relies on new technologies to organize and manifest in and as a multiplicity of actors and acts. Guerrilla organization and tactics are a multiplex of techno-political articulation, one that produces and exposes an enmity so profound that the state's ability to identify and combat the partisan is compromised. But the polycentric form that we now associate with network organization and power replaces the transformation in partisan relations that results from the actual incorporation of new technologies into preexisting relations of conflict. In so many words, the guerrilla is the organizational and ontological basis for such a theoretical maneuver to take place, although one absent of a unitary core. Collectivity is ontologically bound to guerrilla organization and tactics in this discourse.

While I explore various guerrilla histories in this book, my theoretical understanding of what radical collectivity is and what it does is also grounded in what Marx calls "cooperation." In chapter 13 of *Capital, Volume I*, Marx theorizes cooperation as an inherently collectivized power motivated by workers' shared condition of exploitation. Although one might typically understand such a condition through its negative effects, Marx offers a radically productive concept of "working with." "Working with" describes a condition in which workers realize their relational capacities for collective labor: "not only do we have here an increase in the productive power of the individual, by means of co-operation, but the creation of a new productive power, which is intrinsically a collective one."[54] Jason Read, following figures like Gilbert Simondon, Etienne Balibar, and Paolo Virno, argues that Marx's concept is predicated on pre-individual qualities that ultimately lead to a trans-individual ontology: "the very things that form the core and basis of our individuality, our subjectivity, sensations, language, and habits, by definition cannot be unique to us as individuals. These elements can only be described as preindividual, as the preconditions of subjectivity."[55] What Marx calls cooperation is thus the condition under which workers articulate these pre-individual qualities in concert, producing a collectivized and relational concept of subjectivity that is "something other than a collection of individuals."[56] Read elsewhere characterizes his ontological argument as a trans-individual condition which "underscores the fact that individuation is always individuation in and of a particular collectivity."[57]

Although contemporary Marxism sometimes stands at odds with post- and decolonial work, I follow Marx's concept of cooperation because it is both rhetorically and politically analogous to post-, decolonial, and queer-feminist figurations of subjectivity. Cooperation and the pre-individual status it asserts are quite similar to Sandoval's cinematographic articulation of political organization that was discussed above. It is perhaps even closer to Judith Butler's reading of Theodor Adorno's *Problems of Moral Philosophy* in her book *Giving an Account of Oneself* (2005). There, she writes:

> Yet there is no "I" that can fully stand apart from the social con-
> ditions of its emergence, no "I" that is not implicated in a set of
> conditioning moral norms, which, being norms, have a social charac-
> ter that exceeds a purely personal or idiosyncratic meaning. The "I"
> does not stand apart from the prevailing matrix of ethical norms and
> conflicting moral frameworks. In an important sense, this matrix is
> also the condition for the emergence of the "I," even though the "I"
> is not causally induced by those norms. We cannot conclude that the
> "I" is simply the effect or the instrument of some prior ethos or some
> field of conflicting or discontinuous norms.[58]

What work like this illustrates is a common figuration of subjectivity—an intersubjective state of becoming that conditions political acts at the sites in which they appear and from which individual subjects emerge. It is a relational process, and one that cannot be escaped. The guerrilla presupposes a similar subjective condition—one that I introduce through a Marxist lineage, but which I ultimately surpass through feminist, post-, decolonial, and queer figurations of subjectivity throughout this text. This subjective condition informs all tactical nuance in the course of this text.

I frame the guerrilla's techno-tactical ability as a collectivized subjective enterprise in each chapter of this book. Inasmuch as the guerrilla offers a tactics for opposing its enemy, it also offers concrete examples of collective self-making. Its practices of making are technologically oriented to the same degree that they are politically oriented. Theorizing guerrilla organization and tactics as a process of collective self-making therefore extends to each concept explored above, as well as their practical implications. Collectivity from this standpoint names a process of "working with," a process of manifesting tactical indiscernibility, and a cooperative ethos that retains the claim to opposition and conflict as principles of its articulation.

Why Cinema?

There is a caveat attached to this book, since much of its body is defined by actually existing guerrilla organization and tactics, rather than by any set of individual projects that are presently situated within DH. Furthermore, it might appear counterintuitive, but much of this book focuses on the politics of cinematic production and representation as they are produced by various guerrilla organizations. On the one hand, these points of focus are historical. The guerrilla organizations that I explore in this book mobilize cinema in particular toward their collective goals. Imagined as acts of agitprop and self-documentation, the importance of these aesthetico-political acts is easily mapped onto questions concerning identity, subjective formation, and collective self-making. On the other hand, the visual aesthetics developed and deployed by each group actualizes the guerrilla concept within a broader history of its techno-political character. The guerrilla turn to cinematic production runs parallel to its description as a networked mode of organization.

Methodologically speaking, my focus on cinema follows two lines of inquiry—one inherent to DH, and one lateral in scope. In her article "Why Yack Needs Hack (and Vice Versa)," Cathy N. Davidson claims that "the coding humanist is also, in many ways, the reification of auteurism and the glorification of individual achievement."[59] While this is a contentious view in DH, it is one that I embrace for its political acuity. If DH is to be inclusive, collaborative, and generative, then its technological practice cannot reify individualizing techno-aesthetic acts that precede it. There are certainly other ways of coding that are possible, and the coder, like the auteur, cannot disavow his relational material ground, nor can the coder be thought as an individual figure.

The collective subject of guerrilla organization and tactics is the antithesis of the auteur. In the same way that it is invoked in DH praxis as a figure that represents a multiplicity of subjectivities and possible approaches, the guerrilla upsets the political economy of cinematic production in at least two ways. First, guerrilla cinematic production is characterized by skill-sharing and critical dialogue. Second, guerrilla cinematic production is characterized by the formation of collectivized cinematic space, upsetting what representation is often meant to accomplish.[60] Guerrilla cinematic production does not ask, "Is this figure represented positively or negatively?" It does not ask, "Does this figure fit a stereotype?" It is rather the production of a milieu from which a collective figuration of the self is actualized. I take this spatiotemporal configuration seriously, and it helps me to articulate a political specificity to DH praxis from a similar standpoint.

The second methodological draw that my focus on cinema brings to DH can be likened to Jussi Parikka's turn to base his media archaeological work in new film history, featured most prominently in *What Is Media Archaeology?* (2012). If one of the primary tenets of Parikka's media archaeology is to understand how "modes of sensation themselves can be seen as historically structured," *Guerrilla Theory* proposes something equally modest: historically structured modes of sensation reflect a multiplicity of subjective formations.[61] Parikka's work leads him to theorize the affective climate of intermedial relations, allowing him to offer a media archaeology of the senses. The guerrilla leads me toward a mediated concept of collectivity, embedded within a political ontology of conflict. It is an affective cinematic turn. Cinema is thus situated in this book as a political modality of the subject in which visual technology is the impetus for its rearticulation as a collective figure.

Perhaps the strongest suggestion that I pose with a turn to guerrilla cinema is to establish its history and practice as prefigurative of contemporary debates regarding the politics of making. If the guerrilla is a practice-oriented figure, it is also a maker-figure. It carves out a territory; it makes weaponized art; it makes subjectivity a collective project. The turn to cinema is therefore methodologically appropriate for at least two reasons. First, the lineages we rely on to conceptualize our acts of making in DH circles are often aesthetically focused, and the politics of critical making is squarely situated in a European avant-garde sensibility. A turn to guerrilla cinema, in contrast to the European avant-garde, allows me to conceptualize the politics of making otherwise. Second, if the guerrilla offers a strong set of tactics for theorizing acts of collective self-making, it also offers a standpoint from which to consider decolonial arguments that are often excluded by the adoption of an avant-garde sensibility, as well as the historical articulation of DH as a method and practice. My intervention in the discourse of making in DH praxis is therefore one that is focused just as much on the production of objects as it is on subjects and political bodies.

Cinema is theorized as a tool in the pages that follow—a tool for making politics happen if and where it is deployed from a guerrilla positionality. To say that cinema is prefigurative of contemporary acts of making is to offer DH praxis a broader and tangential historical depth with which to orient critical work. To say that guerrilla cinema is prefigurative of our contemporary political discourse in DH praxis is to give the guerrilla's invocation in the discipline a stronger basis of articulation, albeit a fractured and contested one.

Why Not Digital Tools?

When I say that I avoid analyzing the use or production of digital tools in this text, I am not motivated by either Luddite nostalgia or utopian visions of a digital-free future. Rather, I want to avoid getting caught up in the forward-consuming frenzy of "innovative" technology without giving up on interrogating a broader swath of DH's digital tool use. As a result, I am motivated by the desire to both expand DH's critical frame and approach its political discourse from a technological position anterior to the discipline's development.

Calling for the production of DH praxis from a position that is not fully imbued with the technologies of the present is a common DH endeavor. It shows up regularly in some of DH's most popular critical texts. Conceptualizing a critical discourse of DH praxis that does not utilize or analyze digital tools is not as widely accepted, yet some scholars gesture in this direction. For example, in an essay titled "Toward a Cultural Critique of Digital Humanities," Domenico Fiormonte forwards three imperatives for DH praxis that turn from the discipline's current foundation in the development and deployment of digital tools to a metacritical frame. Here, Fiormonte writes:

> (a) Stop being obsessed with large-scale digitization projects and "archiving fever" (Derrida), which will only increase our dependency on private industry standards, products, and of course funding;
> (b) *improve and cultivate the margins*—that is, give more attention

to our variegated cultural and linguistic local diversity; (c) help to elaborate a new concept of *knowledge as commons*.[62]

The theory-oriented and culturally situated approach that I develop in this book responds to such imperatives. Imperatives (b) and (c), however, are primary, and address the implications of the first.

Improving and cultivating the margins within DH praxis is not limited to our present technological practices or to an isolated history of the discipline's development. Improving and cultivating the margins necessitates an open attitude toward DH's disciplinary scope. It also requires that we think carefully about the relationship shared between thinking and making in ways that might precede or run parallel to the digital. Fiormonte's comment on linguistic local diversity refers to both the means by which text is represented in digital environments under current Unicode standards *and* data-mining practices that rely on unified text-encoding schemes. However, improving and cultivating the margins of DH praxis is not limited to these concerns. Cinema is certainly one aesthetico-technological apparatus that precedes and expands our concepts of linguistic local diversity, especially where it is mobilized in non-Western and radical political contexts, but DH interventions in critical making also necessitate a much broader vision of handcraft in the same vein. Critical making is not limited to coding, curating, mining, visualizing, and the like because it relies on a multiplicity of design vernaculars preceding the digital. Radical feminist sewing circles are a salient example of a broader approach to critical making in DH contexts, as is small-scale zine making. While this imperative touches on some of DH's central debates (to code or not to code, hacking and yacking, etc.), I favor its intervention because it both underscores intersectional approaches to DH praxis and emphasizes cultural specificity. Fiormonte's imperative foments a historically oriented DH method that also demands a radical grasp—a will to produce new possibilities for DH praxis, as it also forwards a method of situated thinking within a vast disciplinary landscape.

Elaborating a "new" concept of knowledge as commons follows from this set of concerns. Fiormonte does not orient the question of inclusion toward the formation of a stronger, more unified corporate body than the tech sector, for example. It is also not solely concerned with creating more inclusive tools. It is rather formative of a concept of the commons that forefronts radically diverse approaches to knowledge production—one that also delimits the effects of privatization on teaching and learning. Creating access points for a common experience of digital culture and preserving those access points are indeed an interesting iteration of Fiormonte's claim to elaborating a concept of knowledge as commons. Perhaps it goes without saying, but developing a concept of knowledge as commons in this way often leads DH scholar-practitioners *toward* the archive, a path that Fiormonte desperately desires to avoid. Yet, the archive's governing logics are central to this concern, especially as they pertain to the interplay of space and subjective formation. How we preserve knowledge, who preserves knowledge, and where we preserve knowledge are all questions that link knowledge production to its common access and use prior to and beyond the digital. Fiormonte's claim to knowledge as commons points to more. I read it as fundamentally a question of infrastructure and design. At the level of infrastructure, I take Fiormonte's intervention to be akin to two important questions proffered by Michael Hardt in his essay "Reclaiming the Common in Communism": "What would it mean for something to be ours when we do not possess it? What would it mean to regard ourselves and our world not as property?"[63] At the level of design, Fiormonte's work is analogous to Carl DiSalvo's adversarial design: "Design attempts to produce new conditions or the tools by which to understand and act on our current conditions."[64]

It is precisely here that I locate DH's institutional function in excess of a strict definition of its digital tool use. I am not interested in digital tools because the kinds of questions that many DH scholars are currently pursuing are applicable to the very constitution of the contemporary university, regardless of our ability to code, visualize, archive, and so on. For example, if I align Fiormonte's imperatives for DH with Jeffery J. Williams's call for a critical university studies in the face of "our current period of neoliberal antihumanism," the import is immediately apparent.[65] Our current educational milieu is neoliberal in Williams's view "because it reconceives higher education as a mercantile market rather than a public realm apart from the market; it reconfigures those attending as job seekers rather than as citizens; and it aims for an edge in global competition rather than cultural understanding and sympathy."[66] Williams's claim here is in near-perfect agreement with any outcome that might follow from Fiormonte's interest in departing from large-scale digitization projects, improving and cultivating the margins, and elaborating a new concept of knowledge as commons.

Mapping these kinds of constellations is an exercise in guerrilla theory. It points to new insurgencies in DH praxis that broaden the scope of our collective political will. More to the point, forefronting these kinds of conceptual linkages enables DH to enact an ideologically diverse set of tactics for critically analyzing our present circumstances and actualizing alternatives. It asks that we consider who we are as makers as we also strive to produce the common good.

What's to Come

Each chapter in this book dialogues with the next. Prior to offering a description of each chapter, I need to acknowledge two obstacles that this book confronts on every page. The first is to consider the status and function of violence in guerrilla organization and tactics beyond the limits of a liberal democratic framework. When I say that I trace a guerrilla lineage that is adversarial, illiberal, and situational, it pertains to the guerrilla's invocation of violent revolution *as well as* its aesthetic acts. I do this *not* to insist that brutal acts of opposition are necessary for political conflict to carry out its transformative possibilities; I do this to consider its underlying logics. As a result, I work with a concept of violence that is challenging, but one particular to guerrilla organizations that formed during the late 1960s and early 1970s. Ben Morea, for instance, a founding member of Black Mask/Up Against the Wall Motherfucker, argued in a Free Press Report that there is a dichotomy that "is always made between non-violence and violence and that's a false dichotomy. The dichotomy is between living and death . . . Some kinds of violence are living, understand? Some kinds of violence are death. If your violence is because you desire to live and is only directed against people who would prevent you from living, then I don't consider that violence. I consider that living."[67] Jean Genet theorized a similar approach to violence almost a decade later in an essay titled "Violence and Brutality." Writing in support of the Red Army Faction, Genet argued that violence is an inescapable facet of life: "violence and life are virtually synonymous."[68] By contrast, he argues that acts of brutality are avoidable, defining brutality broadly as "the gesture or theatrical gesticulation that puts an end to freedom, for no other reason than the will to negate or to interrupt the accomplishment of the free act."[69] Huey P. Newton's concept of revolutionary suicide functions in the same vein: "there is an old African saying, 'I am we.' If you met an African in ancient times and asked him who he was, he would reply, 'I am we.' This is revolutionary suicide: I, we, all of us are the one and the multitude."[70]

Contemporarily speaking, these attitudes have reemerged. Consider Neera Chandhoke's articulation of revolutionary violence in her book *Democracy and Revolutionary Politics* (2015). "We have to recognize that democracy and justice may not be conceptual siblings," she writes, "and that sometimes violence has to be used to seize justice from states."[71] Analyzing acts of revolutionary violence taken up across South Asia and the Middle East to justify her argument, Chandhoke continues this thought in the very same logic I invoke throughout this introduction: "Violence is not always an unwelcome visitor, or an uninvited stranger who has strayed into our harmonious world, but whose prolonged stay can be brought to an end only if we, in a determined fashion, refuse to extend hospitality. On balance, we have to accept that violence is part of individual and collective lives."[72] Historically speaking, guerrilla invocations of violence find their contemporary correlate in groups like Antifa. Consider Mark Bray's description of Antifa's illiberalism and justification for political violence: "Militant anti-fascism refuses to engage in terms of debate that developed out of the precepts of classical liberalism that undergird both 'liberal' and 'conservative' positions in the United States. Instead of privileging 'neutral' universal rights, anti-fascists prioritize the political project of destroying fascism and protecting the vulnerable."[73]

The question of violence posed in this book is therefore not one based on indiscriminate rage or senseless motivation. It is rather one formative of the guerrilla's ontological condition, and productive of its political insurgencies, organization, and its tactics. These conditions presuppose that democracy and justice may not be conceptual siblings even as we might strive toward their alignment. Similar concepts are required in order to understand the particularity of the guerrilla's position. They lead me back to an intersectional approach throughout the text. They clarify how collectivity coincides with partisan opposition in the formation of collective subjects.

Second, this book confronts the masculinist character of guerrilla organization and tactics in the situations it explores. Guerrilla histories are often characterized by a hetero-masculinist rhetoric, fueled by patriarchal control. The collectives explored in this book perhaps embody this version of guerrilla history to an extreme degree, but the means by which masculinity and patriarchal power function as norms by each group lead to a critical discussion of embodiment in the formation of partisan opposition. My criticism of the figure's reliance on a hetero-masculinist subjectivity allows me to rethink how the guerrilla has been invoked in DH praxis and how its reinvention comments on contemporary politics. The methodology deployed in this book, necessarily so, rejects the guerrilla's dominant hetero-masculinist condition in favor of its role in manifesting a radical articulation of difference in political practice.

Chapter 1, "Protocols for Conflict," offers a genealogy of guerrilla organization and tactics in contemporary critical theory. Its primary focus is to connect the guerrilla's conceptual history with the technological structures formative of its political ontology, but also with those that are thought to supersede it. I take a sustained look at network theory and power in this chapter as a result, tracing Michael Hardt and Antonio Negri's occlusion of guerrilla organization and tactics in their invention of the multitude, and I also look at Alexander Galloway and Eugene Thacker's theorization of network power's ethical bonds via biopolitical control. I bring the arguments presented by these thinkers back to the guerrilla's invocation in DH praxis, arguing that network theorists' attempt to occlude the guerrilla's influence on the productive side of network power results in an anti-realist politics that DH avoids by inviting the guerrilla into its theoretical lexicon.

Chapter 2, "The Maker and the Made," contrasts two politicized maker figures that precede DH's maker turn: the European avant-garde and the Latin American guerrilla filmmaker. The avant-garde represents solitary and individualized acts of making in this chapter. Although many European avant-garde artists are situated collectively in a historical view, that is, Futurists, Dadaists, Surrealists, Situationists, and so on, I argue that the avant-garde is perhaps more closely aligned with the bourgeois concepts of the individual that it opposes, especially in its present co-optation by the alt-right. Inversely, the guerrilla filmmaker, situated in the Latin American Third Cinema movement, offers an example of a collaborative making process that transforms its participants into a collective figure. I forefront the ideological conflicts that inform these contrasts, and trace their conflicts in contemporary acts of making. I critique the European avant-garde via Angela Nagle as prefigurative of contemporary acts of brutality, that is, gamergate, trolling, and alt-right politics more generally. I critique Solanas and Getino's reliance on a hetero-masculinist rhetoric that delimits the guerrilla's political transformation by imposing a male body and subjectivity onto the political actors that claim it. I situate both criticisms as an opportunity to reflect on DH's countercultural ethos and the histories it deploys to organize its politics.

Chapter 3, "The Production of the Commons," explores contrasting styles of cultural preservation. Digital humanities, on the one hand, favors a Creative Commons-style approach to cultural preservation that rethinks the institutional value of representation, publicity, and citationality. I draw from Dorothy Kim and Eunsong Kim's "#TwitterEthics Manifesto," Bethany Nowviskie's "Capacity and Care," and Jessica M. Johnson's "Doing and Being Intellectual History: #Formation as Curated by Black Women," along with a handful of related DH examples. Guerrilla acts of cultural preservation, on the other hand, oppose institutional control full stop where it comes to be aligned with the market and the state. I argue that they function as a kind of critical unmaking, following various strains of DH-related work. I focus on the anarcho-communist collective Black Mask in particular here, tracing its anticapitalist and anti-imperialist aesthetico-political regime through to its acts of cultural preservation predicated on collective concepts of the self. The method that follows from these contrasting styles is also located in Black Mask's aesthetico-political regime. This chapter concludes with a discussion of Black Mask's "decolonial Dada"—a politically informed aesthetic practice that equates cultural preservation with tactical relations of affinity as institutional power is unmade—and its possible implications for knowledge's free dissemination via #guerrillaDH.

In chapter 4, "Guerrilla Theory from the Underside," I situate the political history, aesthetics, and theory of the Black Panther Party within contemporary debates concerning the digital formation of black life. I frame the chapter around Tara McPherson's profound essay "Why Are the Digital Humanities So White? or Thinking the Histories of Race and Computation," and Stefano Harney and Fred Moten's essay collection *The Undercommons*. Both texts offer a concrete vocabulary for co-articulating problems of race and violence as radical politics are affirmed. I explore Aria Dean's proclamation of a productive and collectivized mode of becoming in the production of black social life within digital environments via Fred Moten's figuration of "blackness as nothingness." I further problematize this work by exploring alternative figurations of the archive. First, I investigate Black Panther cinema as an archive of self-defense, articulating collectivized experiences of violence that attempt to preserve the situation as it was, all the way down to its field of vision. Second,

I recount Kodwo Eshun's figuration of museological contest, following Dean, within an Afrofuturist framework. Third, I outline Michelle M. Wright's exploration of horizontal archives. Finally, I situate Jade E. Davis's practice of decolonial Dada as an archival mode predicated on acts of translation. I conclude this chapter by exploring Moten's concept of "debt work," and call for DH to conceptualize acts of cultural preservation as an "undercommons" that forms multiple and overlapping solidarities across a multiplicity of subject positions, across radically difference experiences of oppression.

In this book's conclusion, I examine three contemporary approaches to critical DH work. Each approach I outline is not a pure extension of guerrilla politics, nor is each combination situated within its lineage. They are meant to show what radical political configurations of the present look like, and how the guerrilla ethos is preserved at moments of their application. I offer a brief reading of minimal computing, positioning its "needs-based" economy within the broader discourse of this text. I situate hacking as a form of transformative critique and draw out its inhuman metaphors. I do so to further underscore questions of gender and race where collective subjectivities are claimed in contemporary culture, but also to reassert the importance of economic critique in critical DH work. Finally, I detail a concept of DH as Critical University Studies (CUS), arguing that DH and CUS need each other for three, interrelated reasons: (1) co-articulating the rhetoric and method of both discourses would broaden the awareness and need to refuse the university's continued neoliberalization; (2) DH and CUS's political cohesion would better ground egalitarian visions of the university's future; and (3) developing common organizational models would better oppose institutional and disciplinary inequities. Thinking DH as a form of CUS begins with giving attention to diverse interventions in its discourse, perhaps even prior to the question of disciplinary tool-use.

Neither the agonisms internal to the discipline nor the antagonisms drawn out by guerrilla organization and tactics are resolved at this book's conclusion. My project is one of inherent conflict, but one of productive conflict in the places and times that political subjects come to be articulated. The point is *not* to insist on the universality of guerrilla organization and tactics. It is to insist on addressing the demand that guerrilla organization and tactics place on the concept of the political within the present forms of intellectual discourse. *Guerrilla Theory* stretches this demand to its present limits. DH praxis is its contemporary site of articulation.

Chapter 1

Protocols for Conflict

Friend and enemy take up their places in taking the place of
the other, one becoming, prior to the slightest opposition, the
ambiguous guardian, both the jailer and the saviour, of the
other.

—Jacques Derrida, *The Politics of Friendship*

Maintaining criticality and experimentation means challenging
received traditions, even—perhaps, especially—those that
defined the first generations of Digital Humanities work.
—Anne Burdick, Johanna Drucker, Peter Lunenfeld, Todd Presner,
and Jeffrey Schnapp, *Digital_Humanities*

The tactical valuation of digital humanities work is characterized as both a
politically informed theoretical project and an institutional enterprise. Both
are contoured by material ambition. To adopt a tactical stance is to adopt
an attitude of contingency, perhaps a militant perspective on the terrain of
one's site of action, which ultimately favors momentary gains. It is to get
things done, but also to prioritize the present time and context of one's labor
so as to radically alter its shape. This chapter, as it introduces the arguments
addressed in the totality of this book, favors a tactical DH that utilizes theory
as a political tool—a political tool that focuses its attention on the logics and
organizational structures that make our work critical in and of the present.

I take the following statement as something given, extant in the contemporary history and formation of DH work: the dialectical tension inherent
to our disciplinary trajectories frames DH praxis as a space for productive
contestation. This is apparent in the series of self-imposed dyads DH uses to
define its own disciplinary norms (hack/yack, in/out, big/minimal, distant/
close, tenure track/alt-ac, etc.), but also in criticisms of DH's institutional
influence, particularly its proximity to neoliberal imperatives for university
organization. Perhaps a more fundamental point of tension is thus DH's

privileged institutional status, and subsequently how its disciplinary norms inform institutional power. In the abstract for their 2013 Modern Language Association roundtable, "The Darkside of the Digital Humanities," Wendy Hui Kong Chun, Richard Grusin, Patrick Jagoda, and Rita Raley identify this issue head-on, writing:

> The same neoliberal logic that informs the ongoing destruction of the mainstream humanities has encouraged foundations, corporations, and university administrations to devote new resources to the digital humanities . . . And because there is no sign that these funding streams are going to dry up any time soon, and no sign on the horizon of an increase in funding for the "crisis humanities," there is great potential for increased tension between the "haves" of digital humanities and the "have-nots" of mainstream humanities.[1]

This tension bears itself out internal to DH in the list of dyads above, and it is furthered by the polarities of disciplinary formation, priority, and precarity external to the discipline itself. Conflict and contestation operate as both internal modalities of methodological definition *and* external forces that put pressure on DH's continued expansion. To *have* and to *have not* signifies much more than economic difference.

This is precisely where my turn to theorize the guerrilla's invocation in DH praxis as a political tool, tactical figure, and mode of collective self-making takes center stage. My aim in this chapter is to carve out a space in DH to participate in critical theoretical traditions that preempt and eschew DH's more tool-oriented work, without sidestepping DH's own methodological demands as it does so. As a result, much critical discourse endemic to DH praxis is waylaid in this chapter—I proceed via several theoretical detours that *lead* to a discussion of DH and the critical implications of its guerrilla rhetoric.

This chapter proceeds by recuperating a concept of militancy that operates as an intellectual commitment, revealing its guerrilla roots. I then move to unearth the guerrilla's complex invocation in critical theory, leading up to its invocation in DH. The whole of this work amounts to a genealogy of technologically informed conflict that operates at the level of state power, network power, and concomitantly institutional power as I conclude to read critical DH work in its immanent democratic alternatives to present radical political discourse. The guiding questions for this chapter are twofold: in what ways might radical political concepts change our approach to intellectual labor in DH? In what ways might they alter our attitudes about the function of theory in DH praxis? To pose these questions and to pursue them is both an expression of the guerrilla's critical invocations and an act of generative thinking. To pose these questions as an extension of DH's tactical evolution is to situate them at a remove from the rational calculus of our contemporary institutional state.

To be clear at the outset, I also need to say what I am *not* interested in doing. I am *not* interested in explicating how one becomes a radical by embarking on this project. *Nor* am I interested in affirming the figure's hetero-masculinist iterations. The guerrilla lineage I establish here is theoretically oriented, actualized through a legalistic discourse on territory and power, and critiqued for its abstraction as it is imported into network theory. As the book progresses, I critique guerrilla organization and tactics more forcefully through feminist, post- and decolonial, and queer engagements directly or indirectly situated so as to reimagine their import and scope. Above all, this book explores militant concepts and figures. Guerrilla organization and tactics are not operative unless they are engaged in conflict. Yet, the guerrilla's militancy is not reducible to capricious applications of force. Its militancy is characterized by the refusal to abstract or dissociate its political interventions from the context of its action.

Militant Critique

"The opposite of civility is not incivility, but militancy," write Tavia Nyong'o and Kyla Wazana Tompkins in their "Eleven Theses on Civility."[2] Militancy, the form of "radical-incivility" they invoke, is a collective political enterprise that "undoes the arkhe of subjectivity" by turning us from "individual pain to structural analysis."[3] I begin this section by linking intellectual militancy to the position from which it is theorized—a position of need. What need signifies is contextual. It signifies the desire to radically transform present intellectual discourse, the work required to make space for one's own intellectual traditions, and the will to cede control over the political flow of contemporary life even as it is opposed. To be militant is to enact radical incivility, to put these needs into practice, and to operate in opposition to any individualizing force of oppression that exists as its obstacle.

In a short article titled "The Militancy of Theory," Michael Hardt recognizes a "growing dissatisfaction with the political capacities of critique," proposing, following Michel Foucault, what he terms the militancy of theory.[4] Hardt's militancy intervenes both methodologically and politically. For him, contemporary modes of critique lack a transformative ethos; they cannot dissolve existing hierarchies of power (inside or outside of the university) or offer alternative modes of social organization. It is not enough to analyze the contradictions of a given text, become an intellectual disciple of a given thinker or movement, or rely on our status as experts in order to adjudicate the next intellectual trend. This parallels similar arguments in DH. Amy Earhart's claim, following Matthew Kirschenbaum, that "collaboration, real time scholarship, [and] open access" help us to restructure academic hierarchies is certainly related to this concern for critical lack.[5] For Hardt, though, the difference does not rely on making a distinction between hack and yack (making or critique). Nor does it fully rely on bridging academic institutions with nonacademic bodies. His project is rather to politicize the act of critique if and when it appears and to make critique a form of collective action.

For Hardt, critique should adopt and deploy a tactical presentism, ideally resulting in a collective milieu from which new forms of critique might also produce new forms of life: "the philosophical relation to the present is an active and collective relation, that is, not merely a matter of registering or even evaluating the present but acting on and transforming it. The task of theory is to make the present and thus to delimit or invent the subject of that making, a 'we' characterized not only by our belonging to the present but by our making it."[6] This concept of militancy is akin to contemporary methods of making in DH circles; we simply do not refer to active and collective relations of production as militant in the way that Hardt does. What Hardt proposes is a concept of theory as practice, but one focused on the production of subjectivity rather than the production of digital objects. This is a theme I take quite seriously in this book. It frames numerous instances following this chapter in which I explore how the production of a tool or aesthetic object is inextricably linked to collective acts of self-making.

In their coauthored *The Undercommons: Fugitive Planning & Black Study* (2013), Stefano Harney and Fred Moten practice an insurgent mode of critique by theorizing militancy as a confrontation between preservative and antagonistic powers. On the side of oppression, the militancy of preservation and policy organizes itself against insurgent social life. It is deputized to control and eliminate insurgent black social life in particular as it also commands social reproduction. Following Frantz Fanon and Nahum Chandler, Harney and Moten theorize the militancy of preservation as a problem of value. On the one hand, the militancy of preservation operates under a logic through which black social life is valued in a purely economic sense. Whiteness and its modes of preservation valorize an economic relation in which capital might profit from subjects that it simultaneously excludes. On the other hand, the militancy of preservation operates under a logic through which black life is rendered valueless, both socially and politically. The state routinely and violently controls where and how the expression of blackness is articulated, leading, as Moten notes, to a more pervasive culture of violence and war than lynch law.[7]

To confront this brutal power, Harney and Moten propose its obverse: a concept of the "undercommons," a method and style of life "wary of critique, weary of it, and at the same time dedicated to the collectivity of its future."[8] Rather than simply recuperating a concept of militancy here, Harney and Moten propose a paleonymic concept of militant thought and action in opposition to its statist iterations: an insurgent mode of being, one that is possibly more upsetting to some than the recuperation of militancy itself. As Jack Halberstam notes in his introduction to *Undercommons*, Harney and Moten's undercommons is not a call to arms, but a call to subversion. It is the production of subversive critique (inside and outside of the university) that is both collective and untimely.[9]

On the productive side, then, Stefano Harney calls the undercommons a "militant arrhythmia," appropriating the term in order to characterize it as an irregular blockage of history.[10] Like Hardt, this concept of militancy compels its practitioners to focus on the present and its collective political demands. Unlike Hardt, both Harney and Moten underscore the structural inequalities that prohibit this tactic from appearing as a universal political strategy. The undercommons, and the militant arrhythmia that it provokes, are a necessity of another kind. It is a response that originates in and from a universally contested ontological position—what we might call an ontological priority of violence—and it works to subvert organized powers of oppression. The undercommons is therefore a form of insurgent social life, insurgent black social life in particular, that functions under a logic of general and generative antagonism. The undercommons is not militarized, but Harney and Moten do put a militant lexicon to work in novel circumstances. The undercommons is militant in its intent to disrupt, preserve upheaval, and unsettle the territorializing logic of policy and planning. It is a form of life that acts against the policies and disciplinary powers that would enclose it. It breaks beyond the territory it is given, and subverts the *nomos* of disciplinary power.

This is a feeling and a fact of life that is often pushed to the margins of DH scholarship. One gets the strong sense that Harney and Moten's claim to insurgency greatly expands on the insurgency attributed to Mark Sample's description of DH, being "all about innovation and disruption."[11] The militancy of Harney and Moten's undercommons, similar to theories of intersectionality, acknowledges disciplinary subjugation by refusing it, laying claim to a systemically diverse method of intellectual inquiry *in the first instance*. True to the lineage of many academic disciplines, one can now happen upon any number of sub-DH disciplinary practices that add to the primary category, but similar to intersectional approaches to DH, Harney and Moten's militancy does not disrupt by addition; it cleaves the world to its position and holds its own standard of life.

Finally, Rita Raley also explores a related militant attitude in her book *Tactical Media* (2009), centralizing and furthering insurgency in digital contexts. Her book stems from and builds on various histories of tactical media, offering what is both a challenging and innovative critique of political praxis: the performance of a dynamic and anti-programmatic politics (both inside and outside of the university). Following Geert Lovink and David Garcia, Raley claims that tactical media mobilize various technologies and media to disturb hegemonic power structures, but the "outcomes of those disturbances remain uncertain and unpredictable."[12] In fact, tactical media "requires that its practitioners cede control over its outcomes," rendering it a political practice without command and a revolutionary movement without end.[13] The same conditions stand where tactical media is mobilized as a critical methodology, or, in the language above, a critique of critique. Raley's intervention functions on two planes.

Politically, Raley's work draws out aesthetic modes of resistance to the variances of "postindustrial society and neoliberal globalization."[14] Like Hardt, she is a theorist of the here and now: "tactical media contests the future terrain of the political, but it does so via virtuosic performances deployed and experienced in the present."[15] The militant subject that follows from this mode of tactical presentism emerges from digital networks and responds directly to the axiomatics of capital. Her critique, along with the subjects she focuses on, is malleable, virtually constructed, and centered on processual aesthetic practices. Academically speaking, Raley's work on tactical media intervenes in militant politics and critique. In practicing and performing tactical media, one must militate against the power of command and the lure of dictation. The tactical media practitioner is therefore one who is authorized to act (perhaps she is one who authorizes herself to act), but is not authorized (or does not authorize herself) to control. To phrase this methodologically, a critical engagement with these imperatives requires one to act, but to act in a way that refuses the power of command by hegemonic interests, particularly neoliberal interests, at every level of their articulation. This tenet of tactical media dovetails well with Hardt's claim to militancy above, but it also brings a mode of militant critique to media and technology's place in higher education that supersedes hierarchical disruption. Indeed, this prefigures Raley's contemporary work in digital humanities.

The methodological imperatives inherent to these concepts are far-reaching. Each will be addressed throughout this book. For the time being, I am interested in a theoretical question that is equally political—what is supposedly "guerrilla" about these militant methodologies, and how do they interact with DH? They certainly do not espouse the kind of militarism that some DH scholars reject, but neither do these claims to new forms of militancy emerge from a political vacuum. These theories of militancy share guerrilla roots. The theory and practice of the Red Brigades, Zapatistas, and the Black Panther Party undergird Hardt's theory of militancy, along with various other forms of guerrilla struggle. Harney and Moten reference the Black Panthers in particular as they develop concepts of general and generative antagonism and the violence of innovation.[16] Raley turns to guerrilla tactics in her exploration of tactical media, drawing a one-to-one connection between the performance of tactical media and the networked form of guerrilla organization.[17] Clearly, the turn to militancy in contemporary critical theory is situational and bound to disparate histories and traditions. It is not universalizing, and I do not intend to universalize it. Rather, in exploring what is common to these disparate histories and traditions—what is "guerrilla" about these militant interventions—I am interested in understanding how indulging a guerrilla positionality informs the concepts outlined above, and further, how this might affect the ways in which the guerrilla's invocation in DH praxis is approached.

In doing so, I motivate a discussion of self-making and partisan opposition that extends to every chapter of this book.

Friends and Enemies

A contentious and divisive political relation, wherever it is invoked, prefigures guerrilla organization and tactics: friends vs. enemies. I have already identified how the proclamation of the friend-enemy relation followed from the guerrilla's invocation in DH praxis, but the logic has a much broader and complex history. I begin with a historical analysis of the guerrilla's role in the formation of the friend-enemy relation at the level of sovereign power and subsequently move to analyze its role in the formation of a political theory of networks. I want to underscore my position, however, so that it is not confused. I situate political conflict as a baseline from which present political relations spawn. It is neither a command nor a goal, but it does inform the articulation of both antagonistic and agonistic political forces throughout this book. If and when it is identified in or applied as a political force in DH praxis, the friend-enemy relation directs scholar-practitioners to interrogate its formation and modes of articulation, ideally leading to alternative political concepts.

Historically speaking, the friend-enemy relation finds its most forceful contemporary theorization in the work of Carl Schmitt, who was both a jurist and political theorist aggrandized by the Nazi Party throughout the 1930s. His formulation of the friend-enemy relation facilitated gross justifications for inter-state warfare, and his infamous *Nomos of the Earth* stands as an ode to the European sovereign state, outlining processes of appropriation, distribution, and production that delimit geopolitical difference.[18] For the purposes of the history I provide here, Schmitt's *nomos* defines a "concept of the political," a mode of political division and confrontation located at the heart of contemporary warfare, that is ultimately distinguishable from the operation of politics. As Chantal Mouffe clarifies, to make a distinction between politics and the political is to distinguish "the ontological dimension of antagonism . . . and the ensemble of practices and institutions whose aim is to organize human existence."[19] The means by which political distinctions are made is thus a perception that "many us/them relations are merely a question of recognizing differences," but also one in which "there is always the possibility that this 'us/them' relation might become one of friend/enemy."[20] In other words, where difference inspires politics, one cannot eliminate the potential for difference to revert to irreconcilable conflict. Schmitt is thus primarily interested in exploring the ontological dimension of antagonism, and subsequently mobilizing it as a force of political control.

As a primary means of doing so, Schmitt claims that partisan opposition originates in a process of othering—conceiving of one's enemy as "existentially something different and alien"—so that war is possible.[21] The enemy is cast as the *hostis*, the public antithesis and enmity-bearing body to its opposi-tion. The means of conceiving of another in this way are many, but the enemy is always one who threatens the unity and integrity of the state. Schmitt's *nomos* is thus intimately tied to the ways in which one is conceived of as an enemy via geopolitical difference, intending to delimit who the enemy is and what he is capable of. The common feature to all partisan formations is their telluric condition, however—partisans are tied to the land, they fight territo-rial wars, and are consistently localizable. Given that borders fix territory in Schmitt's political, the loss of this primary feature would result in a potentially uncontainable threat to state power. As a play between states, friends and enemies are corporate bodies, immanent agglomerations of both individual and universal however and wherever territorial boundaries are parsed. As a play between non-state actors and states, the enemy is much more difficult to locate and define.

In the interplay of his political, non-state actors accept Schmitt's claim to division via existential difference. Guerrilla warfare in particular relies on it. However, the political relations that manifest when non-state actors foment a legitimate claim to partisan conflict against the state upset Schmitt's terms for division and enmity leading to war. Non-state actors are diffuse, and they rely on a multiplicity of tactics that refuse both centralization and homoge-neity as organizational principles. More than this, non-state actors turn the partisan demand back on to the state. Where guerrilla organization and tactics manifest, what appears is an asymmetric force of opposition that names the state as its absolute enemy. This threat is so powerful, in fact, that Schmitt reconfigures the friend-enemy relation in his *Theory of the Partisan* in order to account for the emergence of political conflict mobilized by non-state actors. There, the *hostis*-making drive that prefigures his political is still present, but it is under threat by the co-development of guerrilla warfare and industrial technologies. Concerned with the rapidity of industrialization, Schmitt turns to the figure of the guerrilla to underscore the dissolution of clear partisan division through what he terms "irregular war."

The historical development of regularity and irregularity is interesting from Schmitt's perspective. Where he focuses on open space (the ocean and the air) and piracy to describe conditions of irregularity impertinent to war in more popular texts, his *Theory of the Partisan* focuses on guerrilla fighters and their effect on territorial integrity. According to Schmitt, "the partisan of the Spanish Guerrilla War of 1808 was the first who dared to wage irregular war against the first regular modern army."[22] True to form, the most important feature of the Spanish Guerrilla War for Schmitt is that the Spanish partisan "risked battle on his own home soil," resulting in a "*theory* of war and enmity that logically culminates in the theory of the partisan."[23] The guerrilla is a partisan in the strict sense (one who demands absolute political division, but also one who radically upsets the basis of political division), and guerrilla warfare is, as G. L. Ulmen notes, a "small war" mobilized toward "total war"

within and around the boundaries of a given state.²⁴ Again, regularity refers
to the state's hold over the land and its law of the land, and irregularity is
largely a refusal of fixed territorial boundaries. The guerrilla moves at will and
in many directions at once; it creates its own lines of authority and segments
territory to its advantage.

Diametrically opposed to Schmitt's *nomos*, the guerrilla embodies territory
in a fluid and processual movement. The refusal to adhere to fixed territorial
lines of division is indeed a refusal of the homogenous corporate body in
favor of the production of a diffuse mobile body, but the mediating factor that
allows for the partisan to exceed its telluric condition is technology advancement. With rapid advances in "technical-industrial" progress, the partisan
begins to develop more sophisticated and more effective tactics for destabi-
lizing the state's sovereign power. By incorporating more advanced forms of
technology into its repertoire of resistance, the partisan is reincarnated: the
telluric partisan becomes a motorized partisan, nomadic in its constitution
and use of force. Here, Schmitt writes:

> Even the autochthonous partisan of agrarian origin is drawn into the
> force-field of irresistible technical-industrial progress. His mobility is
> so enhanced by motorization that he runs the risk of complete dislo-
> cation . . . A motorized partisan loses his tellurian character. All that's
> left is a transportable, replaceable cog in the wheel of a powerful
> world-political machine [*Weltpolitik treibenden Zentrale*] that puts
> him in the open or invisible war and then, depending on how things
> are developing, switches him off again [*abschaltet*].²⁵

In so many words, the identifiable and localizable features that are endemic to
Schmitt's political are compromised by the co-articulation of guerrilla warfare
and technological progress. More than this, the agile and diffuse movement of
a novel techno-political body undermines the centralized and stalwart body
of the state.

What ultimately manifests Schmitt's political is a complex and proleptic
political ontology. The figure of the motorized partisan, characterized by a
techno-tactical novelty, fundamentally alters the way in which friends and
enemies are parsed. In existential terms, guerrilla warfare brings what is other
inside the state's territory as individual or non-state actors use the state's infrastructure against itself. This concept of the political is dialectical. Where the
guerrilla appears, the state exists in a perpetual condition of crisis, a condition
that preemptively anticipates its threat to its borders. Where the guerrilla
becomes motorized, its organization and tactics anticipate new technological
developments and mobilize them toward a position of total opposition. The
guerrilla is an antagonist to the regularity of sovereign power and an affirmative political subjectivity for those who adopt it. The guerrilla undermines
territorial boundaries *and* the distribution of political difference by producing

partisan opposition through a diffuse and mobile political subjectivity. These features are an enduring challenge to political theory and praxis, and are ultimately mobilized toward liberatory ends.

A Democracy of Network Powers

Contemporary theorists of the guerrilla form typically focus on how it alters political forces and subjects, making the body of guerrilla organization a central concern as political relations are parsed. At the same time, the guerrilla's adoption of industrial technologies prefigures the discourse and political use of digital technologies, even if we don't always recognize it as such. What remains consistent as both points of focus overlap is the guerrilla's status as a marginal and existentially different entity by comparison to the regularity of the state form. Perhaps this is a nascent intuition in DH praxis. For the DH scholar-practitioners who have invoked the guerrilla, the figure's outsider status is easily grasped, as is its will to disrupt. In the course of this section and the following, I show how network theory reinvents the guerrilla's partisan logic so as to co-opt it for theorizing novel ethico-political regimes. I direct the conversation to a liminal position. I work to underscore the political realities that precede DH's invocation of the figure, allowing me to demonstrate DH's alternative to this discourse in later sections.

While it might not be immediately apparent, the formation of Schmitt's political, but primarily his concern for the guerrilla's ontological irregularities, informs the political mobilization of network power. Alexander Galloway characterizes the guerrilla as an asymmetric force of opposition that "encounters the power center not as equal, but as an unholy monster, seemingly formless and ungovernable."[26] Simon Critchley defines urban guerrilla struggle in the United States and western Europe as a force of "active nihilism," or a political position governed by pessimism, leading to dubious political projects: "the active nihilist," opposed to the passive nihilist, "finds everything meaningless, but instead of sitting back and contemplating, he tries to destroy this world and bring another into being."[27] Michael Hardt and Antonio Negri theorize the guerrilla as a figure of crisis with a Deleuzean twist, describing its form and organization "as a pack of wolves, or numerous wolfpacks that counterinsurgency forces have to hunt down."[28] Quite clearly, the guerrilla's contemporary characterization is one of complete and intentional othering. The guerrilla is a sacrilegious monster, a suicide squad, and a social predator, absolutely opposed to the unified body of the state. It is, to be succinct, inhuman. The guerrilla is a body without borders, a figure without content, and a subject of collective harm.

Paired with its technologized character above, the subjectivity derived from a theoretical treatment of the guerrilla underscores that the crisis of Schmitt's political is much more complex than a dispute over territory. The figure is a political subject that presents an alternative to homeostatic institutions, unitary corporate organization, and the simple binary between friendly and hostile states. Representative of the guerrilla's partisan demand—that of becoming an absolute enemy within and beyond the state form—guerrilla organization and tactics are an art of making difference and collectivity political, technological, and ontological alternatives to state power. Its process of othering inherent to political articulation consequently manifests in a genealogy of both present and futural political forms.

What Schmitt's focus on partisan conflict and guerrilla organization so deftly demonstrates, and what contemporary scholarship proves, is that arguments over territory quickly lead to ontological arguments concerning the figures that inhabit it. Where new technologies and new media are concerned, scholars are perhaps more comfortable speaking in the language of protocols, networks, and asymmetry than in the language of friends and enemies. The reason for this is simple. Although the techno-political language of networks is a genuine outgrowth of these partisan debates, the friend-enemy relation is thought to be surpassed by it. Thus the turn to networks is a predictable outcome. In the instances when Schmitt refers to diffuse technologized bodies in and beyond state lines, the historical conclusion is the flow and organization of networks. Where network theory immediately precedes DH's command of the digital, concerns for territory are almost universally replaced by the ontological status of networks and the subjects who inhabit them. Partisanship is not a question limited to territory in this discourse; it is focused on the production of collectivized political subjects.

The premise of this section is gestural, but clear-cut: network theory intentionally and preemptively sidesteps friend-enemy relations in contemporary political discourse to its advantage. It does so through two political improvisations. First, network theory doubles down on the concept of a diffuse and agile political subject, relying on the claim that collectivized political figures have advanced beyond our ability to adequately frame them by any preexisting protocol for political conflict. In doing so, network theory aims to produce consistent conditions of ontological irregularity so as to reframe political relations. And second, in its attempt to influence the tenor and flow of political resistance, network theory favors ethico-political regimes that demand ontological expansiveness, transforming the guerrilla's political characteristics into unsuppressed strategies for revolution. Through this transformation, network theory aims to reconfigure partisan relations via consistent conditions of deterritorialization.

One does not have to search very hard to confront these claims. Let's recall Paolo Virno's definition of guerrilla organization and tactics that sits at the root of autonomist Marxist iterations of network power: guerrilla organization and tactics require "a high level of social cooperation, a freedom of movement in enemy territory, [and] a capacity to cope with a multiplicity of variables in the course of action"; "guerrilla action . . . exercises direct power, a decentralized and diffused power, as pluralistic as the enemy's power."[29] Similar to Schmitt's definition of the figure, Virno's definition of guerrilla action points to a set of characteristics common to revolutionary subjectivity in the autonomist tradition that ground asymmetric flows of political resistance. If direct, decentralized, pluralistic power can be harnessed on a larger scale, it could reconfigure political relationality in total.

Understanding the guerrilla's treatment in Michael Hardt and Antonio Negri's *Empire* trilogy is foundational to this end. Across their trilogy, Hardt and Negri theorize networks as both a relation of power and a relation of production prefigured by guerrilla organization and tactics. The reason for this is simple. Hardt and Negri argue that the organizational and tactical qualities of the guerrilla model are "viewed best as *transitional forms* that reveal above all the continuing and unsatisfied desire for more democratic and independent forms of revolutionary organization."[30] What demands such a transition? Early in *Empire* (2000), Hardt and Negri follow the development of network power and organization through to a triumphant (and perhaps premature) conclusion:

> Resistances are no longer marginal but active in the center of a society that opens up in networks; the individual points are singularized in a thousand plateaus. What Foucault constructed implicitly (and Deleuze and Guattari made explicit) is therefore a paradox of a power that, while it unifies and envelops within itself every element of social life . . . at that very moment reveals a new context, a new milieu of maximum plurality and uncontainable singularization—a milieu of the event.[31]

The development of this so-called milieu follows from the techno-political production of network power; when the network's imperial power is internalized, a democratic event emerges that also produces a networked democratic body. Hardt and Negri's characterization of network power is thus twofold.

On the one hand, the pair characterize contemporary power relations as diffuse and decentralized iterations of Empire—an expansive neo-imperial force that aims to be all consuming. Empire holds as its constant project the incorporation of new modalities of production, new subjects, and new expanses (physical or virtual) that it must control.[32] Framed in this way, Empire is also an economic power, one in which its technological character takes precedent, and one that matches diffuse flows of capitalist modes of production. Take the assembly line as an example. Under a Fordist model, production takes place in a single location: the factory floor. Each worker completes a specific job in a vast, but physically connected, routine of production. Under a post-Fordist model, production is diffuse and mediated by lightweight, mobile technologies. Physicality is no longer the defining character of production, but rather cognitive processing (human and digital) that relays the material flow of information across disparate locations and times. As these centers of power and modalities of production expand, the tension between internality and externality (inside and outside) becomes magnified. Power is no longer territorial; it is supraterritorial. Resistance to Empire allegedly follows suit. The questions that follow are straightforward. What happens when sovereign power is coterminous with the organization and flow of networks? What happens when all forms of life are transformed into capitalist forms of life? The tension here is not simply one of inclusion or assimilation, but of the control mechanisms inside various sovereign institutions once all externalities are assimilated.[33]

On the other hand, Hardt and Negri theorize a novel form of resistance that attempts to limit the depth and flow of sovereign power through "the constitutional formation of limits and equilibria, checks and balances, which both constitutes a central power and maintains power in the hands of the multitude."[34] Enter their radically democratic vision of the network. Taking the American Revolution and the U.S. Constitution as innovations in modern sovereignty, Hardt and Negri argue that network power developed as an immanent political power, opposed to absolute sovereign power, "by developing new languages and social forms that mediate between the one and the multiple."[35] Network power is said to eliminate transcendental iterations of power (absolute sovereign power) by way of its immanence—its diffusion among pluralistic mechanisms of social control that demand heterogeneity in organization and outcome. What results is thus the formation of a collectivized political subject as agile and diffuse as Empire's networks—a subject that ultimately transitions *from* the guerrilla form *to* that of the multitude. This signals network theory's first improvisation.

Hardt and Negri double down on the concept of a diffuse and agile political subject, relying on the claim that collectivized political figures have advanced beyond our ability to adequately frame them by any preexisting protocol for political conflict. Counter to Schmitt, Hardt and Negri are not interested in speed or the partisan's telluric condition. Where they reconstruct various histories of guerrilla organization and tactics, they claim that "guerrilla forces continually create tighter articulations between the political and the social," leading to the contemporary condition in which the guerrilla "presupposes *the political nature of social life* and adopts it as an internal key to all movements."[36] Hardt and Negri's focus on the conflation of political relations with social life is intentional—it creates a scenario in which *life itself* might be conceived of as a site of political contestation and resistance. In Hardt and Negri's view, "this presupposition is basic, in fact, to the concept of biopolitics and the biopolitical production of subjectivity."[37] What does this mean?

Sociopolitical conflation augurs the production of a political milieu in which democratic resistance is located in the very materiality of one's being. Biopolitics signifies a vitalist bent in Hardt and Negri's work that inaugurates a strategy for managing the democratic flow of life, perhaps even prior to creating the political conditions for it to appear. The pair argue, "biopolitics is a partisan relationship between subjectivity and history that is crafted by a multitudinous strategy, formed by events and resistances, and articulated by a discourse that links political decision making to the construction of bodies in struggle."[38] Biopolitics is mobilized to describe a political modality of production that actualizes "a form of power that regulates social life from its interior, following it, interpreting it, absorbing it, and rearticulating it."[39] How the production of our sociopolitical milieu comes to be harnessed ultimately defines the character of sovereign power and its resistances. To be clear, in framing the guerrilla as a transitional political form, transitional *to* a situation in which politics and sociality are coextensive, Hardt and Negri reaffirm their democratic vision of network power, the production of "a new milieu of maximum plurality and uncontainable singularization."[40] If subjectivity and history now interact on a biopolitical level, the network appears as a form of sociopolitical organization intended to produce more mobile, more creative, and more humanitarian forms of life prior to their control by Empire. The point for Hardt and Negri is not to lay claim to existential difference, as the guerrilla does. It is to be the networked obverse of Empire, to make Empire the multitude's "photo negative," leading to a political situation in which "there is no conflict here between reform and revolution."[41]

Networks of Control

Network theory's second political improvisation clarifies Hardt and Negri's claim to biopolitical production. The multitude's ontological constitution allegedly creates the theoretical potential to favor the ethico-political control of subjectivity itself, continuing to transform guerrilla organization and tactics into unsuppressed strategies for revolution. Alexander Galloway and Eugene Thacker demonstrate this potential clearly and succinctly in their coauthored book *The Exploit: A Theory of Networks* (2007).

There, Galloway and Thacker further define the kind of agility and decentralization articulated by Schmitt above through a more contemporary understanding network relations: "*Networked power is based on a dialectic between two opposing tendencies: one radically distributes control into autonomous locales; the other focuses control into rigidly defined hierarchies. All political regimes today stand in some relation to networks.*"[42] Galloway and Thacker are clear to argue that "networks, by their mere existence, are not liberating."[43] They do not forward a naive techno-political optimism here. The oppositional tendencies upon which network power is based, however, become a problem of control that splits in two directions. Does the network match or extend statist institutions of power and management? Can the network act as a counterpower to such political forces?

For its part, the guerrilla represents the autonomous end of this discourse and is characterized as an asymmetric force of relation: "In conventional warfare, a networked insurgency will fail every time; however, in unconventional warfare (suicide bombing, hostage taking, hijacking, etc.), the insurgent is able to gain some amount of influence."[44] The guerrilla's tactical attributes make its political function clear. Guerrillas maximize their impact where they are and with what they have, knowing that their enemy's power is greater. Yet, as the network form takes over, the guerrilla's asymmetric qualities are reinvented in a language of customs and relations that sanitize the networked interaction of their absolute partisan stance. Galloway and Thacker begin this project by asking an important question in a familiar language: *Is there a 'nonhuman' or an 'unhuman' understanding of networks that would challenge us to rethink the theory and practice of networks?*"[45] What does the inhuman signify here?

To invoke the inhuman is to appeal to an alternative force of political control. It is to seek out principles of networked interrelationality and principles of political organization that offer new protocols for understanding how the constitutive function of difference operates. It is to invoke an "other" in political discourse, but an other that exceeds the boundaries of the guerrilla's subjectivity. Hence, the criteria that Galloway and Thacker establish for their definition of protocols mirror guerrilla organization and tactics as they also work to surpass them: protocols emerge through autonomous interconnected agents; they must be robust, flexible, and accommodate a high degree of contingency; they manifest internal antagonisms that guide their operation; they are universal and total; and they are radically horizontal and distributed properties of organization and control.[46] The radical possibilities inherent to Thacker and Galloway's definition of network protocols are extensive. The figures that manifest such possibilities are more focused. Where the network operates as a counterpower to Empire in its new protocological form, the guerrilla is replaced by another inhuman figure that would ensure absolute political transformation: the swarm.

Galloway and Thacker move quickly here. To state their project concisely, the swarm signifies a transmogrified political body—a body without borders and a body without content—that eliminates any identifiable markers formative of the friend-enemy relation. This is what the inhuman itself affords and what the swarm is intended to manifest. "Perhaps it is not possible for a network to be an *enemy*," the pair write.[47] "*If 'control' in conflict is ordinarily situated around a relationship of enmity (friend-foe, ally-enemy), and if this relation of enmity structures the organization of conflict . . .*" Galloway and Thacker ask, "*what happens when enmity dissolves in the intangible swarm?*"[48] In this iteration of political relationality, difference is alien—wholly foreign in such a way that refers to neither human identity nor subjectivity. It is "other," entirely so, akin to a messianic promise or apocalyptic event. Control in political relationality—the definition of protocols they invoke above—thus follows from an inhuman condition of difference.

Perhaps the most complex point Galloway and Thacker make to this end is precisely how the network as swarm exists as a subject "without a face," and thus a subject that lacks a primary condition of recognizing one's enemy.[49] On the one hand, defacement functions as a guerrilla tactic for political resistance in Galloway and Thacker's view. Riffing on Schmitt's figuration of friend-enemy relations, the pair argue that the guerrilla is an "*instance of faceless enmity*" as "*asymmetrical guerrilla tactics deface the honor of war.*"[50] While this conjures up a form of guerrilla organization and tactics, "going underground" in Galloway and Thacker's argument, the network's priority motivates a concept of productive and intentional othering that is all its own.[51] If one's enemy is radically inhuman, a diffuse body irreducible to a face, enmity is allegedly evacuated from the political relation and replaced with that of an ethics. Following a Levinasian same/other distinction, Galloway and Thacker's messianic promise is fulfilled by Levinas's stance that "a self does not set out, *avant la lettre*, to identify a friend or foe according to pre-existing criteria."[52] "A self" rather calls out to subjectivity, binding one by a responsibility to honor shared ethical imperatives and to preserve life prior to any identitarian form of difference. Galloway and Thacker ask, "If the Schmittian notion of enmity (friend-foe) presupposes a more fundamental relation of what Levinas refers to as 'facing' the other . . . what sort of ethics is possible when the other has no 'face' and yet is construed as other (as friend or foe)? What is the shape of the ethical encounter when one 'faces' the swarm?"[53]

Galloway and Thacker's response to these questions unsurprisingly parallels Hardt and Negri's biopolitical claim. Theorizing the network's liberatory potential as Galloway and Thacker do de-prioritizes enmity from political relations at the same time that it favors inhuman protocols for networked interrelationality. The swarm implicates its other through an ethical obligation as it renders our most primary categories of recognition inoperative. To "deface" oneself is to become inhuman, to evacuate subjectivity from identitarian forms of difference, and thus create a space for the ethical demand to replace relations of enmity. This eventually results in a radically abstract concept of the political relationality, one reductive to a political ontology of "life resistance."[54] Like biopolitical forms of partisanship, life resistance defines a political relation in which "(1) life is what resists power, and (2) to the extent that it is co-opted by power, 'life itself' must be resisted by living systems."[55]

With the space of the political encounter radically deterritorialized and the political subject evacuated of its particularity, network theory's biopolitical incursions into political relationality hinge on a condition of ontological expansiveness. The network is simultaneously the space in which a person forfeits her identity in favor of new protocols for political control and the mechanism by which she dissolves into an agile and diffuse body of resistance, that is, the swarm or the multitude. The political improvisations that network theorists perform to manifest this condition of political thought are not without their critics.

Intentionally so, Harney and Moten's focus on insurgency and subversion materializes from the underside of the autonomist Marxist tradition. It is based on the recognition of material inequality. As such, it demonstrates that the prioritizing conflict within democratic political relations is not simply a speculative or abstract maneuver. It addresses historico-political realities that are productive of our present political conditions. As they argue, the autonomist Marxist tradition owes a debt to black radical thought as it simultaneously borrows from and obscures "a global politics of blackness emerging out of slavery and colonialism, a black radical politics, a politics of debt without payment, without credit, without limit. This debt was built in a struggle with empire before empire, where power was not with institutions or governments alone, where any owner or colonizer had the violent power of a ubiquitous state."[56] The claim here is that it is not possible to think a concept of Empire or the multitude without first recognizing the violence of slavery and debt. To do so is to eliminate the brutalities committed on the basis of identitarian forms of difference without confronting them. Alexander G. Weheliye moves a step further, arguing that "bare life and biopolitics discourse not only misconstrues how profoundly race and racism shape the modern idea of the human, it overlooks or perfunctorily writes off theorizations of race, subjects, and humanity found in Black and ethnic studies, allowing bare life and biopolitics discourse to imagine an indivisible biological substance anterior to racialization."[57]

Think also of Byung-Chul Han's *In the Swarm* (2017). There, he argues that the swarm does not constitute a radical collective; it "demonstrates no internal coherence" and "does not speak with a *voice*."[58] In so many words, the networked agglomeration that Galloway and Thacker name the swarm is not a *we*; it is merely a disjointed collection of individuals. Han extends this critique to the ontological dimensions of digital networks more generally, arguing that networks do not manifest radical alterity at all—they act as narcissistic mirrors, delineated by likes and upvotes. "The positivity that is inherent in digital technology," he writes, "minimizes the possibility of having any [transcendent experience of the 'other']. It prolongs only the *same*. The smartphone, like the digital in general, undermines our ability to encounter and work with negativity."[59]

Finally, consider Shaka McGlotten's essay "Black Data." McGlotten mobilizes Galloway's figuration of anonymity that one might experience in/as the swarm in order to "enact a form of Black data that's different from discussions of Black life that would reduce it to lists of bare accountings which are incomplete and would misleadingly suggest that Black life must always and only be subordinated to historical and contemporary traumas or victimization."[60] He cultivates "a notion of Black data tied to defacement, opacity, and encryption," following Galloway's work by valorizing "techniques of becoming dark or opaque in order to better become present in the ways that we want, but without being seen or apprehended."[61] McGlotten's performance of this idea is key: he delivers a version of the work cited here while wearing a black mask—*doubling* rather than erasing the racial contours of anonymity and encryption. As a result, McGlotten's work extends the tactical qualities of Galloway's argument without minimizing the sovereign brutalities that prefigure acts of defacement. He describes "a world in which our identities and movements could become our own, opaque to the securitized gazes of states and corporations," but not eliminated by the abstract erasure of subjects and bodies.[62] His praxis is not a repetition of the same, but the representation of negativity in spite of the subjective indistinction made possible by digital technologies.

Parallel to this vein of thought, my interest in guerrilla organization and tactics does not lie with the precondition of faces. It relies on thinking through protocols for conflict via the structural particularities of collective self-making. If network theory's goal is to replace relations of enmity with a political relation of another kind, perhaps a revised ethical relation via Levinas, all that is evident here is that ontological expansiveness rises to the level of an imperative. "*The concept of resistance in politics should be superseded by hypertrophy*," Galloway and Thacker write, allowing subjects to embody abstract inhuman qualities in the effort to create political counterpower writ large.[63] While certainly not a *nomos* in Schmitt's sense, the network is positioned here as an ontological principle of restraint (like a natural law as opposed to a geopolitical one) that would disallow partisan conflict from manifesting as a productive valuation of the protocological.

Again, my concern, following these debates, lies with the interstitial qualities of the friend-enemy relation as it forms a collectivized subject in its particularity. It is a turn that endeavors to understand how "us/them," friend vs. enemy, becomes we. The antagonism produced by the exclusionary tendencies of autonomist Marxist discourse and network theory more generally demands such a turn. The claim here is not that networks are wrong, or that some other organizational form should hold a privileged place in and among contemporary technological production. Rather, the question becomes, why do we obscure the partisan roots that inform the political development of networks? What do we lose when we do so?

The Guerrilla in DH Praxis

What does this debate have to do with digital humanities? This is perhaps the question that looms largest thus far. DH's political ethos, clarified in its embrace of concepts like generativity, inclusivity, and collaboration, is realized in networked iterations of its tool-use, infrastructure, and organization. But critical strains of DH praxis have avoided reducing the political to the interplay of disembodied subjectivities and their ontologically expansive imperatives for political action. DH has left the door open to a line of political thought, militant in its articulation, that refocuses its attention on the intimacies of collective action as a precondition of its democratic will. DH's invocation of the guerrilla, contrary to its co-optation by network theory, therefore offers insight into its own disciplinary formation, and further, the degree to which such academic debates sustain each other as institutional power transforms.

What I have identified so far is a complex play between two differing political tendencies. With network theory, we see the desire to eliminate partisan conflict with the intent to control the flow of resistance to our most coercive institutions. With the guerrilla, we see a claim to the necessity of conflict when political subjects emerge from a position of exclusion to a dominant institution, regime, or discourse—both share and claim democratic roots. The point here is not to ponder over the swarm's ability to exist as an enemy, or that of eliminating guerrilla organization and tactics from political discourse in favor of theorizing ideal ethico-political circumstances. It is rather to show how the guerrilla reemerges in DH praxis as a figure that mobilizes inhumanity toward a tactical confrontation with the institutions of its oppression.

Before I can address the host of political figures inherent to DH praxis as they compare to the guerrilla (makers, digital avant-gardes, and so on), I need to clarify the methodological import of the work analyzed above for DH. How political subjects are formed and organized directly relates to the politics of disciplinary formation and power. This is what tracing the guerrilla's connection to Schmitt's political and its subsequent reinvention by biopolitical iterations of democratic discourse allows. Where Schmitt is concerned with preserving the status of the sovereign state, network theorists conceptualize resistance as a demand for bodies without borders and figures without content, theorizing the guerrilla out of existence while also co-opting its generative power. Theoretically and politically, critical iterations of DH have embraced the guerrilla for what it signifies (the oppositional, the maroon, the fugitive, indebted to the legacies of queer theory and critical race studies), but also for its tactical innovations. The democratic potential of theorizing the guerrilla concept within DH praxis is thus not a question of war or militarism, as it exists in relation to statist institutions of power. It rather relies on theorizing protocols for conflict within and against institutions that reproduce structural brutalities. It is, in the lineage of intellectual militancy above, to delimit and (re)invent the subject of political action from particular positions of need.

The guerrilla represents a micropolitical discourse in DH. It prioritizes alterity and modes of intellectual inquiry that demand context-specific tactics for political engagement. This is precisely what the architects of #transformDH appear to refer to when they invoke guerrilla organization and tactics and further articulate their project as a desire for collectivity. It is what underlies various calls for the production of a guerrilla DH that favor anonymity, cryptography, and digital anarchy. The micropolitical focus in DH, by virtue of its guerrilla roots, signals an activist methodological approach to intellectual inquiry that spans the divide between theory and practice. This approach is small-scale and always subject to a position of relative instability.

Let's reconsider Natalia Cecire's brilliant comments from "In Defense of Transforming DH" here. To position the guerrilla as a heuristic for DH praxis is to draw "not only on the sometimes aggressive affects of the much-deprecated Theory but also the activist dimensions of the little-t theories (gender, queer, critical race, disability) that have emerged from it, and which have been associated with personal and professional risk and often literal bodily harm." Cecire continues:

> It's true: this is not a language that comports very well with the dom-inant rhetorics of digital humanities, which emphasize openness, collaboration, and inclusiveness—which are, in short, liberal. But as I understand it, that's really the point of #transformDH. A liberal, inclusive, always-collaborative, never-oppositional digital humanities is a digital humanities that can afford to be above the fray, a digital humanities for which theory is, well, theoretical, mere yack, and not a tool for activism or indeed survival.[64]

In contrast to the assumed democratic guarantee of network power, Cecire's description of #transformDH points to a concrete method of political non-neutrality. It is a mode of radical incivility, framed as disciplinary definition. It functions on at least two planes.

First, think back to Chantal Mouffe's *Agonistics*. Characterized by the figure of the adversary, "the opponent with whom one shares a common allegiance to the democratic principles of 'liberty and equality for all' while disagreeing about their interpretation," Mouffe describes a process in which internal disagreement is channeled toward democratic horizons.[65] Agonism is the democratic production of solidarity through difference, absent the elimination of contest. Cecire's adversarial stance performs a similar political function—she preserves a kind of militant incivility in the effort to forefront theoretical tools for activism—diversifying DH praxis as political needs are met. She does not eliminate democratic thinking from DH work; it is rather the opposite. Her stance forwards a democratic ethos as it stems from legacies of exclusion that simultaneously produce liberatory horizons for their subjects of practice. Second, she invokes the guerrilla in order to signify a protocol for conflict that radically upsets the institutions of its exclusion as it also points to an alternative figuration of the political. This is precisely where democratic desire and political antagonism meet in DH's invocation of the figure. Where Cecire identifies activism, survival, and risk as political principles for DH work, she points to a radical ethos for which the guerrilla's antagonism holds generative utility. It stands in for total opposition to material inequality. This position is only supported by DH invocations of guerrilla organization and tactics that call for extralegal intervention or provoke friend-enemy logics.

The most pressing question of this chapter—how the guerrilla's invocation contours DH's methodological transformation—can now be addressed on a larger scale. Consider Galloway's description of DH method in a conversation with David M. Berry titled "A Network Is a Network Is a Network: Reflections on the Computational and the Societies of Control":

> Digital humanities faces a number of challenges. First and foremost it has defined itself as a community of tool users favouring empirical and positivistic methods. This has the dual advantage of both bringing more scholars into the fold and endowing them with powerful new technologies. But at the same time it exacerbates what we might call the Zuhandenheit problem [ready-to-hand]: tools get used unconsciously and without critical reflection. With this waning in critical reflection, and as the digital humanities expands, the ideological infrastructure will become more emboldened.[66]

Galloway's claim is certainly an overly generalized reflection on DH praxis; it does not accurately describe the values of DH's most critical work. In fact, it speaks to a methodological condition that much critical DH work subverts. Take Chun, Grusin, Jagoda, and Raley's work cited in this chapter's introduction as a preemptive response. If network power operates in its sovereign iterations across a multitude of its own institutions, the "dark side" of DH addresses political tendencies that the guerrilla's invocation is meant to confront. If, as they argue, "the same neoliberal logic that informs the ongoing destruction of the mainstream humanities has encouraged foundations, corporations, and university administrations to devote new resources to the digital humanities," they pose a question vital to DH's continued critical praxis: what conflicts exist "between DH as a strict tool-and-interface-based practice and the institutional logics of the new neoliberal networked universities"?[67]

Look to Rosi Braidotti's iteration of this question. In her argument, DH's role in university reformation functions as a supra-disciplinary power. In its critical valences, it is a "nomadic shift" toward a radical mode of inquiry, agile and mobile in the face of disciplinary territorialization:

> What are the codes and modes of re/territorialization of these new, supra-disciplinary fields of knowledge? How do they escape from epistemic accelerationism? To take the two pillars of the posthumanities—the environmental and the digital humanities— what meta-patterns of institutional development can we detect in their recent exponential growth? What can make them nomadic and "critical"?[68]

When Braidotti names DH as a pillar of the post-humanities, she is looking to politicized forms of DH praxis that refuse their stalwart institutional function, "the majoritarian meta-pattern" that would literally accelerate and subsume "the becoming-minoritarian of knowing subjects and knowledge practices" into a monolithic whole.[69] This is embodied in postcolonial DH methods "that re-think transnational spaces and contexts," but also in decolonial DH work in which "the critique of western imperialism and racism provides an added critical distance—an extra layer of dis-identification—that positions these posthuman critical thinkers closer to the dispossessed and the disempowered, adding that many of those are neither human nor necessarily anthropomorphic."[70]

How does DH refuse the will to territorialize and subsume its minoritarian interventions, to divide and distribute radical difference under the institutional logics of new neoliberal networked universities? Indulging the guerrilla's significatory performs something useful. It responds to this question by posing an alternative immanent position to its networked counterparts—a position from which to contextualize disciplinary power and its concomitant nomadic shifts. It demands tactical protocols for political relationality, adaptivity, and organization that do not command a predetermined end. To deploy guerrilla organization and tactics as a politically motivated theoretical tool is to draw out the productive collective potential that emerges from its agonistic and antagonistic tendencies.

The question of network theory's role in the production of a materially specific, conflict-driven political ontology is therefore perhaps less important and less interesting at this juncture. Indeed, in his interview with Berry, Galloway's frame of reference and interest in network power is substantively different, even if it reproduces similar problems. Ethical forms of network power like those theorized in *The Exploit* and the *Empire* trilogy may contravene Galloway's indictment of DH as a positivistic method, but they are conceptually aligned with universalizing tendencies in critical theory that exclude material facts in which their political import would confront subjective obstacles or actually existing structural inequality.

The contrast that I draw between figures like the multitude and the guerrilla, or the network and guerrilla organization, approaches DH's critical praxis from an alternative point of entry. *Guerrilla Theory* inverts the supposed priority of digital tools over critical reflection in DH praxis. It does so by refusing to remove the guerrilla's significatory power from the political constitution of networked organization. It is a study of the political logics at work in our present disciplinary practices, collectively made and collectively contested, as new protocols of conflict are grasped at. It applies the critical turn that is formative of its politics via three future-oriented interests: (1) identifying productive agonisms that are internal to the order and operation of DH praxis; (2) forefronting disciplinary antagonisms that are formative of a meta-political perspective on DH praxis; and (3) positioning DH within a constellation of intellectual work that refuses to exclude the material realities of radical difference from their conceptual lineage.

The need for this approach is embedded in the internal conflicts formative of DH praxis, and those that it compounds as it expands. Now apparent, my disciplinary focus is not one of congruity and agreement; it is rather an attempt to articulate a political concept through which DH's infrastructure might be maximized and its digital focused broadened. My approach is predicated on an active and collective relation to our present disciplinary circumstances as it also draws out the contestatory dynamic that shapes disciplinary power, disciplinary formation, and ultimately what "counts" as DH theory and practice. To conclude this chapter, I perform a reading of this dynamic as it pertains to recent methodological evolutions in DH praxis, ultimately enacting a type of militant work that opens this chapter.

Internalities

In July 2015 in her keynote address at the Keystone Digital Humanities Conference at the University of Pennsylvania, "What's Next: The Radical, Unrealized Potential of Digital Humanities," Miriam Posner captured a critical attitude that speaks to DH's continued disciplinary transformation. She describes DH's internal order as something malleable and heterogeneous, open to criticisms that would defy an undivided summary of its method:

> Digital humanists have heard numerous recent calls for the field to interrogate race, gender, and other structures of power . . . To truly engage in this kind of critical work, I contend, would be much more difficult and fascinating than anything we have previously imagined for the future of DH; in fact, it would require dismantling and rebuilding much of the organizing logic that underlies our work.[71]

The demand to centralize difference and rethink DH's disciplinary power is a constant process, but it is safe to say that the political undercurrent that is formative of so many diverse approaches to DH, #guerrillaDH included, has boiled over. Both the practical and theoretical concerns forwarded by politicized DH work are at the forefront of the discourse. Rather than erase the discipline's need for inclusivity, feminist, post-, and decolonial approaches to DH have produced much-needed spaces of contest in DH praxis, directing our attention to its infrastructural dimensions. Dismantling the hierarchical formations that are common to academic labor, as well as the inequities they are founded on, are primary organizational issues in these interventions. Posner concluded her talk with a statement on inclusion and collaboration, imploring those in attendance to understand that

> it's incumbent upon all of us (but particularly those of us who have platforms) to push for the inclusion of underrepresented communi-

ties in digital humanities work, because it will make all of our work stronger and sounder. We can't allow digital humanities to recapitulate the inequities and underrepresentations that plague Silicon Valley; or the systematic injustice, in our country and abroad, that silences voices and lives.[72]

DH, as it were, would model the future that the university, and indeed institutions of all kinds, should strive for. By distinguishing itself from other disciplines and corporations, DH's call for inclusion will serve as a model, differential and pluralistic, but nonetheless aligned by its distinguished status.

As if in response, Adeline Koh, Sara B. Pritchard, and Michelle Moravec created a viral hashtag in August 2015, inspired by #ILookLikeAnEngineer: #ILookLikeAProfessor. The hashtag was created to address both implicit and explicit bias in the academy by allowing academics to collectively share selfies that deviate from the white male, tweed-wearing, bearded professor archetype. Koh, Pritchard, and Moravec later wrote a manifesto that appeared on *Inside Higher Ed*, "We Look Like Professors, Too," offering an immanent critique of the professorial stereotype: "we look like professors because we are professors."[73] What they point to is thus the very inequities that Posner identifies with a more focused point of criticism: the university itself.

Placing these arguments in dialogue with each other offers an example of politicized DH work that intervenes *within* our institutional milieu, intuitively contesting the context and play of DH's supra-disciplinary power. Posner's address forwards an inclusionary exuberance that is holistically framed. The rhetorical gesture here is clearly both an invitation and a moral claim. We need diversity. We need it because it signifies a certain state of health. It keeps the discipline in good condition, free from the tech sector's problems with underrepresentation that lead to substandard working conditions. With more diversity, DH forms a more perfect union as it charts new disciplinary paths and new pedagogical visions. Indeed, the nationalized rhetoric I rely on to describe Posner's political claim is embedded within it. In no uncertain terms, Posner calls on DH scholar-practitioners to establish justice as a foundational methodological principle, contrasting it with systemic injustices perpetrated by governments across the globe. By envisioning an inclusive politics for DH, Posner positions the discipline as a type of networked model for both intellectual labor *and* governance, well beyond the scope of research or teaching.

Although it extends beyond disciplinary concerns for DH in particular, Koh, Pritchard, and Moravec's intervention addresses concerns like Posner's from the underside. It is characterized by public dialogue over the identities that inform academic titles, ideally resulting in a more diverse vision of "the professor," but it also manifests an adversarial condition inherent to processes of inclusion in our contemporary institutional milieu. Their social media campaign proclaims: #ILookLikeAProfessor! I am a professor, too. I am already within the hospices of the institutional structure but am not counted as a peer "who *also* deserve[s] respect."[74] Fundamentally, Koh, Pritchard, and Moravec's viral hashtag points to an underlying tension between institution and discipline. If the inequities of our institutional milieu prefigure our approach to DH, a political vision like Posner's is doomed to failure. Bodily diversity and institutional bodies stand radically opposed.

Where DH is an exemplar in this discourse, the discussion of the subject and body of diversity as it is motivated by imperatives for inclusivity functions on two planes. On the one hand, Posner's argument invokes a discussion of the discipline's relation to its institutional body via the holistic effects of inclusivity. On the other hand, Koh, Pritchard, and Moravec motivate a discussion of marginalized subjects via an identitarian model that are invoked as necessary components of stronger and sounder work, but not afforded the kinds of institutional privileges of their title, rank, and responsibilities. Diversity might contribute to the health of an institutional body, but does the institution respect the diversity it requires? Does the institution deserve the health that it claims to need diversity for?[75] This is stated more forcefully by Moya Bailey, Anne Cong-Huyen, Alexia Lothian, and Amanda Phillips: "Are our institutions embracing [women, people of color, queer and trans scholars, activist scholars], or are they consuming [them] in the name of diversity?"[76]

This is perhaps one way in which the democratic problem inherent to the discipline mirrors that of states or governments. To the disciplinary point, this debate is representative of a democratic problem that is also central to DH's exponential growth and its protocols for addressing conflict: who's in and who's out? I do not broach this question in its typical iterations here—I am not interested in rehashing arguments over whether or not one should know how to code, fabricate, or build a large-scale platform. What juxtaposing Posner's work to Koh, Pritchard, and Moravec underscores is that fact that when inclusivity is broached, exclusivity inevitably *precedes* and *exceeds* the gesture. Knowledge production remains a primary concern as inclusionary and exclusionary logics duel, but it is not one wholly fixated on digital tools. It also pertains to cultural diversity, to subjects of knowledge production, and how variegated approaches to DH further the discipline without demanding that it form a unified whole. Jessica M. Johnson frames the tension evident between the approaches above in her interview with the *Los Angeles Review of Books* as follows:

> I think there needs to be a conversation about equity within the academy, not just about digital things, but about how folks who are people of color or queer people of color are organizing and creating knowledge in the 21st century, and how the academy can support them in that regard. I think it means changing the way we teach, the kinds of things we put on our syllabi; I think it means appreciating things that are not considered digital tools as digital tools, like social

media as a literacy, as also scholarly production, protecting and com-
pensating intellectual work before it migrates from Tumblr and into
our classrooms. I think it means making the university accountable
for making sure that people have access to digital tools.[77]

This is perhaps what Posner refers to when she claims that diversity will make
DH work stronger and sounder. At the same time, perhaps part of managing
a platform has nothing to do with digital tools as we currently conceive of
them. Johnson's move to expand DH's scope beyond the rigidity of its current
tool-use is therefore as much of a threat to DH's current disciplinary order as
it is a potential path toward novel forms of inclusion and collaboration. It is
proof of a radical democratic problem that is part and parcel of the difference
between who's in and who's out.

For the purposes of my work here, I use these examples in order to describe
agonistic tendencies *within* DH. The political internalities of the discipline,
although not fully contrasted, are evidence of an adversarial logic that motivates and preserves DH's democratic potential. Agonism exists simultaneously
at the level of tools, platforms, centers, labs, departments, schools, and the
university itself. The very same issues are approached through a differential
articulation of politics, predicated on material inequality as it pertains to the
subjects who inhabit the discipline. They are not resolved by mere agreement
over the need for diversity or over the needs of those who bear the burden of
making intellectual labor stronger and sounder.

Inversely, the interventions above showcase a movement from us/them to
the production of a "we," albeit from different sides of institutional and disciplinary power. The "we" that is invoked is both a collective iteration of DH
and a collective iteration of the university, but one that is also contested. It,
implicitly so, names a *potential* enemy through affirmative acts of self-making
and self-representation. The agonistic tendencies that inform the discourse
become united in opposition through an antagonistic play of political forces.
Who's in and who's out thus shifts to a different political register. How might
multiple axes of difference produce a collective concept of our institutional
positions and privileges without homogenizing difference?

An agonistic model extends the institutional problems I pursue in the
course of this chapter. How might conflict become participatory for DH in
a manner that maintains the difference that informs it? Radical difference in
DH requires multiple and overlapping solidarities in the face of institutional
power, on the one side, and disciplinary difference on the other. What the
agonistic model points to in the short term is therefore a means of formalizing
politics of difference as a tactical DH method. It points to the need for a political order that maintains participation across overlapping solidarities that
also preserves radical difference at an infrastructural level. As I will make clear
below, the agonistic approach I rely on to parse the movement from us/them

to "we" relies on producing sites of participatory conflict without eliminating the formative political qualities that ground its logic.

Externalities

In the introduction to her book *Technologies of the Gendered Body* (1996), Anne Balsamo writes that the body

> is a social, cultural, and historical production: "production" here means both product and process. As a *product*, it is the material embodiment of ethnic, racial, and gender identities, as well as staged performances of personal identity, of beauty, of health (among other things). As process, it is a way of knowing and marking the world, as well as a way of knowing and marking a "self."[78]

Gender, but I would include race following this definition of the body as well, is "*both* a determining cultural condition and a social consequence of technological deployment."[79] I cite Balsamo's work here for its affinity with arguments like Koh, Pritchard, and Moravec's above, but also because its function parallels DH's disciplinary discourse from an external view—parallel for its focus on technological facets of humanistic inquiry, but external since it doesn't prioritize digital tool use in its method or production. Balsamo prioritizes a hermeneutic that is more closely focused on the discursive formation of the self. She is interested in understanding technology's effects on the body and subjectivity, rather than applying a digital tool to the body or subject as a means of inquiry. She analyzes subjects who already perform this activity.

Apart from DH method, Balsamo's hermeneutic is perhaps more closely aligned with Marx's argument in the *Grundrisse*, often cited by Michael Hardt, that "production thus not only creates an object for the subject, but also a subject for the object."[80] Where Hardt cites this claim for its biopolitical contours—for precisely how the production of subjectivity is defined by its sociopolitical relations—Balsamo's focus on production bears out the connection between bodies and their function as objects of knowledge. However, the two approaches go hand in hand. What techno-political forms of life produce the body as an object of knowledge? How does the technological production of body inform the subjectivities that it bears out?

Galloway's indictment of DH looms large here. Do we make work external to DH's disciplinary development subject to the tools we use in response, or are other possibilities available to us? If DH functions as an empirically focused, tool-based practice that enforces positivistic methods, then the processual work that Balsamo advocates for, as well as Hardt's focus on production, is antagonistic to DH praxis. If DH demands tool use over discursive analysis, antagonism emerges as well. The terms of its invitation into DH praxis take priority over its inclusion. However, preliminary responses to DH's positivism are clearly located in Johnson's argument above; it can be traced even further to what James Smithies names as a virtue of Balsamo's work by producing a post-foundational DH in his article "Digital Humanities, Postfoundationalism, and Postindustrial Culture"; and it can be easily identified when Fiona Barnett asks, "What would it mean to reorient our origin story away from one with a set of specific, often-cited scholars and conferences and toward a set of projects that mobilizes the conflicting possibilities of hardware and software, bioware and biology, proceduralism and possibility?"[81] To repeat, the *critical* contours of DH praxis do not often resemble Galloway's vision of the discipline. Yet, the performance of Balsamo's hermeneutic as DH method renders the antagonisms of its adoption productive of new alliances with our tools *and* overlapping solidarities with technologically oriented work outside of DH praxis. It motivates a disciplinary transformation that prioritizes mutual risk while it simultaneously reconfigures the praxis upon which the discipline is established. It does so in opposition to a positivistic frame.

Balsamo's work takes priority here not simply as an example of disciplinary formation, however. Her work reminds us of the processual qualities inherent to our practices of self-making, which are explored in earnest throughout this book. Where I spend much of this book focused on subjects of making in guerrilla discourse, Balsamo's focus on the gendered body directly pertains to the role of the maker and the made as a question of infrastructure, echoing the work explored above.[82] Balsamo describes her project as one where she "starts with the assumption that gender functions as an organized system of differentiation that grounds relations of power and knowledge," but one that also focuses its "attention on the ways in which the meaningfulness of gender identity is *reproduced* in the application of new technologies."[83] Gender grounds the articulation of power and knowledge within the institutions in which it operates. Its ontological dimensions are concurrently reproduced via new technologies. Production creates an object for the subject, but also a subject for the object. This is in part how gender frames our most intimate modes of recognition, but also how it becomes reproduced via digital tools.

Positioning work like Balsamo's to intervene in the conceptual formation of DH praxis is a transformative act. It is generative of alternative frameworks with which to guide DH praxis in the present. It also motivates a future-oriented task. The task for the present refers to DH's response to gender and subjectivity's co-articulation in politically focused theoretical works that also operates within a digital register. The second refers to the meaningfulness of gender identity as it is *reproduced* in the application of new technologies that are also invited in to DH praxis. How the two cohere is a question of their processes of exchange. How the two are preserved is a question of DH's institutional position. As a matter of fact, where subjectivity and the body are at stake, small-scale technological application has large-scale implications. The question of infrastructure in this discourse is therefore a minimal occupation with macropolitical influence.

Steampunk's alignment with DH praxis is perhaps the clearest extension of Balsamo's focus in the discipline, pointing toward a broad range of inhuman potential. Roger Whitson, for one, approaches the politics of subjectivity and bodily formation through what he terms nineteenth-century DH, theorizing the steampunk aesthetic as a mode of becoming that is out of step with contemporary socioeconomic forces. The political vision that Whitson ascribes to these technophilic subjectivities is simultaneously queer and committed to a kind of inclusive liberalism: "steampunk contests the technological orchestrations of community and challenges the digital humanities to imagine alternative, perhaps queer, forms of association."[84] Following figures like Henry Jenkins, Joshua Green, and Sam Ford, Whitson is concerned with a democratic ethos of participation, valorizing the fact that "queer and transgender steampunk performers have their own platform on social media sites," and therefore their own heterotopic communities.[85] More than this, Whitson is concerned with the anachronistic adoption of various technological apparatuses in order to curate both individual and cultural identity in steampunk communities. The most conspicuous omission from this work, however, is an answer to precisely how the anachronistic adoption of various technologies creates temporalities of technological practice that also resist the grip of capitalist exploitation across steampunk's spectrum of subjective concerns.

Despite this vacancy, Whitson's work is important because it represents a community of DH scholar-practitioners who purposefully open the door to a much broader discussion of the subject and the body in and beyond DH praxis. Similar to Braidotti, we might follow Lori Emerson and call the gambit of work cited here a crucial convergence of DH with the post-humanities.[86] It might also be described as the convergence of tactical infrastructures, articulated by David M. Berry as a process concerning "how infrastructures become institutions, and more particularly how tactical infrastructures can be positioned to change or replace institutions."[87]

The Laboria Cuboniks collective's manifesto, *Xenofeminism: A Politics of Alienation*, is an apposite correlate to Balsamo's work on this register outside of a DH context, extending the inhuman potential of the steampunk ethos. How the collective moves from micro to macro in a method for large-scale impact is a question of gender's function as an organized system of differentiation within an accelerationist ideology. Perhaps this is not a position that Balsamo herself would espouse, but the collective nonetheless demands the technological transformation of gender and the body with attention to reconfiguring its rational structure. Gender, here, is also a question of its meaningfulness, specifically in its ability to seize technologies of production that are coextensive with our most intimate modes of production. Helen Hester, a member of the Laboria Cuboniks collective, describes the import of this argument as a form of "*social reproduction against the reproduction of the social as it stands.*[88] I cite the third paragraph of the collective's manifesto here in full:

> The real emancipatory potential of technology remains unrealized. Fed by the market, its rapid growth is offset by bloat, and elegant innovation is surrendered to the buyer, whose stagnant world it decorates. Beyond the noisy clutter of commodified cruft, the ultimate task lies in engineering technologies to combat unequal access to reproductive and pharmacological tools, environmental cataclysm, economic instability, as well as dangerous forms of unpaid/underpaid labour. Gender inequality still characterizes the fields in which our technologies are conceived, built, and legislated for, while female workers in electronics (to name just one industry) perform some of the worst paid, monotonous and debilitating labour. Such injustice demands structural, machinic and ideological correction.[89]

Laboria Cuboniks proposes something much more than tinkering with the symbolic order of computing in this paragraph. This, much like the rest of the collective's manifesto, calls for transforming technocracy via its infrastructural formation at both ideological and intimate levels.[90]

First, xenofeminism is a mode of collective self-making that attempts to de-link subject/object formation from real subsumption. The task reads something like, how do we adequately address the structural inequalities of our contemporary condition without reproducing capital's incursion into the realm of subjectivity? How do we become subjects of making within our contemporary socioeconomic milieu without replicating the conditions of our disenfranchisement? This is a variation on what Steven Shaviro understands to be at the heart of accelerationist ideology, "Audre Lorde famously argued that 'the master's tools will never dismantle the master's house.' But what if the master's tools are the only ones available?"[91] Xenofeminism infiltrates the organization and flow of capitalist forms of life in order to radically redefine the power/knowledge regime in its favor.

The collective's second important feature follows from the first. Xenofeminism is a mode of collective self-making that attempts to produce a liberatory infrastructural model that coheres with the techno-political flow of contemporary life. It is again to follow Shaviro, but also to recall Balsamo's work, a means of engaging "in *alliances* with our tools, as Bruno Latour would say, rather than seeing them as flawless instruments or prosthetic extensions of our will."[92] Laboria Cuboniks is explicit on this issue:

> Today, it is imperative that we develop an ideological infrastructure that both supports and facilitates feminist interventions within connective, networked elements of the contemporary world . . . We want to cultivate the exercise of positive freedom—freedom-to rather than

simply freedom-from—and urge feminists to equip themselves with the skills to redeploy existing technologies and invent novel cognitive and material tools in the service of common ends.[93]

Xenofeminism's political is thus one of generative contradiction, elsewhere defined as a form of "xeno-hospitality."[94] It encourages the simultaneous production and reconfiguration of digital tools as capital affords while also declaring such acts to be revolutionary. It is a tactical incursion, asymmetric and profuse. It infiltrates and replicates itself within the institutional bodies that also motivate capital.

Xenofeminism's scope and application are antagonistic to DH in several ways. Most prominently, the scope of its political work is far broader that many DH scholars would claim of the discipline. Adopting it would necessarily compel DH to bear at least some of the burden of transforming technocracy. Furthermore, while its focus on infrastructure and gender is quintessentially cyborg, it also places transformative demands on the maker that are expressly political, underscoring a position of non-neutrality in its ideology. Any act of making, especially those that are critically inflected, must forward a political position in and at multiple sites of contest, including that of the body. It dialogues well with other processual iterations of DH praxis, and demands that one consider what about DH might be transformed as it is invited in. Indeed, what one makes of these kinds of antagonisms is not simply a question for xenofeminism, it is a question of disciplinary constitution where the maker is considered equal to, or even in priority to, what is made.

The formation of a "we" at this intersection is thus predicated on the technological reformation of the body and subject, but it also underscores the antagonism between DH as it is currently practiced with what DH could potentially become if its performance were shifted. It recalls debates for diversity and inclusion, but only as it is predicated on the agonistic play of disciplinary power. It is nomadic, but it does not sacrifice subjectivity to an abstract ontological expanse. The process of inviting these histories of collective self-making into DH praxis therefore rests at a partisan divide. It demands a level of criticality that is equally focused on its own disciplinary articulation as well as the institutions that house it. It also demands an articulation of theory and practice that is not wholly defined by making and using digital tools. What all three bodies of work cited in this section remind us is that any consideration of institutional bodies and bodily difference is macro and micro, abstract and intimate. Manifesting any collective that would follow rests at the intersection of both.

Guerrilla Theory as Provocation

This chapter is an overview of the concepts and politics that I explore in more concrete contexts throughout this book. The theoretical problems that this chapter elicits are undoubtedly controversial and difficult to engage. But again, the point here is to think politically, to develop a context from which one might make politics happen in a different way. Moving forward, I am committed to thinking the politics of difference at the intersection of techno-political experimentation and uncompromising political demands.

What *Guerrilla Theory* ultimately proposes is a tactical DH method that unearths agonistic and antagonistic political forces at many of our most popular sites of disciplinary formation. It does so to question the institutional and disciplinary power of DH praxis as it evolves. My primary task is to address both arenas of discourse: that of articulating partisan relations and technologized modes of subjective constitution in tandem. I do not reduce all political concepts to the friend-enemy relation here, nor do I conflate guerrilla organization and tactics with its logic. I do insist on tracking their contemporary development and play.

My approach is predicated on an active and collective relation to our present disciplinary circumstances as it also draws out the contestatory dynamic that shapes disciplinary power, disciplinary formation, and ultimately what "counts" as DH theory and practice. It results in a political demand that prioritizes the very same mode of hospitality evident in DH's invocation of guerrilla organization and tactics as it also favors agonistic political principles with which to influence our present disciplinary relations. The two logics are coextensive, directing dueling political forces that are endemic to disciplinary formation toward radical democratic ends.

A note from Adrienne Shaw's queer approach to game studies in "The Trouble with Communities" is an apt place to conclude: "Communities are not simply about finding commonalities that eclipse difference," she writes, "they are about finding camaraderie despite difference."[95] Shaw continues, "The trouble with communities is not that they are not inclusive; no community can be all things to all people. The trouble with communities is that too often we speak as though the goal is to create one great community rather than providing a space for multiple communities to exist."[96] Although Shaw has a different techno-aesthetic milieu in mind, this note is particularly helpful where DH continues to forward its critical ethos. If the guerrilla operates as a theoretical tool, manifesting absolute opposition to sovereign powers, its political transformation is to enact collective work through disciplinary configurations that do not subsume difference. Its contradictions propel and challenge this demand. This is its collective potential; it is the liberatory possibility that the guerrilla evokes.

Chapter 2

The Maker and the Made

Articulating a need for a feminist corrective in the digital humanities has come at a much slower pace, perhaps because the instrumentalism of a "tool" seems much less blatantly anti-feminist than the instrumentalism of a gun.
> —Elizabeth Losh, "What Can the Digital Humanities Learn from Feminist Game Studies?"

Making lies far beyond thoughtless production and supporting the vision of those who manage.
> —Daniel Charny, "Power of Making"

"Theory," Chela Sandoval writes, is "capable of enabling the development of a common community of understanding that can, in its collective will, further politically oppositional goals."[1] Sandoval's argument is predicated on three observations that identify ideological conflict as both obstacle and an opportunity for theory to realize its collective will. First, she argues, "critical and cultural studies in the U.S. academy, and the theoretical literature on oppositional forms of consciousness, difference, identity, and power, have been developed as divided and racialized, genderized, and sexualized theoretical domains."[2] Disciplinary division operates as a territorial enterprise in this argument. Demarcating knowledge and limiting its institutional boundaries via a narrow spectrum of disciplinary enclosures masks methodological affinity-making. It obstructs the formation of common political goals beyond the divisions that disciplinary power imposes. Second, "insofar as academic disciplines generate divisions in this way," Sandoval writes, "they continually reproduce an apartheid of theoretical domains."[3] What Sandoval negates in this claim must be made clear. She takes aim at the territorial division of knowledge and its rigid disciplinary organization, arguing that it instrumentalizes theory in its will to police. Oppositional forms of consciousness are needed for theory to realize its collective potential from a plurality of political positions. And third, Sandoval concludes her dialectic by making the political stakes of her argument clear:

> Social actors committed to egalitarian social relations, who are seeking the basis for a shared vision, an oppositional and coalitional politics, and who seek new inner and social technologies that will ensure that resistant activity not simply replicate the political formations that are linked to transnational cultural expansion, must self-consciously recognize, develop, and harness a dissident globalization, a methodology of the oppressed, which is composed of technologies that make possible differential social movement.[4]

Conflict is retained in the production of oppositional coalitional politics because differential social movement refuses totalitarian logics. Sandoval's dialectic does not reveal a fundamental unity as theory furthers politically oppositional goals. It preserves difference as common responses to oppression are articulated. When theory is collectivized, difference inheres in the technologies that make differential social movement possible. The production of subjectivity concomitantly exceeds its reduction to indurate disciplinary control as new inner and social technologies are pursued. To further politically oppositional goals is to preserve a concept of differential articulation that undergirds dissident globalization.

I open by articulating the dialectic that underlies Sandoval's *Methodology of the Oppressed* (2000) so as to make three observations of my own. The first clarifies oppositional logics for which the guerrilla stands in, operating as a metaphor for collective acts of dissent. The guerrilla's protocols for conflict favor modes of collective self-making that produce new modes of relationality, new modes of knowing, and new modes of being. Its tactical allegiances situate alterity as both an antecedent to political opposition and an opportunity to reconfigure the terrain of its action. Agonistics—the contested status of political opposition that is internal to cultures of resistance—define the guerrilla's status as a politically motivated theoretical tool. Antagonism—the division between friend and enemy that motivates absolute conflict between groups—is the origin of guerrilla organization and tactics, but not its final goal. Collectivity—a political ontology in which the individual is never identical to itself—is a feature of the guerrilla's organization and tactics that points toward liberatory horizons. How the guerrilla mobilizes each feature of its being is a question of its context, application, and modes of production. Each component part can be explained by the interplay of who makes collective acts of dissent possible, and what those acts of dissent look like.

My second observation homes in on DH's methodological priorities, particularly its focus on making and tool use. "Humanities disciplines and methods themselves," Bethany Nowviskie reminds us at the conclusion of her essay "On the Origin of 'Hack' and 'Yack,'" "are not either/or affairs.

The humanities is both/and."[5] The dialectical feature of Nowviskie's argument is also predicated on methodological difference—how making might coexist with theoretical work in the humanities—and points to a collective problem that extends beyond our institutional goals. Think of Matt Ratto and Stephen Hockema's "FLWR PWR: Tending the Walled Garden" here. The divide between the individual and collective extends to the conceptual tools that present-day critical maker cultures deploy in the formation of their method: "critical making is an elision of two typically disconnected modes of engagement in the world—'critical thinking,' often considered as abstract, explicit, linguistically based, internal and cognitively individualistic; and 'making,' typically understood as material, tacit, embodied, external and community-oriented."[6] The elision that Ratto and Hockema identify might be restated philosophically. Critical making allegedly moves from a statement like "I think therefore I am" to another possible variant: "we make therefore we become." The link between the individual and the collective is, as always, a tenuous one. It demands a response to more politicized questions. If making is a catalyst for collectivity, what material constraints guide its modes of production? If the tool and its subject realize alternative political visions of the world, what is the extent of maker culture's disobedience?[7]

My third and final observation is located in the subjective character that critical making and tool-use presume. The both/and, community-oriented logic that delimits both humanistic inquiry and maker culture's incorporation into academic labor is not limited to the object of one's practice. It also refers to the production of subjectivity—the recursive arc between the maker and the made that "not only creates an object for the subject, but also a subject for the object."[8] This fact extends to DH's internal order, the latitude that scholar-practitioners have to hack instead of yack and vice versa, and the collective will that emerges from DH's demand that one must "be making" if one wants to participate in DH work. Who one must be and what one must do in order to realize the both/and, community-oriented logic that delimits the tool-object relation is equally historical as it is political. Political opposition, embodied in the production and use of technologies that make differential social movement possible, obviates the situation wherein the tool could be presented as an "alternative to activism."[9] It disallows the tool to appear as a neutral solution to sociopolitical problems or as a means of sidestepping predicates of oppression, that is, "gender, race, class, or imperialism."[10] Making's subjective character places theory on an equal footing with practice, and vice versa.

Against any false bisection of theory's collective will, overcoming the territorial division of knowledge presumes the production and use of new technologies. Critical making realizes politically oppositional goals if and when its conflicts preserve differential social movement. Theory and making are two sides of the same process. The critical work of this chapter is thus aimed at the production of subjectivity—the maker as something made—and the political lineages that draw its politics to a head. Tool and object are subordinated to these concerns. As a result, I take a step back in this chapter. I position the guerrilla as a heuristic for theorizing processes of self-making that are derived from practices of collective becoming. I focus exclusively on productive confrontations across lines of ideological conflict. What I propose in the pages that follow is not necessarily a #guerrillaDH in the sense of a maker culture, but a critical evaluation of DH's political undercurrents alongside a paleonymy of guerrilla organization and tactics focused on collectivized acts of making.

This chapter proceeds as follows. First, I trace a brief genealogy of maker ideologies that parallel critical DH praxis. I analyze the rhetorical contrast between individual and collective articulations of maker culture's production-based political ideology, limiting my focus to avowedly leftist iterations of its practice. This leads me to connect DH's adoption of maker culture with the European avant-garde traditions that undergird it. Second, I draw out maker-related acts that are endemic to avant-garde aesthetics. I argue that the subjects of these movements often failed to produce a partisan alternative to the bourgeois subject, revealing its reactionary undercurrents. Third, I position the Latin American Third Cinema movement as a political alternative to DH's reliance on European avant-garde concepts and figures. I unearth the guerrilla's demand to become something existentially different in this contrast, to enact a process of productive and intentional othering, so as to better understand the subject position that actualizes this demand. Finally, I argue that guerrilla organization and tactics meet significant limitations in the body they project onto the subjects of their practice. I ultimately return to Sandoval's method and clarify the collective organization of oppositional political goals.

The contrast between the European avant-garde and the Latin American guerrillas of the Third Cinema movement offers DH scholar-practitioners a glimpse of what collectivity from a guerrilla standpoint looks like. It is one that does not simply present a nuanced deviation from the norm, but a set of intentionally mediated acts that forward a collectivized and production-based aesthetico-political regime. My reading of avant-garde aesthetics is neither holistic nor deeply rooted. It is partisan and tactical, realizing a guerrilla ethos even as I combine guerrilla organization and tactics with avant-garde aesthetics in later chapters.

Making Disobedient Subjects

"Whether or not the *real* radical philosophers march or protest or run for office in addition to writing inscrutable tomes—this is a question we can, perhaps, leave aside," argues Ian Bogost. "Real radicals," he concludes, "*make things*."[11] Although Bogost offers a crucial challenge to humanistic scholarship and method by forwarding such a claim, his radicalism demands critique. Why are we concerned with naming so-called real radicals? What does this mode of identification give us? Bogost's suggestion cannot be that by making things one becomes a leftist thinker or radical political actor. Nor can the suggestion be that making things shapes one into a radical pedagogue. He is keen to cite Urustar's creation of playable pixel art (work that the Genoa-based brand consultancy modeled on Bogost's own books), Alexander Galloway's project to create a computerized version of Guy Debord's chess-variant, *Le Jeu de la guerre*, Fergus Henderson's culinary philosophy of nose-to-tail eating, and Hugh Crawford's direction of a class project reconstructing Henry David Thoreau's wooden hut featured in *Walden*—yet his examples valorize individual recognition over collective political will.[12] The men who hold the title of "real radicals" function as a kind of maker vanguard, a collection of individuals who should be emulated for their political acuity. Unequivocally, Bogost argues that making is a necessary condition for radical politics to actualize. The difference between making things and making politics happen, however, is decisive.

Let's recall Hardt's militancy of theory. Our "philosophical relation to the present is an active and collective relation, that is, not merely a matter of registering or even evaluating the present but acting on and transforming it. The task of theory is to make the present and thus to delimit or invent the subject of that making, a 'we' characterized not only by our belonging to the present but by our making it."[13] The political work that Hardt names is predicated on subjective transformation, on remaking our sociopolitical milieu into a collective iteration of our desires. Its method prioritizes acts of collective self-making driven by context and need. Making objects is subordinated to making a subject of revolutionary praxis that produces a parallel culture. The questions that follow from Hardt's militancy are perhaps related to Bogost's political will, but are characteristically different in their rhetorical effect. How do we make a radically democratic alternative to the present? How do we nurture its collective realization?

The contrast between Bogost's and Hardt's respective claims to radical politics draws a rhetorical divide between the one and the many, the who and the what, the means and method of political making. It bears out a mereological problem that foregrounds the ontological arguments of the previous chapter. The political bent that motivates these arguments—which subjective figures best embody potential alternatives to statist iterations of power, institutional oppression, and disciplinary force—is a tactical concern, but one that ultimately gives way to questions of process and becoming. Some of the best contemporary work in DH follows in this line of thought. The creation of #transformDH is one such example that demands political clarification of maker form and method writ large. #transformDH implies that action is at its core. The activist DHer transforms the discipline. But what the activist DHer makes, often by her very presence, upsets the institutional milieu in which she persists and from which she emerges. She does so by making her presence known, making inclusive archives, visualizing inequality, rewriting the grammar and syntax of our digital languages, and more. In doing so, the activist DHer realizes the political ontology of the culture, serving as a constant reminder of what is at stake.

Rachel Rose Ulgado and Sarah Fox draw this point out in a position paper titled "Critical Design in Feminist Hackerspaces." These spaces are, as they note, like other hackerspaces in terms of the technology they contain, but they are also "cognizant of cultural norms that they feel are most detrimental to diversity and are committed to creating environments that limit barriers to entry."[14] Feminist hackerspaces are inclusive spaces, but also antagonistic spaces: "They were established in reaction to traditional hackerspaces and designed to provide opportunities for traditionally marginalized people to be empowered and supported in high-tech contexts."[15] The feminist hacker is therefore a kind of maker. She makes space, she makes things, and she makes things in opposition to myriad forms of exclusion perpetrated by the confluence of patriarchal and institutional power. The feminist hacker is oppositional and embodies the contradiction that is endemic to the space she makes.

Michael Dieter and Geert Lovink follow another critical approach in their coauthored manifesto, "Theses on Making in the Digital Age." There, Dieter and Lovink draw a distinction between the maker-as-individual and the maker as a pluralistic anticapitalist force of production. On an individual level, Dieter and Lovink argue, "it is no exaggeration to claim that the maker-as-individual is a key figure of today's neoliberal ontotheology."[16] On a collective level, the maker is "situated within the project-led and precarious economy," likened to Anonymous, and claims to "emerge at a time when the theoretical project of '68 transitions from the work of negation ('unmaking') to embrace a vitalist position."[17] Dieter and Lovink's maker is one who manifests new media (sometimes from old, dead, or zombie media) but one who, following Galloway, "governs a set of possible behaviors within a heterogenous system."[18] As such, Dieter and Lovink's maker is a multitudinous governing power, a figure of production that develops a maker ethos based on the "positive contribution of the many."[19] The maker's task is to produce protocols that inhibit real subsumption at the level of subjectivity, both individual and collective.

Chris Csikszentmihalyi follows this set of concerns. He claims that much of what constitutes the maker ethos can be found in various subcultures that precede it—do-it-yourself efforts are apparent in illegal moonshine production, community gardens, home auto repair, and so on. Csikszentmihalyi goes on to argue that what makes the maker movement unique is its opposition to "private mass producers," favoring a collective ethos over cults of individualism.[20] Like those cited above, this description of the maker figure offers a tentative response to Alan Liu's intervention in DH cited in the introduction: "How the digital humanities advance, channel, or resist the great postindustrial, neoliberal, corporatist, and globalist flows of information-cum-capital . . . is a question rarely heard in the digital humanities associations, conferences, journals, and projects with which I am familiar."[21] It recalls Adeline Koh's question as well: "How much does digital humanities work, through the way it is processed and organized through computational models, actually follow the Fordist logic of modularity?"[22]

Contrary to so many critiques of DH praxis, DH, certainly in its adoption of maker culture, is not absent of a politics. That being said, how DH draws on maker culture to refine its critical insurgencies is open to critique. In his introduction to *Making Things and Drawing Boundaries*, for example, Jentery Sayers argues that DH *could* center maker cultures that "unlearn and deprogram prototypical whiteness," and that "practitioners *could* [emphasis added] yield the floor to the social justice, decolonization, and intersectional methodologies at work in the circuits of collectives such as #*TransformDH, AbTec, FemTechNet*, and *HASTAC*, as well as projects like *Diaspora Hypertext* (by Jessica Marie Johnson)."[23] When Sayers's claims are paired with the anticapitalist ethos of the select makers cited above, the political work that opens this chapter is perhaps even more relevant.

It is Carl DiSalvo, however, who offers a design-oriented solution to the confluence of ideologically distinct, but nonetheless liberatory goals, of leftist maker cultures: adversarial design. Adversarial design is founded on productive political conflict. It "expresses bias and divisive positions, it provides opportunities to participate in disputes over values, beliefs, and desires; and it models alternate socio-material configurations that demonstrate possible futures."[24] Framed as a collective enterprise, adversarial design's internal modes of organization demand agonistic interplay. "What makes a collective agonistic," DiSalvo writes, "is the extent to which it produces an open space of contest where conflicting values and practices can be acted out."[25] Stated in subjective terms, the adversarial designer mobilizes conflict toward collective horizons of political becoming. The object that one makes is a recursive apparatus that also affects the subject of its production. The maker and the made are co-articulated.

The collective that DiSalvo presumes in his figuration of adversarial design is perhaps more difficult to realize than any object it might produce. Agonistics is not collectivity's equivalent. Joint political action presupposes a more primary question: are we individuals who collaborate in order to better our personal standing in the world as it is, or are we building an active and collective mode of relation *in the first instance*, determined to produce a world we desire? DiSalvo's work gives ideological conflict both context and a method for its collective political actualization. The recursive arc between the maker and the made is what motivates the both/and, community-oriented logic that produces agonistic politics. As such, a politics of collective becoming is coeval with a politics of making insofar as radical alterity is centered in the elision of individual and collective political will.

Going Ballistic

The theory/making debate that persists in DH praxis is contoured by the politics and method of prior countercultures. DH's will to center making in its discourse shapes its critical insurgencies—maker culture provides an avenue for DH to position itself as a new intellectual counterculture in and of the present—by invoking countercultures of the past. What gets prioritized, what traditions are invoked, and how consensus is built form a discourse of politically oppositional goals that amplifies the rhetorical divide between the one and the many, the who and the what, the means and method of political making. Perhaps more pointedly, the countercultural ethos that undergirds our acts of making, critical maker cultures, and DH's imperative to produce, centers a debate over the cultural politics of collective becoming that departs from institutional goals.

Consider the following list of DH-related projects that align themselves with the European avant-garde as a window into the countercultural ethos of DH making and tool-use. Although they are not fully aligned with the field, Garnet Hertz and Jussi Parikka situate avant-garde art practice like readymades and bricolage as an aesthetic precursor to circuit-bending and do-it-yourself tinkering in "Zombie Media: Circuit Bending Media Archaeology into an Art Method." There, Hertz and Parikka argue that making offers a point of opposition to "the political economy of consumer capitalism."[26] One can learn and refine similar skills by subscribing to *Readymade Magazine*. Directions for making one's own readymade can be found at MoMa .org.[27] Speaking to DH's history more directly, Steve F. Anderson embarks on an avant-garde recovery project in his article "Aporias of the Digital Avant-Garde" in *Digital Humanities Quarterly*. There he argues that avant-garde aesthetics "may be productively understood as a processing ground for some of the most compelling issues in contemporary digital culture."[28] Similarly, Roger Whitson traces his own genealogy of DH praxis within avant-garde traditions back to Gregory Ulmer, arguing that "in Ulmer's work, the avant-garde proposes an elegant solution to the 'hack/yack' and 'critical making' debates of the past few years: artists make in order to create alternatives to the existing social order."[29] Bill Enders invokes Guillaume Apollinaire's work (a forefather of Surrealism) in his "A Literacy of Building: Making in the Digital Humanities" to argue that "rooted in images and tools . . . is the power to remake the world."[30] As if to draw a parallel to Whitson and Enders's work, Holly Willis argues in a special DH issue of *Visible Language* that avant-garde aesthetics "suggest models for critical forms of moving image writing" by providing "examples of critical visual work that integrate space, time, and the methods of design to produce new ways of knowing."[31] The Mina Loy: Navigating the Avant-Garde project, led by Suzanne W. Churchill, Linda Kinnahan, and Susan Rosenbaum, is explicitly defined as "an experiment in collaborative, public digital humanities scholarship."[32] Churchill, Kinnahan, and

Rosenbaum have also recently called for the formation of a "digital flash mob to form a new, feminist theory of the avant-garde" called "*en dehors garde*" that attempts to dissociate avant-garde politics from the "'martialised,' oppositional stance associated with the historical avant-garde."[33] Finally, Kevin L. Ferguson has used medical imaging software to visualize cinema as "summed images," calling his work Digital Surrealism and Surrealist Slices, to expand the visual spectrum of DH-related work.[34]

On its face, DH's avant-garde turn is perhaps not a surprising one. Where the European avant-garde remediates industrial material in order to make something new, its aesthetic ethos is matched by the do-it-yourself ethos of contemporary maker culture more generally. It favors a heritage of bricolage, *detournement*, and readymades, realized by what is ready to hand. However, the ideological conflicts that define the European avant-garde as countercultural forces of production extend beyond the academic contexts in which their aesthetico-political regimes are claimed. While defined by aesthetic tool-use, avant-garde conflict typically takes opposition to the institutions of bourgeois life. It does so along familiar dyads: proletariat/bourgeoisie, art/religion, rationality/irrationality, individual/collective, and so on. These conflicts continue to shape the cultural politics of collective becoming in the present. How they might be channeled as solutions to contemporary cultural debates, academic or otherwise, bears this point out.

In 1909, the Futurists exalted "movements of aggression" and marveled at the "beauty of speed."[35] In 1918 Tristan Tzara equated art and politics, claiming: "the new artist protests: he no longer paints."[36] In 1924, André Breton disavowed the rational grip of progress and civilization by championing an aesthetic automatism, meant to reveal the "actual functioning of thought" underneath and beyond social control.[37] And in 1967 Guy Debord explicitly refused capital's abstract transformation into the concrete image, arguing that "the more readily [the spectator] recognizes his own needs in the images of need proposed by the dominant system, the less he understands his own existence and his own desires."[38] As if to confirm Schmitt's concern for political asymmetry and technologies of speed, the European avant-garde attempted to develop an aesthetic that fused art and life via revolution, grounding its work in political critique, automation, and war.

But how is political division parsed by such invocations? In what sense is the fusion of aesthetics, politics, and technology made to be a tool of political becoming? The work produced by the European avant-garde elicits such questions. As is evident in their photographic and cinematic movements, the camera is adopted as a technology of interruption and disorder. Its purpose is to disrupt, rearrange, and threaten. Furthermore, as avant-garde photographic and cinematic practice captured both pure movement and disjointed composites, it was meant to fracture the veneer of social order by revealing a complex of uncontrollable forces, some of which are mechanized, and some which are thought to be natural even as they are mediated by new technologies. In the wake of World War I, movements like Cinéma Pur extended these aesthetic interventions as the camera was mobilized to capture the natural movement and force underlying the industrialized world.[39] The camera is thus a revelatory apparatus in this context; it refocuses one's attention on the antinomies of industrial life, as well as the perceived natural forces that undergird it.

Intentionally so, conflict arises via avant-garde acts of revelation. The avant-garde weaponizes the camera in pursuit of differential consciousness. The avant-garde's critics perhaps best articulate the camera's ballistic character. Walter Benjamin, for example, famously argued that the increased use of technological devices in all facets of life is tantamount to the multiplication and generalization of war. This claim is derived from war-driven technological innovations like the atomic bomb, radar, and sonar, but also the mechanization of aesthetic production, infiltrating both high and popular culture. He likens the work of the Dadaists to "an instrument of ballistics," hitting the spectator "like a bullet."[40] He also claims that Dadaist aesthetic interventions are a cause of the increased demand for film—they are distracting to the eye and ward off contemplation because they assault the viewer—and produce a physical shock effect wherever film is screened, limiting the artwork's auratic function.[41] The link between ballistics and the camera is consequential, politically and technologically. As Dadaism inspires the increased demand for film, its ballistic effect is characterized as one of mindless absorption, disallowing any form of productive revolutionary uptake.

By contrast, Benjamin vaunts the work of Surrealist thinkers like Breton in his essay "The Last Snapshot of the European Intelligentsia." Praising Surrealism's disruptive use of technology, Benjamin argues that the movement was

> the first to perceive the revolutionary energies that appear in the "outmoded"—in the first iron constructions, the first factory buildings, the earliest photos, the objects that have begun to be extinct, grand pianos, the dresses of five years ago, fashionable restaurants when the vogue has begun to ebb from them. The relation of these things to revolution—no one can have a more exact concept of it than these authors. No one before these visionaries and augurs perceived how destitution—not only social but architectonic, the poverty of interiors/enslaved and enslaving objects—can be suddenly transformed into revolutionary nihilism.[42]

The political acuity that Benjamin ascribes to Surrealism relies precisely on its perception of bourgeois life—a consciousness only made available by an alterity of sight—that reveals the politics of its decadence and decay. Surrealism's will to disorient the experience of bourgeois life in the city, particularly its dreamlike navigation of the street, taps into a subjective character that Benjamin reproduces in his figuration of the flâneur.

In a discussion of Surrealism, photography, and cinema, for instance, Susan Sontag extends components of Benjamin's work, reading Surrealist photography and cinema in these instances as weaponized flâneurial practices: "The photographer is an armed version of the solitary walker reconnoitering, stalking, cruising the urban inferno, the voyeuristic stroller who discovers the city as a landscape of voluptuous extremes."[43] Like the Futurists and Dadaists before them, the Surrealists articulated new aesthetic imperatives while also championing revolution. Contrary to Benjamin's enthusiasm for the practice, however, Surrealism is not formative of a political concept or critical aesthetic process for Sontag. Surrealism is best characterized as a "bourgeois disaffection"—a kind of class tourism that fetishized poverty in its effort to transgress bourgeois norms.[44] As a result, the weaponized flâneur is characterized by his solitary constitution—a lone wolf who reconnoiters the cityscape, observing the effects of industrial life at a familiar remove.

Paul Virilio explains the coevolution of war and new photographic technologies more concretely. At the opening of his *War and Cinema* (1984), Virilio notes that "the 1914–18 war compounded a new 'weapons system' out of combat vehicle and camera," linking the production of new technologies to the aestheticization of war and speed.[45] In fact, he links the production of cinematic technologies to the production of the Gatling gun and Colt revolver, describing how the crank operation of these weapons inspired Etienne-Jules Marey to create a chrono-photographic rifle, allowing "its user to aim at and photograph an object moving through space."[46] Like Benjamin, Virilio later linked the European avant-garde to histories of technology and war in his book *Art and Fear* (2010), characterizing Futurism, Dadaism, and Surrealism as totalitarian regimes in the guise of artistic movements:

> Avant-garde artists, like many political agitators, propagandists and demagogues, have long understood what TERRORISM would soon popularize: if you want a place in "revolutionary history" there is nothing easier than provoking a riot, an assault on propriety, in the guise of art. Short of committing a real crime by killing innocent passers-by with a bomb, the pitiless contemporary author of the twentieth century attacks symbols, the very meaning of a "pitiful" art he assimilates to "academicism."[47]

The dynamic at play here is complex, since Benjamin's claims against Dadaism above are inherent to Virilio's critique. For both thinkers, certain European avant-garde adoptions of new technologies and use in aesthetic practice are characterized by a fear-mongering ideology that contributes to the subjugation of human beings, rather than their liberation. For Virilio in particular, the European avant-garde in aggregate is simply playing with technologies it cannot understand, solely as a means to transgress. Any political claim to aesthetic production on its part is a self-interested incursion into revolutionary history. Where the European avant-garde interrupts, it spreads terror. Where the European avant-garde reveals disorder, its art destroys any claim to transcendental aesthetic quality, subjugating politics to the transgressive act.

The cultural conflict that informs avant-garde aesthetics is perhaps best stated more specifically. The will to destroy art and civilization is not a universal imperative, but rather is aimed at the market, the state, and a host of institutional powers that perpetuate bourgeois cultural norms. The European avant-garde's infatuation with the camera's revelatory power—the tool that becomes a weapon of consciousness-raising—produces an ideological break with bourgeois life that defines its countercultural ethos. The subject produced—the conflicted political landscape that makes avant-garde subjectivity possible—seeks out a position of absolute distinction to its enemy. Conflict is sustained in the objects of avant-garde art. Systemic modes of oppression are revealed in the cultural division of power that informs avant-garde acts of making.

Mere Antagonism

The inherent connection between the camera and the gun gives definition to the figure that operates it. The critical arguments discussed above cannot be dismissed as simplistic, moralizing diatribes against countercultural forces of production. The underlying argument against European avant-garde political formation operates on two planes. First, the production of subjectivity informs the means by which a tool is instrumentalized. The camera's function as a revelatory apparatus is defined by its weaponization as the avant-garde names its enemy and proclaims its difference. Second, the degree of difference separating the avant-garde from bourgeois life is dependent upon its world-making power and collective ethos. Absent these qualities, what the avant-garde produces is limited to mere antagonism, a reflection of one's individual incongruity that is weaponized by the will to transgress.

The contemporary relevance that these arguments pose for DH praxis may seem obscure. However, the relationship shared between ideological conflict, the production of subjectivity, and the tool-use evident in avant-garde countercultures speaks directly to the politics of contemporary maker culture and method. If the theory/making debate is contoured by the politics and method of prior countercultures, its contemporary cultures of production inherit the ideological conflicts of the past. The first epigraph that opens this chapter draws this point out. By claiming that DH is slow to articulate a need for feminist politics, "perhaps because the instrumentalism of a 'tool' seems much less blatantly anti-feminist than the instrumentalism of a gun," Elizabeth Losh draws a comparison between DH and game studies, retaining the theory/making divide that animates much DH debate, as she also manifests a politics of conflict, subjectivity, and tool-use that connects DH method to a broader set of cultural issues.[48] These conflicts ultimately lead back to the avant-garde antinomies noted above.

First, Losh traces DH debates that result from its maker invocations to prior debates in game studies. She writes:

> Many debates in the digital humanities recall debates already rehearsed in game studies. For example, significant cohorts of digital designers, programmers, and architects must collaborate and compete with those who identify exclusively as critics and theorists within the research community. Questions about which group can speak with the most authority in public fora can be difficult to resolve, particularly when plainspoken discourse and highly technical skills prized by builders and makers are devalued by the academy. Much as DH purists have called for "more hack, less yack" or lionized "builders," designers of classic games are often the keynote speakers at game conferences and serve as celebrity attendees.[49]

Losh's claim to feminist game studies places a demand on DH to consider prior histories and methods as it develops its own standards and norms. Collaborative work that prioritizes acts of making is immediately political and correlates to other disciplines. At the same time, the disciplinary concerns that Losh brings to the table via the DH/game studies comparison is circumscribed by a broader culture of harassment that must be addressed at the overlap.

Second, Losh warns: "Much as feminist bloggers have been victimized by Internet harassment for taking a stand against particular forms of aggressive online conduct accepted as normative, feminist game critics might sometimes find themselves targeted for challenging the hypermasculinity of existing user behavior."[50] This warning is neither idle nor easy to dismiss. Our disciplinary debates over maker culture and method are paralleled by cultural issues that define what gets made, who gets to make, and how the interpretation of these acts is policed. The tool/weapon conflation in this discourse is both metaphorical and actual. Tool use makes possible worlds. The worlds that our tools produce are circumscribed by conflicting desires that allow for harm, alienation, and brutality. The character these forms of harassment have embodied in contemporary culture is the explanatory link between the countercultural ethos that DH praxis embraces and the avant-garde antinomies that undergird it.

Although my argument may seem abstract, Angela Nagle's fascinating *Kill All Normies: Online Culture Wars from 4chan and Tumblr to Trump and the Alt-Right* (2017) makes this point clear. At the book's opening, Nagle develops a persuasive genealogy of alt-right transgression that passes through the European avant-garde aesthetico-political regime. She locates the avant-garde's "transgressive sensibility" in the work of Choderlos de Laclos and the

Marquis de Sade, but also Surrealism and Situationism, adeptly tracing European avant-garde politics to contemporary acts of brutality perpetrated online by Pepe meme-posting cyberbullies and Gamergate trolls.[51] "Just as Nietzsche appealed to the Nazis as a way to formulate a right-wing anti-moralism," Nagle writes, "it is precisely the transgressive sensibility that is used to excuse and rationalize the utter dehumanization of women and ethnic minorities in the alt-right online sphere now."[52] De Sade's transgressive "values of libertinism and individual sovereignty" are formative of this position, as is the infamous Surrealist motto adopted from William Blake: "Sooner murder an infant in its cradle than nurse unacted desires."[53]

Let's take Gamergate as an example of how aestheticized acts of transgression realize a brutal reactionary politics. In Nagle's reading, "Gamergate brought gamers, rightist chan culture, anti-feminism and the online far right closer to mainstream discussion and it also politicized a broad group of young people, mostly boys, who organized tactics around the idea of fighting back against the culture war being waged by the cultural left."[54] The acts of *detournement* (memes, viral videos, etc.) utilized to combat feminist influence on gamer culture were certainly meant to harass (Nagle sums up these acts on pp. 16–24), but also to render the subject of the so-called feminist incursion immobilized through abject visuals. The weaponized flâneur certainly takes on a host of objectionable characteristics in this instance, but definitively emerges from a condition that Nagle calls, following Baudelaire, "*an oasis of horror in a desert of boredom*," now almost exclusively perpetrated by the alt-right, and easily characterized by a more generalized nihilistic culture that informs its politics.[55]

Losh's equation of tool-use with the instrumentalization of a gun perhaps now comes into clearer view. The political undercurrent that informs DH's maker ethos traverses multiple academic disciplines from which DH might refine its own conceptual lexicon (theory, game studies, etc.). However, its countercultural invocations bring ideological conflict to the fore. The recursive arc between the maker and the made is equally bound to navigate ideological conflicts as critical methods are pursued. Some of the most dominant contemporary correlates to European avant-garde countercultures duplicate a kind of bourgeois disaffection that fails to distinguish itself from its opposite via collective, world-making power. This failure is rooted in countercultural transgression, but its tactics are ultimately backward-looking and brutal. Countercultural transgression morphs into a reactionary politics of mere antagonism.[56]

This brief characterization of maker countercultures presents DH scholar-practitioners with a contradiction that is not easy to reconcile. The avant-garde concept does not inherently refashion the subject against bourgeois norms and values in its will to transgress, and it sometimes lapses into a reactionary political stance. Its claim to alterity, revelatory perception, and ultimately liberated political consciousness is just as susceptible to reactionary co-optation as it is to liberatory political will. Yet European avant-garde politics draw out a fundamental point of tension where the maker and the made are co-articulated: what is the difference between indulging a bourgeois disaffection and realizing a partisan demand via techno-political solutions? How does this difference affect the desire to center radical alterity in the elision between the individual and the collective?

If DH is to further a radical sensibility in its proclivity toward critical making—one that it has already invoked—then it demands a lineage that offers a tactical point of contradiction to those that would co-opt it. It requires a robust archive of critical figures from which to draw on as it articulates its political positions. Losh frames such a critique through a powerful provocation: "What would it mean to move from a paradigm of tool development to a paradigm of process and performance in which the network of power formations moves from ground to figure?" I push this provocation further. If DH *could* center social justice, decolonization, and intersectional methodologies in the formation of its maker culture, it requires the very corrective that the guerrilla signifies in its praxis. The guerrilla's invocation in DH praxis is tantamount to a desire for complex opposition to corporate individualism, competition, and value as it boasts feminist, decolonial, and intersectional modes of critique. The contemporary focus on producing radical alterity via the technological apparatus is therefore its most formative partisan demand.

This is precisely where the guerrilla contrasts with the European avant-garde as a mode of political becoming. The guerrilla enacts these modes of techno-political transformation at the site of conflict within a globalized discourse. What I want to add, particularly as it pertains to questions of DH's political figures and lineages, is a position from which the combination of avant-garde method and guerrilla politics is recognized and extended for its techno-tactical novelties. This project begins in the pages that follow, and extends to chapters 3 and 4. It prioritizes a decolonial method that takes aim at the imperial formation of bourgeois life.

A Decolonial Turn

If guerrilla organization and tactics stand to the left of the European avant-garde, they do so because absolute political division is the guerrilla's primary political demand. This is perhaps also a pitfall, but guerrilla organization and tactics are consistently mobilized as a collective mode of self-making that stands in direct opposition to the bourgeois subject. The guerrilla is another name for collective processes of absolute transformation in the face of absolute opposition. It is a radical democratic desire; one that seeks justice to its cause solely on the terms it establishes.

The decolonial turn that guerrilla organization and tactics enact centers its attention on issues of language, identity, culture, and consciousness. Contemporary decolonial method augments these concerns. In her essay "Indigenous Movements and Decolonial Feminism," for example, Maria Lugones characterizes decoloniality as a process of "moving together [and] defying colonial cartographies, seeking autonomy from the nation state, enriching the communal senses of self, designing practices of self-government that place all members at the place of deliberation and decision making and accord each the power to participate."[57] It is, at every step of its articulation, a subjective enterprise: "The long process of coloniality begins subjectively and intersubjectively in a tense encounter that both forms and will not simply yield to capitalist modern colonial normativity. The crucial point about the encounter is that the subjective and intersubjective construction of it informs the resistance offered to the ingredients of colonial domination."[58] The collective subject that Lugones's decolonial method theorizes is coalitional and conflict-driven, anticapitalist and antimodern, since political engagement is made at the "fractured locus of the colonial difference."[59] Guerrilla organization and tactics duplicate this.

We can think of Chela Sandoval's characterization of differential oppositional consciousness as an analogue to this type of collective political making. In Sandoval's view, feminists of color who embody a differential oppositional consciousness are itinerant figures who enact coalitional and conflict-driven ideologies simultaneously—they are diffuse and mobile "weavers," migrating "between and among" sites of contest and coalition.[60] Feminists of color invoke their experience as a form of "tactical weaponry" through a motorized metaphor akin to the guerrilla's telluric condition, likened to the "clutch" of an automobile.[61] U.S. third world feminists push this political point even further in Sandoval's view, enacting a "tactical subjectivity" that finds its articulation in an illiberal style.[62] Citing an unpublished manuscript by Aida Hurtado, Sandoval underscores Hurtado's claim that "women of color are more like urban guerrillas trained through everyday battle with the state apparatus," contrary to their "free-spirited" experimentalist white liberal counterparts.[63] Citing Cherríe Moraga and Gloria Anzaldúa's *This Bridge Called My Back*, Sandoval underscores an iteration of guerrilla politics that comports with DH rhetorics focused on questions of need and survival: U.S. third world feminist struggle is "guerrilla warfare," a "'way of life' [and] a means and method for survival."[64] This claim is further contoured by Moraga's understanding of affinity making, which is codified in a language friendship: "Our strategy is how we cope . . . how we measure and weigh what is to be said and when, what is to be done and how, and to whom . . . daily deciding/risking who it is we can call an ally, call a friend (whatever that person's skin, sex, or sexuality)."[65]

What Sandoval describes is something of a feminist corrective within a broader theoretical lineage of radical political organization, structural inequality, and violence. She reorients guerrilla discourse from ideal political critique to political need, from tool to process, and from ontological expansiveness to embodied realities of everyday life. It is a shared lived experience and a shared ideology that compels joint political action. These characteristics form the connective tissue that links conflict to collectivity—they are the originary mode of connection that precedes any potential form of "working with." Sandoval's cinematic turn, to recall from the introduction, bears this point out. The guerrilla signifies a political position "that apprehends an effective oppositional consciousness igniting in dialectical engagement between varying ideological formations" in this passage, but one that is ultimately "cinematographic," a mode of political engagement that serves as "a kinetic motion that maneuvers, poetically transfigures, and orchestrates while demanding alienation, perversion, and reformation, in both spectators and practitioners."[66] Much deconstructive work is necessary for Sandoval's corrective to take place, but her tactical metaphors and cinematic turn are a first step toward articulating a decolonial alternative to the avant-garde discourse discussed earlier.

I perform this turn by looking to guerrilla cinematic practice as a critical act of making. I make three, interrelated interventions that speak back to DH's countercultural ethos as maker culture is claimed. First, I offer a historical context in which to think the guerrilla's partisan character and contentious political logic. This complicates DH's adoption of the figure. Second, I complicate the figure's connection to critical race studies and queer theory. The guerrilla, here and elsewhere, is not and should not be endorsed wholesale. There is much to critique by way of gender, race, and class. Third, the turn I take toward the Latin American Third Cinema movement offers a different vantage point from which to conceptualize DH acts of making and its avant-garde lineage. If, as Emily Apter argues, guerrilla organization and tactics are "indispensable to theories of political collectivity that seek to supplant bourgeois individualism with a new notion of the group or ontological set," Third Cinema's decolonial ideology produces a collective subject that also opposes bourgeois iterations of the self full stop.[67]

With the Camera as Our Rifle

Born out of anticolonial struggle across Latin America in the 1960s, the guerrilla filmmakers Fernando Solanas and Octavio Getino outline political and aesthetic principles for producing partisan opposition to imperialism in their coauthored manifesto "Towards a Third Cinema." The history of their Third Cinema concept is simultaneously long and short. Long, on the one hand, because Solanas and Getino chart their political intervention back to the colonization of Latin America, focusing on Argentina's own struggle for sovereignty. This history is explored more fully in the pair's film *La Hora de los Hornos / The Hour of Furnaces* (1968), where Solanas and Getino offer a partisan view of history. There, they argue that Latin America was economically disenfranchised, perpetrated by colonial power, and thus continues to operate under a shroud of false consciousness: "In the same year as [Simón] Bolivar consolidated independence in Ayacucho, [Bernardino] Rivadavia signed a trick-loan in Buenos Aires with the Baring Brothers Bank. British banks took over the national banks that issued the country's currency and, in the name of free trade, their manufacturers invaded internal markets."[68] Solanas and Getino's claim underscores the politico-economic connection that runs throughout this chapter. Where Argentina's independence was stalled, colonial power transformed. The colonial grip on Argentina's economy created a condition in which one believes oneself to be free, but remains indebted to local and foreign iterations of colonial power. This, for Solanas and Getino, is a situation that led to contemporary coups and revolutionary struggle.

The short view of history that Solanas and Getino offer is a situational one. Solanas and Getino cite both rural and urban guerrilla struggle in Brazil, Cuba, and Vietnam, relying heavily on the political theory produced by Fidel Castro, Che Guevara, and Mao Zedong. Solanas and Getino cite their work as the impetus for a revolution in cinematic production, but also for a revolution in identity formation and meaning. Most pointedly, they liken the use of handheld cameras to the use of guns in this context, and proclaim a militancy of cinematic production:

> In this long war, with the camera as our rifle, we do in fact move into a guerrilla activity. This is why the work of a film-guerrilla group is governed by strict disciplinary norms as to both work methods and security. A revolutionary film group is in the same situation as a guerrilla unit: it cannot grow strong without military structures and command concepts.[69]

Figures like Benjamin and Virilio would undoubtedly interpret Solanas and Getino's turn to guerrilla organization and tactics as a new permutation in the generalization of war. However, Solanas and Getino's invocation of military structures and command concepts motivates a much larger aesthetico-political concern. Third Cinema is "the decolonisation of culture."[70] It assumes that "culture, art, science, and cinema always respond to conflicting class interests," and that the state and capital are always already techno-fascist assemblages.[71] Solanas and Getino's decolonial stance is reminiscent of Frantz Fanon's anticolonial stance in this sense, particularly with the sentiment that the colonized necessarily adopt a posture of absolute opposition to colonial power: "For [the colonized] there is no compromise, no possibility of concession. Colonization or decolonization: it is simply a power struggle."[72]

Beyond Fanon, the guerrilla principles of Solanas and Getino's Third Cinema movement stand at an inverse to the European avant-garde's reactionary undercurrents. Although the camera and the gun are linked in both movements and mobilized as a technology of political becoming, Solanas and Getino shun revolutionary ideals that prioritize abstract aesthetic output over collective political process: "Ideas such as 'Beauty in itself is revolutionary' and 'All new cinema is revolutionary' are idealistic aspirations that do not touch the neo-colonial condition, since they continue to conceive of cinema, art, and beauty as universal abstractions and not as an integral part of the national processes of decolonisation."[73] The defining difference between the European avant-garde and any concept of a Third Cinema guerrilla is therefore the notion that Third Cinema refers to the construction of subjectivity in absolute contrast to imperial culture. The process of decolonization described here, which is both aesthetically oriented and technologically driven, is therefore better understood as a response to what the Peruvian sociologist Aníbal Quijano calls the coloniality of power. Where state power and transnational capital coalesced over the long twentieth century, Quijano argues that "after the colonization of America and the expansion of European colonialism to the rest of the world, the subsequent constitution of Europe as a new *id*-entity needed the elaboration of a Eurocentric perspective of knowledge, a theoretical perspective on the idea of race as a naturalization of colonial relations between Europeans."[74] This led to a "new world intersubjectivity" in Quijano's view, one that revolved totally around "European or Western hegemony."[75] This mode of intersubjectivity is predicated on a racial-economic order that works to enfranchise European values while it simultaneously disenfranchises Latin American autonomy. This intersubjective relation is precisely what Solanas and Getino oppose, and what the guerrilla turn is intended to remedy.

Although Solanas and Getino take the camera as gun to be the medium of one's political transformation, their process of decolonization via guerrilla organization and tactics is theorized most forcefully as a problem of identity and language. Following a logic quite similar to Quijano's, Solanas and Getino argue that when one attempts to express oneself in a colonial situation, one necessarily relies on imperial command:

> Just as they are not masters of the land upon which they walk, the neocolonialised people are not masters of the ideas that envelop them. A knowledge of national reality presupposes going into the web of lies and confusion that arise from dependence. The intellectual is obliged to refrain from spontaneous thought; if he does think, he generally runs the risk of doing so in French or English—never in the language of a culture of his own which, like the process of national and social liberation, is still hazy and incipient. Every piece of data, every concept that floats around us, is part of a framework of mirages that is difficult to take apart.[76]

This claim is reiterated over and again in *La Hora de los Hornos / The Hour of Furnaces*. If the colonized subject is to transcend the condition of his sub-human status to that of his human status, he must think in the language of the colonizer. This is to say; the entirety of his ontological ground is permeated and delimited by the colonial situation. Where the coloniality of power is operative, there is also complete control over the bodies and subjectivity of colonized people because every iteration, every piece of data informing the situation, is organized around a system of oppression and dependence.

This point needs to be highlighted for its alignment with the contemporary turn in DH praxis to decolonize aspects of the discipline. Extending beyond Sayers's work discussed earlier, Jacqueline Wernimont calls for a DH practice of decolonization in her 2017 MLA presentation and blog post "Remediation, Activation, and Entanglement in Performative (Digital) Archives" that is praxis-oriented. In a critique of a Scalar book that she directed and helped create, *Performing Archives: Edward S. Curtis and the "Vanishing Race,"* Wernimont alludes to decolonizing data and the logic of the spreadsheet, much like the question of language above, precisely because the archive's infrastructures are performatively linked to questions of subjective formation. *Performing Archives* is focused on an "attempt to perform an idea about Native American being, in the sense of performing his idea of what 'Indianness' was," but "in its current state the Curtis project is a really excellent example of small and incremental difference on the top of essentially the same repressive and violent structures."[77] Although Wernimont focuses on a different literature set and decolonial heritage, it seems that the colonial problem is quite similar. Where Solanas and Getino grapple with decolonizing the logic and language of the colonizer so as to perform guerrilla subjectivity, Wernimont grapples with decolonizing the logic and language of the archive so that Native American subjectivity might speak in the manner its subjects choose. Here, it is easy to see that the book's content, as well as its means of publication, are permeated by the colonial situation, while the book's subjects seek to remain in a position of radical alterity to the colonizer's culture and language.

Think also of "The Translation Toolkit," a minimal computing project maintained by Gimena del Río, Alex Gil, Daniel O'Donnell, and Élika Ortega. Situated at the intersection of DH's rapid global expansion and small-scale community-making efforts, the "Translation Toolkit" addresses "the complexity and sensitivity of the issue of multilingualism" and "touches on the large scale problems of economic inequality, colonial history, and political issues that have shaped the world we live in and, by extension, the landscape in which we work."[78] The toolkit is thus an "attempt at drawing attention to the need to acknowledge the linguistic diversity that *already* exists in the field of DH" by "translating and preparing multilingual resources whether at conferences, in editorial and authorial journal work, [or] website and resource developments."[79] Though perhaps not a hard-line decolonial project, the "Translation Toolkit" remains a DH resource that maximizes linguistic autonomy as it simultaneously resists coloniality's intellectual reinscription. The toolkit allows for spontaneous thought at a remove from colonization's dominant languages and cultures.

The decolonial work that Solanas and Getino demand is perhaps a step or two ahead of the archival and translation work discussed above. Yet the subjective valences of Solanas and Getino's project are clear in their intent: the figure that operates the camera must undergo a process of intentional and productive othering. The same is true for any figure that would utilize technologies of differential social movement as a decolonial project. Opposed to their assimilation in and by neocolonial powers, Third Cinema practitioners combine the guerrilla concept with an aspiration to create a novel definition of the self: "the cinema of the revolution is at the same time one of destruction and construction: destruction of the image that neocolonialism has created of itself and of us, and construction of a throbbing, living reality which recaptures truth in any of its expressions."[80] This is its liberatory process. Third Cinema destroys the world-making power of imperialism and reveals an unforeseen living reality from which to refashion oneself.

Collectivity against Hetero-Masculinity

The political ontology that Solanas and Getino imagine follows at least two modes of collective self-making. First, the collective feature of Solanas and Getino's Third Cinema is one predicated on skill-sharing and technological dexterity, much like contemporary maker movements. Michael Chanan argues that in Solanas and Getino's own cinematic practice, specifically their work on *La Hora de los Hornos / Hour of Furnaces*, "the film crew needed to operate with a radical conception not only of the content of the film but also of the production process, including the team's internal relations, the role of the producer or director, and of individual skills."[81] Hito Steyerl continues this line of thought in her essay "Is the Museum a Kind of Factory?" There, she describes Third Cinema's collective making process as a kind of post-representational seeing, drawing specifically from Solanas and Getino's *La Hora de los Hornos / Hour of Furnaces*. Steyerl writes:

> Today, cinematic politics are post-representational. They do not educate the crowd, but produce it. They articulate the crowd in space and in time. They submerge it in partial invisibility and then orchestrate their dispersion, movement, and reconfiguration. They organize the crowd without preaching to it. They replace the gaze of the bourgeois sovereign spectator of the white cube with the incomplete, obscured, fractured, and overwhelmed vision of the spectator-as-laborer.[82]

The collaborative spirit of Solanas and Getino's work is predicated on a diversity of skills to actualize a diversity of subjective blockages to imperial power. It is a means of producing a communal ethos in tandem with its political ideology, and one that also destabilizes individualized subjects and acts. One could phrase this differently by adopting the language of contemporary maker culture. The Third Cinema's collaborative ethos is its protocological demand, while the decolonization of culture is its prototypical novelty.

Following his argument above, Chanan goes on to note that Solanas and Getino's own film "was designed to be stopped in the projector to allow for discussion and debate—designed, in other words, to disrupt the normal passive relationship of the spectator to the screen."[83] The cinematic apparatus is therefore the vehicle through which the guerrilla is brought into contact with a potential network of collaboration. This is its post-representational moment. Here, the spectator and the guerrilla become something liminal. The collaborative effort of the collective is brought into contact with its audience, extending its collective body to a network of political actors. Third Cinema is thus conceived as a process through which

> guerrilla film-making proletarianises the film worker and breaks down the intellectual aristocracy that the bourgeoisie grants to its followers. In a word, it democratises. The film-maker's tie with reality makes him more a part of his people. Vanguard layers and even masses participate collectively in the work when they realise that it is the continuity of their daily struggle. *La hora de los hornos* shows how a film can be made in hostile circumstances when it has the support and collaboration of militants and cadres from the people.[84]

The problem of theorizing guerrilla organization and tactics' techno-political character in this discourse therefore rests on connecting the practice of partisan division with what a body can do. The figure who operates a given technology and the technology itself are an assemblage through which partisan distinctions can be made, productive conflict can come to the fore, and novel modes of relation can take place. The political subject that Solanas and Getino imagine is a radically diffuse assemblage composed of small guerrilla units and Latin America's proletarian masses. It is not faceless, but composed of many faces—one of the guerrilla's strengths is that it gets lost in the crowd. The camera's ballistic character, concomitant with its operation in this manner, is what produces affinity and opposition across lines of political difference.

Third Cinema's production as a revolutionary aesthetic can therefore also be likened to what Foucault calls a technology of the self, specifically the division between *exomologesis* and *exagoreusis*, or the denial of self through either martyrdom or obedience to a master.[85] The re-habituation of the self in this context is uncomplicated. Through an extreme denial of imperial desire, one is remade in the collective vision of an assumed good. Mao Zedong calls this practice "spiritual unification," and guerrilla warfare "the university of war."[86] Carlos Marighella names it as an apprenticeship in "the revolutionary method of action," developing his "seven sins of the urban guerrilla."[87] In a more diagrammatic fashion, Solanas and Getino's turn to guerrilla organization and tactics is also a means of thinking the productive contrast between the one and the many—what Galloway and Thacker think in relation to the swarm or what Hardt and Negri think as a pack of wolves. With each collection of figures, multiplicity is an indivisible quality—*one* cannot comprise the entirety of a swarm or a pack, nor is a swarm or a pack reducible to any individual subject. Collective figures are irreducible to any single component part.

This description of Solanas and Getino's work is perhaps the closest in character to those of the radical maker cultures recounted in this chapter's opening sections. The will to democratize both the production process and the critical analysis of the work augurs a practice of critical making akin to that valorized by Ratto and Hockema, but also by Lovink and Dieter, forefronting the positive contribution of the many. Solanas and Getino's politics are more complex. The subjective character of Solanas and Getino's work, defined by its decolonial stance, invokes the guerrilla so as to create a "we"—a subject that belongs to the present because it is of his making—fully imbued with its partisan spirit. The maker and the made in this discourse are the result of a collective-making political process that mobilizes cinema to foment absolute division to its enemy in all aspects of life.

The second problem of self-making rests on how Solanas and Getino think the relation of the guerrilla to the population that supports it. Solanas and Getino's idea of the Third Cinema movement mirrors this description of guerrilla organization and tactics, but their emphasis on cinematic practice clarifies the modes of social cooperation that the guerrilla relies on. To reuse some terminology from chapter 1, the argument can be reframed as follows: guerrilla organization and tactics bear the friend-enemy concept for Solanas and Getino, while the camera is its technology of production. The friend-enemy concept is what differentiates the decolonization of culture from imperial power, while Third Cinema deploys the camera to preserve life through power. Rather than a faceless swarm, a pack of wolves, or an unholy monster, Solanas and Getino mobilize the guerrilla as the face of a collaborative public enemy that manifests within a populist milieu. This is the primary feature of its transmogrified political body.

As politically salient as this concept may seem, I approach the guerrilla's figuration of the body in this discourse through heavy criticism. I do so because I confront the guerrilla's greatest deficiency at this juncture. As the guerrilla extends its collective body to the spectator via the cinematic apparatus, the collective body it produces is universally grounded in hetero-masculine subjective features that are linked to colonial power. The maker's recursive arc is consistently codified as a masculine enterprise in Solanas and Getino's work, as is the body it produces.

At the introduction of *La Hora de los Hornos / Hour of Furnaces*, political and subjective becoming are claimed as processes of becoming men. Over scenes of police beating men and women in the street, Solanas and Getino mix quotes by Che Guevara and Frantz Fanon, solidifying the film's masculinized discourse: "A long war. A cruel war. Impunity. The price of becoming men. A people without hate cannot triumph . . . colonized man frees himself through violence."[88] This is a common trope in Solanas and Getino's film. The pair go on to critique European paternalism, citing it as the source of Latin American inferiority. At the same time, they reinscribe the claim to masculinity as a source of mutual recognition by following a dialectical inversion of the gendered marker. Quite clearly, the colonized subject, in tandem with the spectator, is interpellated as a male-gendered subject. This subject is tantamount to an ontological condition that "gives" a body to the figures it interpellates: guerrilla filmmakers, spectators, and so forth.

On the one hand, we can read this condition through its colonial valences—what Nelson Maldonado-Torres calls misanthropic skepticism, or a colonial logic that "posits its targets as racialized and sexualized subjects. Once vanquished, they are said to be inherently servants and their bodies come to form part of an economy of sexual abuse, exploitation, and control."[89] Where the colonial subject inhabits a subhuman status, where his body is crafted into an object of and for exploitation, his path toward liberation is delimited by hetero-masculine colonial contours. If one wishes to become human, one must first become a man. The transformative power of such a demand offers the possibility of ontological equality within a colonial logic, but it also passes the colonial project forward. In a feminist context, this is precisely what Maria Lugones has termed the coloniality of gender, or "the intersection of race, class, gender and sexuality in a way that enables . . . the indifference that men, but, more importantly to our struggles, men who have been racialized as inferior, exhibit to the systematic violences inflicted upon women of color."[90]

This is more than a contentious moment in the guerrilla's theoretical history and actual implementation. This form of brutality is gendered as guerrilla subjectivity actualizes itself through cinematic interpellation and political conscription, reinscribing sex/gender regimes inherent to colonial power. It is important to underscore the fact that these acts are also recalled in the guerrilla's invocation outside of its original context. If the guerrilla underscores a debt to queer theory and critical race studies, both figurally and tactically, then these acts must be addressed as they travel. The guerrilla is simultaneously a force of division and a force of unity whether it is utilized as a politically motivated tool or a conduit for making objects and subjects of revolution. It is rife with agonistic tendencies that magnify the difference of its participants as it also seeks out productive alliances.

Failures of the Subject, Failures of the Body

The ideological conflicts that animate the entirety of this chapter revolve around the most fundamental claim posed by the acts of critical making discussed above, academic or otherwise: "we make therefore we become." The question of who we are as makers is imperative at the conclusion of this chapter. It demands an unflinching look at our politics of self-making and the conditions through which subjectivity is continually refashioned. Between the avant-garde and the guerrilla, DH practitioners are met with a failure of the subject and a failure of the body. One cannot escape the bourgeois culture it opposes; the other cannot escape the gendered power of its colonial condition. One heritage presents us with an art of remixing and repurposing delimited by reactionary lapse, while the other presents us with a skill-sharing workshop delimited by heteronormative expectations of the body. These failures are not grounds for dismissal. They are an opportunity to reconceptualize their interplay.

When Sandoval writes that theory is "capable of enabling the development of a common community of understanding that can, in its collective will, further politically oppositional goals," her call to create new inner and social technologies is predicated on decolonial lineages that retain conflict within collectivized figurations of the political.[91] If DH could "unlearn and deprogram prototypical whiteness," if its "practitioners *could* [emphasis added] yield the floor to the social justice, decolonization, and intersectional methodologies" via its critical maker cultures, it necessarily invokes a host of radical methodologies that exceed institutional goals.[92] The demand to produce, undergirded by the inherent connection between making and being, is continually contoured by the theory/making interplay. The failures, antinomies, and possible points of connection between DH's countercultural precursors are thus an opportunity to combat multiple oppressions while simultaneously enacting the collective work that the guerrilla signifies in its praxis. If the guerrilla is a theoretically motivated political tool, its use complicates, supports, and supersedes the countercultural ethos that motivates DH's maker turn.

How the two cohere is perhaps a question of agonistics. It is also a question of ideological formation across multiple iterations of oppositional consciousness—some of which must be opposed in their entirety. The cinematic histories briefly explored in this chapter are not mere examples of aesthetic tool use. They are, in Sandoval's argument, acts of political transfiguration that motivate the dialectical interplay shared between theory and practice—the both/and, community-oriented logic that also inspires DH's maker culture. They are opportunities to consider, evaluate, and reimagine a plurality of differential articulation as institutional goals and cultural production overlap.

The final step in realizing theory's ability to build a common community of understanding that aligns politically oppositional goals is to consider how collective desire might manifest as coalitional modes of connection. This is precisely what decolonial method demands. Where difference is retained as new technologies of differential social movement are sought after, collectivity cannot operate as a homogenizing force of political connectivity. Sandoval's feminist corrective in guerrilla discourse makes this clear.

How DH might take up this position in the continued evolution of its critical insurgencies is both provocative and generative. If our maker cultures are to produce a kind of collective power that demands the coalition super-session of present ideological conflicts, this is, perhaps, as Judith Butler would argue, done so situationally: coalitional political work "cannot be figured in advance"; it is radically contingent and tactically oriented.[93] Where irrecon-cilable difference motivates a concept of "working with," coalition across difference becomes a collective political imperative. As Butler argues, this is an advantage: "perhaps a coalition needs to acknowledge its contradictions and take action with those contradictions intact."[94]

Chapter 3

The Production of the Commons

Satanically, indeed, more initiative is in a sense demanded here
than in the old-style war: it seems to cost the subject his whole
energy to achieve subjectlessness.

—Theodor W. Adorno, *Minima Moralia*

Should we not be suspicious of postmodern critiques of the
"subject" when they surface at a historical moment when
many subjugated people feel themselves coming to voice for
the first time?

—bell hooks, "Postmodern Blackness"

Issue one of *Black Mask*, the first in a series of ten pamphlets produced by
the eponymous collective, appeared in the Lower East Side of Manhattan in
fall 1966. Announcing Black Mask's first public action against the Museum
of Modern Art (MoMA), the magazine proclaimed: "A new spirit is rising.
Like the streets of Watts we burn with revolution. We assault your Gods . . .
We sing of your death. DESTROY THE MUSEUMS . . . our struggle cannot
be hung on walls. Let the past fall under blows of revolt."[1] The collective's
message was clear. Destroy elite gallery spaces. Destroy MoMA. This was not
a battle *for* the museums, or an argument in favor of including minoritarian
art forms in elite archives; Black Mask's was a battle for liberation—the redis-
tribution of living culture outside of centralized institutional controls—in
the face of the museum's enclosure. It was to be the beginning of a cultural
revolution, global in scope, and one harkening back to the Dadaist anti-art
movement.[2]

I begin with Black Mask's call to destroy the museums because it approaches
cultural preservation differently. The contrast between the collective's call
and contemporary DH imperatives for cultural preservation could not be
starker. DH favors a Creative Commons style, sometimes modifying corporate models of attribution, sometimes building its own tools in the effort to

produce knowledge as commons. The museum—indeed GLAM (galleries, libraries, archives, museums) spaces of all kinds—stands in for a concept of the commons that is often global in scope and institutionally aligned. To begin from a position of political negativity signals a need to unmake institutional control. Black Mask's will to refuse and pivot toward an alternative horizon of thought and action emerges from a situation in which the common good is positioned beyond any existing instrument of care. Where the collective calls to destroy what is so in order to manifest the new, it valorizes the collective itself—revolution as being—and positions collectivity as the bridge between exploitative institutional cultures and a future culture free of capitalist exploitation, wars for imperialism, and racist power structures.

While I do not recapitulate Black Mask's call for destruction, I do pursue two concepts of the commons in what follows, one valorized by DH praxis, and one originating from an avowedly anticapitalist culture of resistance. We should remember that the commons encompasses two spheres of human need. It refers to "the common wealth of the material world—the air, the water, the fruits of the soil, and all nature's bounty," but also to "those results of social production that are necessary for social interaction and further production, such as knowledge, languages, codes, information, affects, and so forth."[3] DH's concept of the commons is easy to articulate given the critical work I have covered so far. The discipline's focus on generativity, inclusion, and collaboration are the fundamental markers of its methodological transparency. It is perhaps best articulated by Cathy N. Davidson's concept of a Humanities 2.0: "a humanities of engagement that addresses our collective histories and concern for history" via emergent digital tools.[4] Anticapitalist figurations of the commons operate on a related level, extending concepts of knowledge as commons to modes of social formation. They are perhaps best articulated through what Silvia Federici and George Caffentzis identify as the formation of "autonomous spaces from which to reclaim control over our life and the conditions of our reproduction."[5] These spaces may be digital, they may be physical, but they are fundamentally opposed to capitalist alignment.

The dialogue that follows is predicated on these contrasting styles of producing and preserving the common good. Black Mask's collective political work is the processual ground and figure through which this dialogue takes place. I position Black Mask's tendencies for cultural preservation as an antagonist to critical DH figurations of the commons and draw out their implications for its acts of collective self-making. The two are ultimately linked via concepts of refusal and disgust, as well as intersectional critiques of preservation that bear out an alternative political potential. I forefront Black Mask's will to destroy what is, comparing the collective's illiberal style to DH-related concepts of critical unmaking, and I explicate its project via subjective will. This chapter concludes with a discussion of Black Mask's decolonial Dada—a politically informed aesthetic practice that equates cultural preservation with tactical relations of affinity—and its possible implications for knowledge's free dissemination via #guerrillaDH. Let's recall that thinkers like Simon Rowberry, the authors of "The Digital Humanities Manifesto 2.0," and Alex Gil *all* invoke the guerrilla in reference to knowledge's free movement in technocratic spheres. Decolonial Dada realizes the will to preserve unsuppressed access to sites and objects of cultural heritage in the contrast between publicly recognized labor and subversive tactics for producing alternatives to ossified institutional power.

The Living and the Dead

Black Mask's history is as interesting as it is enigmatic. Loosely affiliated with the Italian American filmmaker Aldo Tambellini, the collective was best known for its violent rhetoric and political analogue to Tambellini's black aesthetic, an art concept that was synonymous with primitivism and abjection. As described by a founding member, Osha Neumann, Black Mask had many names (The Motherfuckers and The International Werewolf Collective), and saw itself as a collection of "urban guerrillas swimming in the countercultural sea of freaks and dropouts (we didn't like the media term 'hippies') who had swarmed the cheap tenements of the Lower East Side of New York."[6] The collective's most vocal member, Ben Morea, "was the only white person offered honorary membership of the Black Panther Party, by Bobby Seale, and was asked to run for Vice President of the US in 1968 by Eldridge Cleaver, who ran for president with the Peace and Freedom Party."[7] As Gavin Grindon notes in his essay "Poetry Written in Gasoline," Morea "respectfully declined both."[8]

Of all the collective's statements and acts, it is clear that Black Mask was motivated by a will to make and sustain actually existing alternatives to the present social, economic, and political order. The collective proclaimed destruction because it was a necessary step toward realizing a more liberatory human condition. Preservation was thus always a partisan task in Black Mask's work, and was guided by the interplay between living out our creative capacities and combating the powers that would co-opt them. Institutions like the museum stood in the middle, marking a distinction between enclosed and common forms of cultural preservation. I cite Black Mask at length:

> The Vietnamese are fighting against the destruction of their culture as well as their land. The African revolutionaries have always been concerned with the preservation of their culture in the face of colonialism. And in this country the black man is becoming more aware of his culture, among others, the birth of jazz is no mean achievement. As well as the Mexican, Puerto Rican and Indian seeking to preserve theirs.
>
> Obviously, none of these people are concerned with the museums, but neither are we (other than seeing them destroyed). They

are involved with a living culture which is what we hope to see rise throughout America, a living culture which comes from the creative spirit of man. With this we can change the stultifying classrooms, the inhuman city, the concept of work when it is unnecessary and every-thing else which is crushing life instead of allowing it to fully grow. This cannot be achieved without revolution, but neither can it be achieved without the creative force. Sure: Close the warplants or the pentagon or city hall or the precinct station—but don't stop there, let their culture fall too.[9]

As Black Mask's rhetoric indicates, the call for MoMA's destruction was not a call for destruction's sake—it was intended to create the conditions for social reconstruction via an egalitarian ethos. It was to actualize an anti-institutional sensibility—expanding one's definition of what art could be against institu-tional validation—while also paralleling anti- and decolonial opposition at alternative institutional sites. The museum would be re-created as a pastiche of its ruins, realized in the performance of collectivized aesthetic acts, and as a multiplicity of autonomous spaces wholly disentangled from the market and the state. The debate over the museum's destruction is therefore grounded in a larger debate motivated by a dichotomy of sociocultural forces. What is living culture? How is it bound by the dead?

Black Mask's dichotomy between the dead and the living is straightfor-ward. Dead culture refers to modes of production that originate in and are guided by the interests of capital. Living culture refers to human capacities for self-making that both *precede* and *exceed* privatization. Where the state and the capitalist mode of production are positioned as both the base and the limit of our labor power, dead culture persists. Where subjects are able to produce (knowledge, art, etc.) in affinity with each other at a remove from the market and the state, living culture persists. In a piece titled "The Total Revolution" from *Black Mask No. 2*, the collective makes this point clear: "the aesthetic revolution today must be a part of the total revolution. A revolution which will bring about a society where the arts will be an integral part of life, as in primitive society, and not an appendage of wealth. A society where man has control of his life and the economic wealth of his community. A society free of bureaucracy, both totalitarian and bourgeois. A society where 'to each according to his needs' is the rule, not the exception."[10] In a DH terminology, living culture is much closer to acts of collaboration and generative thinking, while dead culture would refer to individualistic and profit-based intellectual endeavors. The power that Black Mask attributes to living culture can there-fore be summed up by its militancy—it is a call to both destroy and reproduce in opposition to institutional hierarchies and economic exploitation from a collective standpoint.

Marx's distinction between dead and living labor clarifies Black Mask's rhetorical link between dead and living culture in a broader political context. In Marx's view, dead labor refers to the means by which labor becomes productive for capital. Living labor refers to one's labor power, or one's ability to work and produce, prior to its conscription into the capitalist mode of production.[11] Dead labor results in atomization, while living labor is the kernel of sociality that is free from capitalist exploitation. The relationship shared between the dead and the living is one that is equally concerned with the subjects that are formative of living culture as it is with the objects of its production. The distinction between dead labor and living labor precedes this relation. As Jason Read notes, the problem of subjectivity that we encounter under neoliberal regimes "is not a matter of the reproduction of a fixed subject, but instead the extraction of wealth from a multitude of subjects that are constituted as basically interchangeable."[12] The collective, by contrast, is the conduit through which revolution might be maximized and living culture realized in the present. It preempts capital's subsumptive movement—to make subjects generalizable for profit's accumulation—as it posits an assembly of subjects who are indistinct from each other and illegible to the powers that would command them.

In light of both Marx's and Read's arguments, Kathi Weeks's description of refusal perhaps best captures Black Mask's position, albeit from a different ideological position.[13] The call to destroy MoMA is a function of the collective's absolute refusal to have its creative energy stultified and generalized by institutions of capital. It is another front on which to refuse the exploitation of labor:

> [Refusal] comprises at once a movement of exit and a process of invention. The refusal can make time and open spaces—both physical and conceptual—within which to construct alternatives. Rather than a simple act of disengagement that one completes, the refusal is, in this sense, a process, a theoretical and practical movement that aims to effect a separation through which we can pursue alternative practices and relationships.[14]

These are the affordances that Black Mask's call to destroy MoMA was meant to realize. The museum and the collective are thus a synecdochal site and figure of total revolution, but Black Mask's invocation of Vietnamese freedom fighters, African American revolutionaries, Mexican, Puerto Rican, and Indigenous anti- and decolonial movements also directs the dead/living dichotomy toward a broader politics of cultural preservation. The collective's call to destroy the museum is a refusal of its institutional standing, capture, and imposition on labor. It would open space for an alternative to the market and the state to manifest itself. Hence, living culture is positioned as freedom from injustice, whereas dead culture secures unjust power. If the commons is to emerge, Black Mask argues, "the total environment" must be reshaped, "physical and psychological; social and aesthetic, leaving no boundaries to divide man. The future is ours, but not without a struggle."[15]

Dead Labor, Living Subjects

Contemporary arguments that favor representation within GLAM spaces are perhaps best explained in contrast to Black Mask's call. Think of the Guerrilla Girls' intervention in contemporary museology as a starting point. In *The Guerrilla Girls' Bedside Companion to the History of Western Art* (1998), the collective upsets the spaces and subjects of cultural preservation by proffering the question: "Why haven't more women been *considered* great artists throughout Western history?"[16] More than a simple provocation, the Guerrilla Girls ask this question so as to "identify and ridicule the powers that be and to drag the misogynists and racists kicking and screaming into the 21st century."[17] As such, the Guerrilla Girls make the gallery into an antagonistic space that centralizes subjects that were thought to be insignificant and interchangeable.

The Guerrilla Girls are also militant in their claim that representation has *always been* linked to wealth patronizing the GLAM sector. As the Guerrilla Girl Romaine Brooks argues, women are not excluded from Western art histories indifferently; wealth is mobilized to exclude difference under the auspices of quality. Wealth is mobilized in this way to protect its investment, building consensus around what rises to the level of artistic talent and what does not:

> In the old days of Western culture, it was patronage and the atelier system. It's not that different now, though patronage doesn't come in the form of royal courts and the Roman Catholic Church, but in the form of gallery owners, collectors, critics and museums who back certain artists. Once enough money has been invested in a certain artist, everyone mobilizes to keep that artist's name out front and consequently in history. The artists who make it in this way begin to define quality.[18]

The collective's work reveals this fact as it (re)historicizes the gallery space, and deploys refusal toward alternative ends. Appropriate space. Redistribute its political economy. The collective does not give specific detail on the effect this has had on the patronage system, but they do claim that they have "made dealers, curators, and collectors accountable," presumably directing patronage in a different direction, rather than undermining it entirely.[19]

Black Mask paralleled this position; however, the collective was not interested in the politics of representation, patronage, or institutionalized histories.

Black Mask's common vision for cultural preservation gained from eliminating elite archives, refusing their cultural effects. The collective's interest in eliminating elite gallery spaces, contrary to groups like the Guerrilla Girls, was not meant to destroy relations of antagonism or aesthetic practice, nor was it meant to silence and ignore. It was rather a call to support anti- and para-institutional sites of cultural preservation that free knowledge from becoming dead. This, in Black Mask's view, was just as much an aesthetic task as it was subjective.

Black Mask's political position was provocative, even in our contemporary context. Brought into DH discourse and method, the guerrilla's invocation is as provocative as it is threatening. It focuses our attention on the politics that motivate acts of making, but also on our spaces of preservation. The GLAM sector's centrality in DH method is undeniable, as is its existence as a performative space. We hold exhibits in our labs, we curate and archive, we digitize physical materials, we debate metadata standards, and we build partnerships with museums on the basis of augmenting their cultural function with new technologies. How is a dead/living dichotomy reflected in this discourse?

DH's focus on the micropolitical aspects of archival and curatorial practices is often framed as a response to historical silence. It does so, analogous to the Guerrilla Girls above, through a politics of publicity, bringing excluded and overlooked histories of preservation to light where rigidly defined gallery spaces, statist and corporate control over the museum, and do-it-yourself sites of cultural preservation stand in relation to one another. This political concern is formative of DH's figuration of the commons. Think of how Dorothy and Eunsong Kim argue in their "#TwitterEthics Manifesto" that we should "move away from the pyramid to a circular system that values process over product" and "allow for a multiplicity of views."[20] There, the pair recognize the need that women and people of color have to make their own networks and spaces for self-preservation—"the dream of building our own structures complements the decolonization of the public spaces that we are invested in"—while also demanding that various institutions dignify this need.[21] DH does not destroy the museum in order to liberate living culture. It explores self-provisioning by other means, augmenting our access to cultural heritage sites, recognizing curatorial exclusions, and developing archival tools for personal use.

Kevin L. Ferguson's essay "To Cite or to Steal? When a Scholarly Project Turns Up in a Gallery" is a good starting point to draw out DH figurations of the commons on an individual level. In the summer of 2016, Ferguson noticed that the content of his scholarly work, which consists of "summed" images of hundreds of films, appeared in a British gallery, attributed to an artist/author other than himself, without recognition of Ferguson's work or method.[22] Ferguson argues that the artist intentionally obscures the broader aesthetic history to which his work refers and offers a robust bibliography referencing similar work. Finally, following a critique of the gallery and the artist, Ferguson makes his method available, offering a tutorial and link to the software he uses to create and archive summed images.

In Ferguson's account, his work appeared in the gallery space as objects alienated from their author's labor, excised from their mode of production, and attributed to another artist. It appeared as dead culture, rarified, commodified, and appropriated. His alternative, which is open and collaborative, is an attempt to liberate the processes by which work like his can be appropriated. He refuses acts of intellectual theft via a transparent politics of citation. For all intents and purposes, Ferguson's claim is one that is formative of living culture. His concerns certainly signal a debate over copyright and attribution, but they are perhaps more fundamentally a debate over the political logics that govern our spaces of cultural preservation, scholarly work included. If DH work is interdisciplinary in both form and method, it traverses institutional boundaries in a way that upsets the logic that governs, separates, and administers them. In DH praxis, this debate spans the physical/digital divide as well.

Digital databases and platforms for cultural preservation are often heralded as a cure to privatized physical sites, especially at a communal level. For instance, in a combination of keynote addresses titled "On Capacity and Care" that were featured on her blog, Bethany Nowviskie follows the Institute for Museum and Library Services by calling for the formation of a "national digital platform" for our cultural heritage. Such a platform would orient the preservation of cultural heritage

> toward sharing, in robust, open access repositories; for the linked and rich metadata that make them discoverable and interoperable; for usable but lightweight VREs or *virtual research environments*, filled with integrated, interchangeable toolsets; for the coordinated policies and agreements that help to shape practice and establish norms; and—at the most basic level—for a strong investment in building and sustaining the *workforce* needed to create and maintain and advocate for it all: for everything that would constitute a true national digital library.[23]

Many of the possibilities inherent in the formation of a national digital platform listed by Nowviskie track with Matthew K. Gold's brief interest in guerrilla pedagogy. It is open, collaborative, and transparent. Indeed, a platform like this would upset the political economy of privatized gallery spaces by fomenting new forms of collaborative interaction, open dialogue, and participatory action. This is motivated in part by thinking the components of the GLAM sector constitutively. It is also an effect of the digital on the physical. Digital access to a national digital platform for cultural heritage would provide unprecedented access to objects and information that are typically limited by physical entry and private interests.

The DH imperative for open and accessible GLAM spaces is a direct challenge to privatizing logics that govern our spaces of cultural preservation; however, it is not meant to fully disentangle cultural preservation from market forces or state sponsorship. This is reflected in DH's Creative Commons style. It negotiates this relationship in two ways. The first refers to the means and methods of providing open and accessible content, typified in Nowviskie's national digital platform. The second refers to the labor that both prefigures those spaces and makes them functional. Where DH aligns itself with institutions that are "best" situated to preserve these imperatives over the long term, the question of labor functions on two planes. On the one hand, there is labor attached to the objects and knowledges that are preserved. This refers to figures like Ferguson, who make aesthetic objects and augment scholarly approaches to DH. It could also refer to the Guerrilla Girls' work on more radical ends of the spectrum. On the other hand, labor allows these sites to persist. This refers to the communal aspects that are endemic to Nowviskie's claim to a sustainable GLAM workforce. It could refer to the production of decolonized spaces that Dorothy and Eunsong Kim call for in their effort to realize open and participatory modes of research. Our sites of cultural preservation inherently connect both forms of labor.

On its face, the dead/living dichotomy that Black Mask fomented might seem totally estranged from this discourse. However, the question of what is dead and what is living (in both objecthood and labor) is formative of the GLAM sector's infrastructure. Jeffrey Schnapp and Matthew Battles understand this connection intuitively in their coauthored *The Library Beyond the Book* (2014). In their eloquent articulation of the library as a living mausoleum, the contrast between the dead and the living corresponds to the status of knowledges interred and the labor that both produces and houses them: "both a cemetery and the livebrary: a place of intensified, deeper sociality and communion, a place of burial and mummification that equals a place of worship and constant renewal, reactivation, and conversation across the centuries."[24] Like the museum, the library both preserves and presents—it inhumes objects of knowledge in order to reactivate them over and again, well beyond the context of their creation or original use. For Schnapp and Battles, the difference between the dead and the living is therefore also a question of how the space of its preservation is administered. While this might take a virtual form, the pair also reimagine the library as a collaborative workspace—a space in which creative force and production meet in the presence of the past. The library as museum is thus a site in which dead and living constantly circulate, perhaps to the indifference of the walls that confine the confluence of this generative energy. The secondary layer to the dead/living distinction is therefore a question of the methods guiding our labor. What supports and what might delimit circulation and reactivation at our sites of cultural preservation? The production of living culture and its institutional capture become a question of living labor's use where creative force is interred.

What Schnapp and Battles's work makes clear is that dead culture and interred knowledge are not identical. Moreover, dead knowledge and dead labor are not equal. Dead culture's unchecked influence ensures cultural production's capture to the indifference of its circulation. Dead culture forces knowledge to conform to a hierarchy of production and preservation, but also to the exclusion of knowledges and objects that the state and/or capital cannot find value in. The living mausoleum does not. When GLAM spaces function under the logic outlined by Schnapp and Battles, they are not a simple commingling. They form productive sites of contestation as well. This is formative to their existence in/as a resource of the commons.

This condition is articulated succinctly in Jessica M. Johnson's blog post for the African American Intellectual History Society, "Doing and Being Intellectual History: #Formation as Curated by Black Women." There, Johnson opens her post with two important quotes. First, she provides an amended quote from the introduction to Mia Bay et al.'s *Toward an Intellectual History of Black Women*: "An intellectual history of black women is, at its simplest, a history of 'black women as producers of knowledge.'"[25] Second, she offers a quote from Alexis Pauline Gumbs's short article "Seeking the Roots: An Immersive and Interactive Archive of Black Feminist Practice": "A black feminist archival project is, at its simplest, a project designed to '*document ourselves now*, in ways that include, affirm, and activate our whole communities.'"[26] The first quote underscores the fact that any debate over what is dead and what is living within our sites of cultural preservation must account for the subjects who are productive of the objects and knowledges preserved. The second quote valorizes an alternative position to that of Nowviskie. What Gumbs describes here is both a refusal to be made dead, placed in an "unmarked grave," and a refusal to be made interchangeable.[27] Black feminist practice accomplishes this through the do-it-yourself construction of alternative structures for cultural preservation. Note that while this is productive of black feminist archives, it also signals a double burden: in order to have their culture preserved with respect to its context and modes of production, black women must also take on the labor of preserving it.

The debate over space and subjectivity in the explication of GLAM labor is intimately combined in this discourse. In advocating neither the total destruction nor the *detournement* of elite archives, Johnson publicizes the need and the expectation for those excluded from elite archives to document their own forms of cultural production. This same concern is consistently echoed in #femDH work, and points to a condition in which subjectivity and space are inextricable.[28] The experiential archives of black feminist practice are representational, haptic, and digitally mediated in Johnson's description, but they also bring publicity to the fore. Johnson articulates the political task in response to these elisions as a public politics of citation, one that does not elide living labor, but enlivens it. She writes:

> A black feminist and radical womyn of color politics of citation is one that acknowledges ways black women's intellectual production has been and continues to be rendered invisible, exploited, or devalued, then both centers the intellectual artifacts created by black women and privileges black women as producers and creators with the sole and extraordinary right to determine their encounters with institutions (i.e. academia, mainstream media, law enforcement vis à vis the surveillance of social media platforms and the internet more broadly) and bodies of thought outside their own circle.[29]

In no uncertain terms, Johnson's claim to citation is not limited to the acknowledgment of one's work; it is a claim to publicity that is also an act of control. A black feminist and radical womyn of color politics of citation determines how knowledge is encountered, reactivated, or referred to. It operates autonomously, reclaims and controls its conditions of social reproduction, and provides resources based on sharing and equal access. Johnson's claim to citation is therefore a public proclamation that mirrors living culture, as opposed to the dead, with a politics that favors accessibility while it also recognizes necessary limitations on an object or an idea's reuse.

The politics of citation to which both Johnson and Ferguson refer, differing but nevertheless public, commands the contemporary ethical debate in DH. Ferguson calls for openness and accessibility via acts of citation, and Johnson calls for recognition via the same. From a political standpoint, these practices can be framed as a refusal to be made dead—a refusal to be made into an interchangeable object of exploitation by socioeconomic forces—while retaining control over a culture's reuse. These practices have a tangible effect on our spaces of cultural preservation, physical and digital, as they also do on the subjects they have historically excluded. Space is reorganized as subjects of exclusion are recognized.

Violence as Living

A return to Black Mask's formulation of dead and living culture is necessary to proceed. Living culture does not simply refer to MoMA's destruction and the reclamation of one's labor within a collective milieu. It is embedded within an illiberal political logic that heightens partisan tension. Its subjective character is coeval with the proclaimed need to destroy the market, the state, and the institutions that allow them to persist. It is a call to sabotage statist cultures— unmake their physical and psychic dominion—so that the new might emerge.

In a Press Conference Report in the *Free Press*, Ben Morea proposes a concept of violence that maximizes the Black Mask's partisan stance where living culture is claimed:

> The dichotomy is always made between non-violence and violence and that's a false dichotomy. The dichotomy is between living and death . . . Some kinds of violence are living, understand? Some kinds of violence are death. If your violence is because you desire to live and is only directed against people who would prevent you from living, then I don't consider that violence. I consider that living. If your violence, like the police violence and the military violence, is directed against others, killing others, that is violence because it's death.[30]

Morea's claim is neither flippant nor unthoughtful. It describes a political condition in which state-perpetrated brutality both prefigures generative acts of resistance and mobilizes acts of collective self-making. His argument is especially incisive where the collective's politics originate, and furthermore in its attempt to foment an egalitarian alternative. Morea's claim is predicated on two assumptions: (1) violence is inescapable, but can be differentiated by productive and destructive acts, and (2) the violence one commits indicates what modes of relation and possible futures exist as live options for one to pursue, revealing the scope and limit of one's collective future.

These conditions are a direct reflection of the collective's anticapitalist ideology, but extend to their aesthetico-political regime well. The call to liberate and reclaim living culture not only recognizes that preexisting brutalities necessitate such actions; it is an essential step toward producing an alternative political economy of free culture and knowledge. It is the promise that living culture remains a common good, and it signifies a desire to reproduce life via collective labor by alternative means. Violence is therefore an access point to a broader set of concerns where cultural production and cultural preservation meet. What must be done to create and sustain a commons that refuses capitalist alignment? How does this correlate to preservation projects that are rooted in liberal ideals as opposed to illiberal politics?

Before I explore these interventions in particular, I want to outline two concepts in contemporary scholarship on new media and DH. While not illiberal in scope, the examples below acknowledge the need to eliminate existing powers in the effort to create liberatory alternatives. Both examples clarify Black Mask's argument, but also its inclusion here. They foreground the political and subjective arguments that follow.

First, Garnet Hertz and Jussi Parikka's claim to European avant-garde aesthetics, featured in chapter 2, functions under a similar logic. Hertz and Parikka introduce their work on "Zombie Media" by claiming that their "archaeology of tinkering, remixing and collage would not start from Duchamp and the historical avant-garde, but from opening up the screen, the technology."[31] Hertz and Parikka presume two forms of violence in the formation of media archaeology as an artistic method. On the one hand, the pair forefront the conditions formative of the anthropocene: our current geological age wherein human impact on the environment is its most dominant threat of collapse. Industrial materials pose a global threat in their accumulation as waste, just as the media have traversed their "speculative opportunity phase" to their "consumer commodity phase," and to their present "archaeological phase," showcasing the fact that "media never dies."[32] Dead media form part of a global network of waste that threatens all forms of life that antedate it. The privatization of living labor persists in the dead object. Its obsolescence is a referent to our accelerated and unsustainable patterns of consumption. On the other hand, Hertz and Parikka advocate for a process of generative disassembly that commits violence to our consumption-based political economy. They do so in the effort to open the screen and technology up to productive afterlives. When dead media are dismantled in order to reuse them in the present, the economic imperative to consume, progress, and forget is refused. This is a form of violence that works to eliminate patterns of consumption that produce environmental collapse.

A second example follows from Fiona Barnett et al.'s "QueerOS: A User's Manual." There, the authors express a "queer impulse to explode" our most common interfaces at the same time that they imagine the user of a QueerOS becoming "one/multiple/nothing" through its use.[33] A QueerOS refuses legibility, disallowing its conscription into our political economies of the digital. As such, "it is necessarily an unreliable system full of precarity, and thus reflects the condition of contemporary queer subjectivity."[34] While a speculative enterprise, the articulation of a QueerOS is an exercise in forming an active and collective relation to the present by first eliminating what restrains it. We must destroy the interface so that an alternative technology of the self might emerge through the collective social relations that follow. Jacob Gaboury's "Critical Unmaking: Toward a Queer Computation" offers further insight into this speculative maneuver. There, he argues, we must "acknowledge how futurity has been colonized by the cultural logic of contemporary technology, and as such [contemporary technology] cannot serve as the primary vector for queer computational critique. Thus, rather than mobilize queerness as a useful technological apparatus, we might deploy it as part of a critical practice of unmaking."[35] In the effort to become one/multiple/nothing via the interface's disassembly, queering the interface does not go far enough. It must be critically unmade, centering the production of subjectivity in a manner that tracks with the dead/living divide. What does it mean to become one/multiple/nothing through the violence and generativity of our most intimate technologies? How might this affect our approach to cultural preservation?

Following these examples, Black Mask's political work is perhaps most impactful *prior* to the formation of a gallery space or archival site. DH's figuration of the commons intervenes at the level of institutional capture. Its common character is generative of political acts. Critique is concomitant with these acts. Framed as a guerrilla exercise, Black Mask's desire to destroy MoMA is more than an anti-art movement within this discussion. It, intentionally so, precludes the turn to publicity as a political tactic. It signifies a will to unmake institutional powers as the collective pivots toward an alternative that refuses any recuperation of the present. It trades on ontological indistinction via collective acts of self-making that are coterminous with its call to destroy. These are the tactics the collective deploys in order to realize the future it imagines—to unmake contemporary institutions of oppression—and realize its own political economy of the commons.

The violent response to dead knowledge and dead labor's production meets a theoretical fork on this point. Black Mask's political does not share a one-to-one correlation with any existing form of DH praxis, and the means by which it establishes its position requires critique. DH valorizes openness, accessibility, and recognition in its vision of knowledge as commons. Black Mask valorizes collective self-making in its attempt to subvert state power and the commodity form. This is precisely where Black Mask departs from DH praxis as it is currently practiced and where its anticapitalist figuration of the commons is made transparent. Its departure is consequential. Where Black Mask forefronts political work that is illegible and oppositional to institutional power, it marks a subjective turn that vaunts performance and lived experience, rather than detourned museology. It does so in order to model liberatory alternatives to both institutionalized forms of cultural preservation and processes of transforming living culture into dead. The subjective turn is synonymous with unmaking the present social, political, and economic order.

Collective Subjects, Performative Acts

In what follows, I ground my reading of the collective's work as a kind of critical unmaking, albeit from a controversial position. Black Mask's political is, at least in part, reliant upon the moving image as it formulates a response to the dead/living dichotomy. Cinematic work that is formative of the collective's aesthetico-political regime gives equal focus to the subject it forms and to the body it imposes; it also reveals potential moral hazards. Its politics are both a model and point of critique. I do not address the question of publicity as a remedy to the collective's politics. Nor do I avoid the ethical imperatives that are inherent to public acts of citation which address these problems. I address these questions in the processes through which Black Mask articulates its subjectivity, fundamentally shifting the public debate, and thus the political terms upon which acts or preservation are situated.

Academic analyses of Black Mask's work are few, but of those that exist, Nadja Millner-Larsen's is vital. In a short article outlining Black Mask's conceptual work, "Black Mask: Revolution as Being," Millner-Larsen writes that "despite [their] attacks on the art institution, Black Mask's members were also involved in New York's nascent expanded cinema and underground film and theatre scenes of the mid-1960s, through their collaborations with the Italian-American multimedia artist Aldo Tambellini."[36] Importantly, Tambellini was not a member of Black Mask proper, but he did, as Millner-Larsen notes, work with the collective on "a series of 'electromedia' performances" that combined kinetic and multimedia art practices.[37] Black Mask's connection to political issues inherent to cinematic practice—to the ontological conditions formative of representation and erasure—is therefore enhanced by interrogating Tambellini's work prior to the collective's connection to Dadaism and decolonial struggle. The collective established itself as a revolutionary body of creative actors, making alternatives to their present context, as they transitioned to a position of absolute refusal.

A U.S.-born émigré to Italy, Tambellini returned to the United States in 1946, and in 1959 he moved to New York City's Lower East Side, where he subsequently cofounded the "underground 'counter-culture' group 'Group Center'" with two of Black Mask's members, Ron Hahne and Ben Morea, along with several other artists. Group Center's legacy rests on its organization: "non-traditional presentation outlets for artists to present their work to the public."[38] As a gallery space, Group Center fomented an ideological position similar to Black Mask's call to destroy the museums. Here, Tambellini notes:

> I wrote at [the time Group Center was founded], "Creation is not the commodity of a status-seeking class. Creation is the vital energy of society. We believe that the 'our system' is an enormous dinosaur extinguishing at a fantastic rate which opposes truth and freedom and that it has squeezed out of man the essential vitality which made him part of the human race." For that reason, "Group Center" consciously and intentionally chose to become a counter-culture, underground group trying to find ways to change and impact that harsh closed-in system.[39]

The rhetorical similarities between Tambellini's description of his countercultural gallery space and Black Mask's first political action are too apparent to miss. It is also an interesting prefiguration of the politics that guide contemporary forms of critical making. Both discourses rally around the maker and the made, locating their import in both the space of the act and the subjects that produce it. The implicit statement seems to be that the generative acts associated with the group are a continuous expression of their collective formation. Making is a form of being, and being together as a collective realizes an alternative to institutional exclusions and capitalist logics.

The feminist valences of this argument should not be elided. Recall Elizabeth Losh's provocation from chapter 2: "What would it mean to move from a paradigm of tool development to a paradigm of process and performance in which the network of power formations moves from ground to figure?"[40] Tambellini's definition of Group Center certainly enacts an aesthetic turn that relocates power formations from ground to figure, but one that also magnifies the antagonisms that inform its relocation. Tambellini seems to suggest that preservative acts wholly opposed to capitalist logics rely heavily on performance and site-specificity by means of their collective will. Group Center's location is in its performance. This is the site and process of unmaking institutional space, and thus institutional power. One cannot conceive of a long-form act of preservation so long as capital's co-optive power lurks in the surround. If one is to truly preserve living culture, one's only option is to refuse, destroy, and rebuild—to unmake what excludes—and embody cultural revolution in one's present circumstances. Perhaps Tambellini's work departs from Losh's provocation here, but it certainly departs from her intersectional work in its racial contours.

Stemming from his work at Group Center, Tambellini chose the color black to act as a base concept and metaphor for hundreds of political and aesthetic projects. Throughout the 1960s and '70s, Tambellini developed his black aesthetic by working with mediums as various as sculpture, poetry, film, and television. At its base, the black aesthetic was meant to signify the violence and abjection in human origin, at times abject and disorienting, as a contrast to knowledge and light. At the same time, Tambellini relied on the rhetoric and aesthetic of the Black Power movement in order to craft his concept: "Black is one of the important reasons why the racial conflicts are happening today, because it is part of an old way to look at human beings or race in terms of colour," Tambellini argued in the October 1967 issue of *artscanada*. "Black will get rid of the separation of colour at the end. Blackness is the beginning of the re-sensitizing of human beings."[41] Tambellini continues, "I strongly believe in the word 'black power' as a powerful message, for it destroys the old notion of western man, and by destroying that notion it also destroys the tradition of the art concept."[42]

Tactically speaking, Tambellini's work moves in two directions at once. First, his use of black as a conceptual tool relies on the notion that black precedes art—black is "the beginning of all things," Tambellini proclaims, "just like we begin with the dark stage, we begin with the black stage in all life."[43] This is a recurrent feature of human life in Tambellini's view. Humans emerge from the womb, we emerge from a cave, we project ourselves into space—all of these instances of becoming are an emergence from blackness.[44] This recurrent stage contextualizes the desire to unmake institutional power, its effects on culture, and subsequently how culture is preserved. Of his present circumstances, Tambellini argues that "man himself is completely in this darkness; he's a moronic human being right now—dictated by the capitalist structure that reduces him completely to an unthinking object."[45] Blackness is primitiveness and lack, but it also prefigures enlightenment via our acts of self-making. The justification for this conceptual maneuver and those like it is rooted in Tambellini's rejection of elite gallery spaces: "I don't even go the god damn museums any more [*sic*], Tambellini exclaims, "I get the creeps, god damn it, I get depressed for months—it reminds me what the fucking black man must feel when he walks in the damn upper class of this society. I see the god damn slums in this country. I know how it feels to be black and walking the streets of white society and as a white man, I feel what this damn ruling class is doing to anybody creative."[46]

For all intents and purposes, Tambellini's conceptualization of black as primitive, concomitant with the feelings of alienation and oppression aligned with African American subjectivity, functions as a kind of cyclical critical unmaking that is meant to reproduce the conditions of human development in order to realize the new. However, his assumptions result in a reactionary stance that exploits racial tension in the effort to abstract universal human experiences from their material ground. In his *The Universal Machine* (2018), for example, Fred Moten recounts the conversation between Ad Reinhart, Cecil Taylor, and Aldo Tambellini in *artscanda* and critiques Tambellini's work. Where all artists utilized the color black in their work as an art concept, Moten notes how Tambellini's work is part of "an old discourse that combines primitivism, futurism, and blackness as the disavowal of physicality."[47] This is, in his reading, a disavowal of the racial dimensions of being that make black life concrete even as Tambellini states his desire to unmake specific institutions of oppression.

The second movement grounds the first in aesthetic practice. Tambellini invokes race in his work in order to subvert state power on a larger scale. Visually speaking, a strong example of this invocation can be traced to his 1966 film, *BLACK PLUS X*. There, Tambellini tries to disavow the signifying power of whiteness by inverting the color of his subject's skin. He does so by projecting the film's negative, representing African American subjects as white-skinned. This cinematic inversion creates multiple effects. It is a clear comment on race in the United States, asking viewers to consider blackness with the same care that they uncritically offer to whiteness. The film's use of close-ups also plays with ideological perspective and affect. Often only parts of the bodies featured in the film comprise the frame. It is as if African American children have been placed under a microscope, but also as if the spectator is moving with and among the children at play, both distancing the spectator *from* and implicating the spectator *with* the subjects depicted on the screen.

Although a set of simple gestures, Tambellini's cinematic work is similar to the performative power he ascribes to Group Center as a whole. Race is a material construct that is formative of social and economic inequity, and cinema can be mobilized to reorient and rearticulate one's perspective and one's subjectivity. Abjection is a conduit to this fundamental realignment. The maker and the made's recursive arc exists solely in unmaking what is so in order to remake what could be. By placing the viewer in and among subject positions she is estranged from, Tambellini's interest in reorienting the viewer's perspective arguably transforms abjection into empathy. It is an attempt to transcend the imperial gaze by allowing white viewers to identify with African American subjects in common terms. Empathy, however, comes at the cost of whitewashing his cinematic subjects.

Subjectivity and Preservation

I want to underscore two features of Tambellini's work at this juncture that reappear with Black Mask—both correspond to his desire to unmake institutional powers as collective subjectivity and para-institutional acts of preservation coincide. On the one hand, the intended effect of Tamebllini's art is to reorient the viewer's perspective (psychologically and politically), destroying the viewer's present frame of reference by inverting it. The art's role in producing a political effect, an act of unmaking that actualizes political becoming, is an extreme example of something like Losh's performative turn, leading to intersectional ambiguity. If Tambellini's work was meant to implicate the viewer with the subjects he sees on screen, is his gaze merely extended, or is imperial power subverted? On the other hand, the racial contours of Tambellini's work are duplicated in Black Mask's aesthetico-political regime. In Millner-Larsen's reading, for example, Black Mask's political, but especially its "electromedia performances," "were entangled in the problem of representational thinking inherent to structures of racism."[48] If and how Black Mask superseded representational thinking of this kind comes to bear on its figuration of the commons and acts of preservation.

Consider Black Mask's rhetorical analogue to this aesthetic maneuver. In the collective's essay "The New Proletariat: Nigger as Class" featured in *Black Mask No. 10—April/May 1968*, Black Mask continues the whitewashing process, failing to adequately understand racialized violence as it seeks to destroy the market and the state:

> The "Negro" revolution (civil rights) gave way to the "Black" revolution (nationalism) which must finally give way to the "Nigger" revolution: the total expression of a new emerging class of dispossessed. There has always existed a dispossessed class (lumpen) but never has it occupied the center of social change, being peripheral to the means of production . . . Now it is exactly these non-workers and automated ex-workers who are the most socially pivotal; it is how the system deals with them and their existence which shall determine its continuance; and conversely it is how we strengthen this consciousness that we succeed. We must expand the possibilities of this class and spread its social view: the question of "Nigger" transcends race and becomes one of class.[49]

In perhaps its most appropriative move in the entirety of its writing, Black Mask claims that with capital's expansion on and over life, all revolutionaries inhabit the disenfranchised position that African Americans hold in the United States, regardless of race. Analogous to Tambellini's ideological claims—a condition perhaps inherited from his certitude that blackness is "a universal force that will 'get rid' of race"—Black Mask massifies African American experience, spectacularizing and then dissolving the particularities of racialized oppression.[50] Again, unmaking is predicated on the idea that blackness can be refashioned as a condition of ontological indistinction, rending its experience from material history, and thus the particularity of its oppression. Where Millner-Larsen argues that Black Mask follows "the more radical implications of Fanon's work," this passage is indicative of the collective's unwitting reproduction of "the white gaze."[51] It is a nod toward thinking race and class co-constitutively, but it is anathema to actual intersectional critique.

This presupposition further contours the collective's claim to cultural preservation. The will to critically unmake racist institutions and to inaugurate a post-representational political milieu lapses into structural erasure. Race here is only engaged in its elision, allowing the concept of class to expand beyond the factory floor as race dissolves into air. The collective is thus a mechanism for making the black aesthetic a living reality, but also of instrumentalizing abstract racialized oppression to its advantage as living culture is preserved.

This observation is compounded when compared to intersectional analyses that are focused on racialized oppression. Think of Patricia Hill Collins's characterization of the "*outsider within*," following from a characterization of black women's work in the post-World War II era. Collins offers an inverse view of race and social formation. In Collins's account, "Domestic work allowed African-American women to see White elites, both actual and aspiring, from perspectives largely obscured from Black men and from these groups themselves."[52] Black women's labor allowed them to see and experience the social reproduction of white life. Their labor implicated them in its reproduction, offering black women an intimate perspective into the social reproduction of white life, but their status as domestic laborers was simultaneously an insurmountable barrier to achieving socioeconomic equity. Collins continues:

> On one level this insider relationship was satisfying to all concerned. Accounts of Black domestic workers stress the sense of self-affirmation the women experienced at seeing racist ideology demystified. But on another level these Black women knew that they could never belong to their White "families." They were economically exploited workers and thus would remain outsiders. The result was being placed in a curious outsider within social location (Collins 1986b), a peculiar marginality that stimulated a distinctive Black woman's perspective on a variety of themes (see, e.g., Childress 1986).[53]

The limit that Collins points to is undergirded by deep socioeconomic brutalities. It is a strong example of how "intersectional paradigms remind us that oppression cannot be reduced to one fundamental type, and that oppressions work together in producing injustice," but it also demonstrates an underlying opacity that limits one's ability to empathize across racial barriers, even when one is within intimate proximity of the barrier.[54] This characterization of black women's labor belies Tambellini's original assumption, as well as Black Mask's generalization of the African American subject position, in two senses: (1) aestheticizing race as a means of destroying racial inequality is a one-sided process, and (2) black women are already intimately aware of the processes through which whiteness is reproduced and are excluded from it. If white subjects are only able to empathize with others if they are whitewashed, the imperial gaze magnifies; it is not subverted.

This is perhaps an undergirding misapprehension that guides Black Mask's reconceptualization of class. Any collective act predicated on generalizing African American experience does not supersede representational thinking in a liberatory mode.[55] The effort to critically unmake institutional power ends halfway. It arguably duplicates racialized brutality by favoring the white subjects who wish to mobilize African American experience as a political tool.

From Unmaking to the Commons

Black Mask's subjective turn and call to destroy was predicated on Tambellini's black aesthetic. The recursive arc between the maker and the made evident in Black Mask's reconceptualization of class duplicates racialized brutalities, but it also points to a generalized condition of refusal meant to produce a revolutionary milieu. In this context, unmaking is a subjective enterprise that creates class consciousness, but it also serves as the fundament of Black Mask's collective aspirations. Unmaking manifests in the interplay between traditional sites of capitalist refusal and the formation of an active underground. Subjectivity operates in erasure for the collective. Publicity is not the proclamation of individual will in Black Mask's view, nor is its goal to create a system of inclusive representation under existing signifying regimes. It is the proclamation of absolute refusal.

What, then, is preservation for? The analogous acts of preservation outlined in the DH contexts discussed earlier operate in parallel with current GLAM spaces. They may evidence a kind of agonistic interrelationality, but public-facing DH work does not aim to eliminate the present. Black Mask's subjective turn marks the will to create and preserve autonomous spaces of living culture that bear out productive antagonisms. It undergirds the collective's eventual vision of the commons. In what follows, I think through the political implications of creating a collective underground meant to preserve the will to refuse as a predicate to DH's own proclamation of guerrilla organization and tactics. This process begins by untangling Black Mask's common goals from its basis in blackness. It demands that the common good find an alternative post-representational basis.

As Millner-Larsen notes, Black Mask "widely acknowledge that they stopped making artwork once the group gained momentum. For them, art's ability to support contemporaneous political struggles had to move beyond the mere representation of oppression."[56] While this may not adequately explain the collective's theorization of a new proletariat, it does point to alternative interpretations of its claim to violence. The ontological argument that informs Black Mask's collective aspirations is coterminous with its interest in cultural preservation. My effort to frame Black Mask's political as a form of critical unmaking focuses on cultural preservation's subjective character—a process in which the subject exists as both the maker and the made—and its collective character, including its faults, is forefronted. Importantly, the subjective turn in this aesthetico-political history is abutted by a perspectival position that grounds the collective's processes for channeling living culture toward the production of the commons. Abjection and violence manifest a perspectival position that is wholly limited to the situation in which they are deployed.

Consider William Haver's concept of guerrilla seeing here. He argues that guerrilla seeing is a site-specific modality of political articulation that requires

> a situating of oneself without a cartographic or perspectival reflection, because haptic, guerrilla seeing exceeds, essentially and at every point, every possible cartography or perspectivism. And therefore is something other, something more, than the reflective subjectivity of every transcendental cartography. Haptic, guerrilla seeing never puts things in perspective. It is the very experience of non-transcendence, of non-neutrality.[57]

In refusing the transcendental gaze, the guerrilla embodies alternative modes of relation, actualizing the power of collective self-making by virtue of its radical positionality. The guerrilla cannot transcend the ontological conflict that is formative of its subjectivity. Brutality precedes its politics, formation, and acts of revolution. For Black Mask, post-representational politics demand that living culture move from the production of aesthetic objects to the production of revolution full stop. The demand to destroy what inhibits revolution—to unmake institutional power in the will to preserve living culture—is a symptom of its perspectivism.

This perspectival position is important for at least two reasons. First, it describes an ontological condition that is necessary for the actualization of the kinds of collective self-making that I have examined throughout this text. In claiming that the guerrilla is in a sociopolitical position of non-neutrality, a kind of embodiment of militant affects in its position of immanent reflectivity, eliminates the cognitive distance that prioritizes the "I" over all other modes of individuation. The haptic quality that Haver attributes to the figure of the guerrilla is the catalyst of its differentiation. Second, this condition realizes the collective situation that guerrilla politics are meant to produce. In Millner-Larsen's reading, Black Mask's post-representational figuration of the subject is a means of *decolonizing* inherited models of subjectivity. She describes this method succinctly: Black Mask's aesthetico-political output ultimately forwards the notion that "to be a Dadaist in 1968 required one to embrace a militant practice of decolonization, a struggle that might only be waged at the level of the aesthetic and the political, the visual and the haptic, the representational and the real, simultaneously."[58]

The collective's will to destroy, to unmake and produce alternatives to the present, is thus grounded in a broader political milieu. It is not limited to Tambellini's black aesthetic, or perhaps most importantly to its own confused articulation of race, as it invokes avant-garde politics and decolonial will. It rather attempts to realize the very basis of critical unmaking—refusing to let the future be colonized by our present comportment to it. The combination of decolonial and avant-garde politics in this discourse is its most generative feature—the act that would push its politics beyond mere transgression and mere antagonism. Think of Tristan Tzara's claim to disgust in his "Dada Manifesto" as a starting point:

> Every product of disgust capable of becoming a negation of the family is Dada; a protest with the fists of its whole being engaged in destructive action: Dada; knowledge of all the means rejected up until now by the shamefaced sex of comfortable compromise and good manners: DADA; abolition of logic, which is the dance of those impotent to create: DADA; of every social hierarchy and equation set up for the sake of values by our valets: DADA: every object, all objects, sentiments, obscurities, apparitions and the precise clash of parallel lines are weapons for the fight: DADA.[59]

Where Tzara's claim to negation is clear at the opening of this quote, its conclusion is its most important feature. *All objects and all sentiments are a potential weapon that can be oriented toward a politics of negation.* The ontological status of disgust is more important than any particular object that would manifest it. This remains true for Black Mask. In the instances that the collective mobilized violence and abjection toward specific goals (destroy the museums!), the point was not to use tools that might visualize an alternative political formation. It was an all-encompassing form of revolution that magnified feelings of disgust that were prefigurative of their acts of refusal. It was to *be* a weapon that produced a desired outcome. Black Mask ultimately instrumentalized this experience so as to grasp at a decolonial problem not fully realized in its acts of collective self-making: under what conditions might subjectivity be rethought, disarticulated, and subsequently rearticulated at an absolute distance from the market and the state's imperial grasp?

Perhaps somewhat predictably, Black Mask's combination of avant-garde and decolonial politics begins with a call to destroy. In an essay titled "Revolution as Being," featured in the collective's final publication, *Black Mask No. 10—April/May 1968*, Black Mask clearly articulates its perspectival position: "To think on Being and to Be revolutionary is to undertake to destroy a great deal of ourselves in the process," the collective writes. "There is no distinction between the subjective and the objective in the revolutionary act. Being must everywhere be the basis of our thought and deed."[60] The collective's primary enemy is America's bourgeois culture—"the structure of sublimation that constitute [*sic*] bourgeois society"—that masks the common good from the masses.[61] This series of arguments undergirds Millner-Larsen's claim to Black Mask's decolonial idea. The discovery of "being" through the revolutionary act is analogous to the decolonial refusal of a European *id-entity*, or speaking in the language of the colonizer. It corresponds to Solanas and Getino's decolonization of culture, but also recalls Maria Lugones's call to move together and defy colonial cartographies via intersubjective relationality. Disgust and refusal are Black Mask's entry points for a collective subject to emerge within the metropole that corresponds to revolutionary struggle worldwide. The subject of revolution eliminates objectivity in thought and action, situating herself among the dispossessed. The "I" does not stand apart from the prevailing matrix of ethical norms and conflicting moral frameworks. In fact, there is no "I" to speak of in Black Mask's theorization of revolution as being. There is only the collective, readied to enact cultural revolution.

This is precisely where Black Mask's concept of the commons emerges. The concept is articulated in three stages, and relies on its subjective turn, specifying its equation of cultural preservation with tactical relations of affinity and its intended effect on the future. "In the pre-revolutionary period," Black Mask writes, collective political relations would manifest in affinity groups, assembled "to project a revolutionary consciousness & to develop forms for particular struggles."[62] This is followed by the revolutionary period itself, where affinity groups are proclaimed to "emerge as armed cadres at the centers of conflict."[63] In the post-revolutionary period, affinity groups "become models for new everyday life. In this way the organization transcends the historical problems of centralism vs. decentralism, by making all structures a dynamic inter-relation of centralist & de-centralized elements: affinity groups coalesce to form large organizations/institutions simultaneously engaging in public struggles for consciousness & maintaining an active underground."[64] The common future Black Mask envisions maintains a commitment to continued struggle, but operates on a clear set of lasting principles: develop "new technological organization of resources, a new distribution of wealth, reestablishment of ecological principles . . . , to create a whole new complex of free relations between people, that can satisfy all our complex needs for change & our consuming desire to be new & to be whole."[65] Unequivocally, the collective forefronts the need to eliminate institutional structures that inhibit one's ability to live as it points toward liberatory futures. But its final provocation, that its tactics result in a dialogic work of common social organization, is paramount.

As such, violence forms two sides of a dialectical process in this discourse. On the one side, violent acts aim their attention at the abolition of bourgeois institutions that allow state-sponsored brutality to persist: "Close the warplants or the pentagon or city hall or the precinct station—but don't stop there, let their culture fall too."[66] On the other side, the collective does violence to itself, abjecting its members' privileged status as it refuses to let its subjectivity undergird the market and the state. The bourgeois individual is as much a threat to the collective's revolutionary ethos as larger forces of social (re)production. The subjective turn in Black Mask's aesthetico-political regime therefore clarifies differing tendencies of preservation. It clarifies the political motivation for conflicting needs to produce the commons. Collectivity arises from abjection and violence against the bourgeois individual. Identitarian difference is subsumed in the course of its destruction as collective models take over. What Black Mask does not adequately address is the distinct status of racialized and sexualized brutality that extends from colonial and neocolonial policy, opening the door to myriad forms of cultural appropriation. Blackness and erasure must be disengaged from each other if blackness solely refers to physicality's deprival.

Decolonial Dada!

The method that follows from Black Mask's political, oriented toward cultural preservation and needs-based reclamation, is the dialectical comprisal of nascent decolonial consciousness and guerrilla perspectivism. If Black Mask's politics operate as a form of critical unmaking, it is because it draws on prior countercultures that give its work context and direction, aligning it with avant-garde and decolonial imperatives for its application. Black Mask's critical offering is a decolonial Dada method that is meant to equate cultural preservation with tactical relations of affinity—"total unemployment and the new man" repackaged in the fight to "liberate ourselves from tight-assed bourgeois life."[67] Gavin Grindon expands on this sentiment:

> In their radical neo-avant-garde claims for art and revolution, and in their accompanying activist-art practices, groups like Black Mask influentially rework the avant-garde iteration of the autonomy of art-as-a-value as a language for general intellect's antagonism to capital. Their neo-avant-garde redeployment of dadaist and surrealist artistic tactics served as a political language for imagining the other identities and ways of living which now seemed possible. In this situation, the

"aestheticization of politics" was not, as in Walter Benjamin's famous formulation, a catastrophe, but a site of radical potential.[68]

This sentiment is predicated on the disgust with state-sponsored brutality and its modes of social organization. It is realized in their negation. Black Mask's will to align itself with Vietnamese freedom fighters, African American revolutionaries, Mexican, Puerto Rican, and Indigenous anti- and decolonial movements is an attempt to both fuse art and life into a common revolutionary practice and learn to preserve it via a host of violent affects.

The questions that follow rest where refusal and world-building coincide. Can the act of meeting public needs coexist with collectivized acts of subversion? What might be desirable about their coextension? If Black Mask's work offers anything truly novel to DH praxis, particularly following my argument in chapter 2, then it certainly lies in the combination of decolonial and avant-garde projects. It lies where publicity and erasure meet in the call for affinity, cultural preservation, and ultimately the production of the commons. If the collective's decolonial Dada were to realize its potential, its first decolonial act would be to eradicate racialized generalization from its ontological ground.

On the productive side of the argument, decolonial Dada is the synthesis of political refusal with collectivized world-building. The concept's ontological underpinnings mirror the arguments over ontological expansiveness featured in chapter 1, and Black Mask's call to destroy MoMA is only one variation of its deployment. Indeed, if subjectivity and space are co-implicated in a decolonial Dada method, the collective features of Black Mask's political demand their recontextualization. Ontological expansiveness, maximized racialized inequality, or any other form of appropriation in the production of abstract political strategies cannot predetermine conditions of refusal, or what comes after. The argument is rather located in a multiplicity of tactics that mirror the guerrilla's invocation as a politically motivated theoretical tool. How is difference prioritized over the will to control? How is context prioritized over universal utility?

Think of DH's own #guerrillaDH as an analogue to this desire. When Simon Rowberry ponders after DH's "Napster moment," he lauds cultures of piracy and bootlegging, claiming them to be formative of a "guerrilla digital humanities [that] can be broadly defined as the application of methods associated with digital humanities to texts still protected by copyright laws."[69] Such an approach relies on "a sleight of hand to avoid detection," and therefore an unwillingness to be made legible to institutional forces.[70] It does violence to institutionalized forces of preservation, particularly the economic imperatives that guide them. But it does so as a form of living. It is a means of liberating interred knowledge made dead.

In his own formulation of a #guerrillaDH, Alex Gil writes: "I fight in the archive, real and virtual, where an important chunk of our collective memories are in danger of disappearing or await patiently. The fight consists of advocacy most of the time, but sometimes, and this is the fun part, building playgrounds on the margins of the law. My heart definitely lurks in bushy hills above the legal gothic where I am forced to make a living, hence the guerrilla in #guerrilladh."[71] He goes on to articulate the need for politicized DH work that does not exist as a public enterprise—work that may inadvertently undermine public efforts aimed at inclusion and representation:

> Of course, much of the work of #guerrilladh is unpaid and unrecognizable by definition, but it counts. The republic of letters we contribute to with guerrilla work is also not the publicly accessible library that we ultimately need, but it counts . . . I hesitate to write these lines because I know that our struggles in the shadow clash with our struggle to have the work of the humanities sustained adequately by our institutions and our patrons, public and private. One possible solution is to deploy derivatives from the shadow work in recognizable channels. Another example of this type of work is the public study of existing shadow and pirate libraries, both the technology and the social phenomenon.[72]

Gil's work operates in the same vein as Rowberry's discussed above. #guerrillaDH operates in erasure, illegible and undetected by institutional power, but open and accessible to those who operate within underground networks. It is violence as living: living knowledge and living labor that are both preserved and made free at a remove from patronage, corporate interests, and ossified institutional power. If #guerrillaDH work appears within an institutional context, it does so in a derivative form—a copy of the living labor that undergirds it.

Perhaps the same is true for the authors of "The Digital Humanities Manifesto 2.0" when they call for a tactics of anarchic remix. Their guerrilla action items advocate for varying degrees of subversion, articulating a logic quite similar to Black Mask's concept of living culture and desire for the commons:

> weak = ignore the well-intentioned "voices of reason" that will always argue for interpreting scholarly or artistic fair use in the most restrictive manner (so as to shield the institutions they represent from lawsuits, no matter how improbable or unfounded); adopt vigorous interpretations of fair use that affirm that, in the vast majority of cases, scholarship and art practice: a) are not-for-profit endeavors whose actual costs far exceed real or potential returns; and b) are endeavors that, rather than diminishing the value of IP or copyright, enhance their value.

> medium = circumvent or subvert all "claims" that branch out from the rights of creators to those of owners, the photographers hired by owners, places of prior publication . . .

strong = pirate and pervert materials by the likes of Disney on such a massive scale that the IP bosses will have to sue your entire neighborhood, school, or country; practice digital anarchy by creatively undermining copyright, mashing up media, recutting images, tracks, and texts.[73]

The argument above draws at least two lines of division that are important to note. First, anarchic remix opposes the commodity form—the situation in which monetary value both precedes and exceeds the creative act. Think of the hard-line stance against the commodification of knowledge that Geoff Cox outlines in his book *Speaking Code* (2012) as a correlate here: "if the legal apparatus . . . sets out to turn information into commodities, then alternatives are required that seek to free ideas from their complicity with these restraints."[74] This sentiment holds true for copyright and Creative Commons alike. Second, appropriation is aimed at large corporations, doing violence to the corporate beneficiaries of living culture. Appropriation among friends is perhaps a common goal. We can think of McKenzie Wark's "RetroDada Manifesto" as an analogue. Beginning "in disgust," RetroDada rearticulates Dadaism for the digital landscape, arguing that "we should make all art and literature and cinema free" since "the medium is as unimportant as we are." "Take any material at all" and "steal only from the best."[75] In this argument, theft from corporations is necessary for producing the commons. Theft among friends in the service of a common goal is an act of solidarity. What originates in a will to unmake institutional power results in an alternative culture with liberatory values that stem from anticapitalist cultures.

#guerrillaDH manifests a desire for a multiplicity of tactics in the production of knowledge as commons. It combines political refusal with acts of collective self-making that build a world with common interests at its heart. This is precisely where publicity and erasure emerge as coextensive bases for tactical relations of affinity, rather than enemy-making difference. The institutional milieu in and at which critical DH concepts of the commons are aimed is one method of resistance. The anti-institutional ethos that anticapitalist concepts of the commons forward produces their own autonomous space that is wholly disentangled from the market and the state. If and when the two meet, tactical demands are not to be confused with universal imperatives for political action

Against Collectivity

In what remains, I want to push the dialectical work of this chapter to its conclusion. I have explored two forms of cultural preservation here, two approaches to producing common good, giving more weight to guerrilla tactics that to those of public DH work. In the effort to extend the political implications of what I have explored, I want to analyze a final alternative, drawing out the political need to reserve differing concepts of the commons in their disjunctive relationality: Sara Ahmed's concept of selfcare as warfare. I turn to Ahmed's work because it speaks to questions of cultural preservation as an alternative to DH's tactical alignment with institutional power and Black Mask's collective demand. She, too, theorizes refusal as a productive political demand, but one that eschews collectivity in its departure from the market and the state.

Ahmed locates refusal in the interplay of resourcefulness and collectivity, particularly in the brutalities of antifeminist sentiment, both large and small, in her 2014 blog post "Selfcare as Warfare." Following a reading of Audre Lorde's *A Burst of Light*, Ahmed writes: "When you are not supposed to live, as you are, where you are, with whom you are with, then survival is a radical action; a refusal not to exist until the very end; a refusal not to exist until you do not exist."[76] In the moment when self-care becomes warfare, refusal becomes a conflicted act of preservation that leads Ahmed in two directions. Resourcefulness, on the one hand, describes the need for refusal in the face of racialized and gendered brutalities. She writes: "Perhaps we need to ask: who has enough resources not to have to become resourceful? When you have less resources you might have to become more resourceful. Of course: the requirement to become more resourceful is part of the injustice of a system that distributes resources unequally."[77] Think of this claim as a more contemporary inflection of Collins's outsider within. Ahmed names structural inequality as a barrier to existing within an abundant world. Her description of resourcefulness could describe something like Johnson's black feminist and radical womyn of color politics of citation as a means of preservation, but it also extends further. Collectivity, on the other hand, is refused as a cure-all to institutionalized oppression. "Collectivity," Ahmed writes," "can work for some individuals as a means for disguising their own interest as collective interest."[78] She continues, "When collectivity requires you to bracket your experience of oppression it is not a collectivity worth fighting for."[79]

When collectivity becomes a mechanism for limiting one's ability to survive, new modes of subjective articulation are demanded, new modes of preservation are demanded, as is an alternative vision of the commons. Citationality reemerges as an act of affinity-making that is both insurgent and subversive. In a blog post titled "White Men," for example, Ahmed's work parallels contemporary concerns for publicity in DH as acts of care, but she does so by espousing citation networks that form the basis of a self-provisioning common. She writes:

> Citationality is another form of academic relationality. White men is reproduced as a *citational relational*. White men cite other white men: it is what they have always done; it is what they will do; what they teach each other to do when they teach each other. They cite;

how bright he is; what a big theory he has. He's the next such-and-such male philosopher: don't you think; see him think. The relation is often paternal: the father brings up the son who will eventually take his place. Patriarchy: it's quite a system. It works.[80]

Citation practices that operate as a mode of weaponized self-care defend against their own erasure, especially in the face of the homogenizing power of colonial thought. They do so because they perform an alternative archive of thought that is not organized by patriarchal legacies of exclusion and white supremacy. The question of how erasure refuses its original exclusion is precisely the decolonial problem. It turns the dichotomy between life and death into a dialogue of oppression and resistance without homogenizing subjective differences that inform it.

What if a guerrilla figuration of the dead/living dichotomy was theorized from this position? The guerrilla's invocation in DH praxis is situated where publicity and erasure meet. The guerrilla signifies a refusal to be made dead while also refusing to affirm economized iterations of the self—something it shares with Ahmed's claim to self-care as warfare. It signifies the will to produce critical acts of unmaking as something beneficial—a path toward realizing a commons. The guerrilla also forwards a political position in which refusal actualizes variant practices of collective self-making. Although this might preclude a politics of publicity, it demands that a politics of care inform its action. If the production commons is tantamount to experiments in self-provisioning from differing sites of need, the relational character of its political project also binds it.

Where DH's focus on publicity meets its guerrilla invocation, perhaps the most productive outcome is located in a politics of refusal, contoured by the recursive effects of decolonial work. It is a transformational moment. The guerrilla forwards a radical articulation of this demand at the same time that it reveals its capacity to oppress, dominate, and wound. The anticapitalist commons it works to realize is differential to the point of fault, but the dialectical play of contemporary debates over cultural preservation allows for a multiplicity of tactics to emerge, shifting partisan lines of affiliation, and redefining what it means to live.

Chapter 4

Guerrilla Theory from the Underside

We are witnessing an information revolution—a revolution that is leading global transformation. People of African descent have always played pivotal roles in the history of technological revolutions—sometimes as innovators and inventors, more frequently as laborers—and whose labor permitted the wealth that spurred further technological advances. The social consequences of today's information revolution include suffering and economic insecurity for African Americans and others in the African Diaspora, and also dislocations among others in society. Our communities have been digitally divided, but we are dedicating ourselves to serve as a bridge over the river of that divide.

> —"The Next Movement in Black Studies: 'eBlack Studies,'" Abdul Alkalimat, et al.

One could perhaps say that certain ideological conflicts animating present-day polemics oppose the pious descendants of time and the determined inhabitants of space.

> —"Of Other Spaces: Utopias and Heterotopias," Michel Foucault

The challenge that Tara McPherson issues at the conclusion of her profound polemic "Why Are the Digital Humanities So White? or Thinking the Histories of Race and Computation" resonates perhaps even more forcefully today than at its publication in 2012: "Politically committed academics with humanities skill sets must engage technology and its production not simply as an object of our scorn, critique, or fascination," she writes, "but as a productive and generative space that is always emergent and never fully determined."[1] The question that motivates McPherson's polemic, and thus its conclusion, frames technological use and production as both an open horizon and a groundless foundation; a processual space that belies first philosophy and final cause. Her method is equally forceful. McPherson draws out logics of modularity that are prevalent in hardware structure, software architecture, and the social field by co-articulating critical histories of race and UNIX design in the United States in the mid- and late 1960s. She argues that technological development characterized by discrete "simple parts," "connected by clean interfaces," is implicated in the brutalities of racial segregation.[2] Furthermore, these brutalities are extended by contemporary logics of financialization. Both strategies are mobilized toward separation and containment: "if the first half of the twentieth century laid bare its racial logics, from 'Whites Only' signage to the brutalities of lynching, the second half increasingly hides its racial 'kernel,' burying it below a shell of neoliberal pluralism."[3] McPherson's call to action is contoured by an equally critical claim: epistemologies structured by computer culture must acknowledge—"the greatest hits of structuralism and poststructuralism" must acknowledge—that "race, particularly in the United States," fundamentally shapes "how we see and know as well as the technologies that underwrite or cement both vision and knowledge."[4] Importantly, McPherson argues that modularity molds fields of action, spheres of thought, technologies of the body, and epistemologies of perception to its sovereign jurisdiction. Modularity cordons off, objectifies, and apprehends as ground overtakes its figure—hence McPherson's call to approach technology as an unfixed space. Fluid political work is not without political conviction. It is a commentary on our operative concepts of the political.

What, then, is the character of resistance? What political transformations are necessary in order to conceptualize space in opposition to logics of territorialization and to their technologies of separation and containment? Let's recall Stefano Harney and Fred Moten's coauthored *Undercommons: Fugitive Planning & Black Study*. At the opening of the text, Harney and Moten evoke Chantal Mouffe's distinction between politics and the political, albeit of a different order. "Politics," they write, "is an ongoing attack on the common— the general and generative antagonism—from within the surround."[5] The political is thus characterized as "the self-defense of the surround in the face of repeated, targeted dispossessions through the settler's armed incursion."[6] Harney and Moten's inversion of these two foundational concepts is quick and intentional. The common, rather than the state, anchors their political work. It is the control mechanism that grounds the figures and tactics of resistance they explore. Any attack on the common is a threat to political order. How politics and the political cohere—how conflict shapes the political— gives purpose to Harney and Moten's intervention. Consider the friend-enemy relation once more. When described by Schmitt, the guerrilla antagonizes the state. It upsets the regularity of the state form by organizing itself as a diffuse and mobile body. It opposes the state's territorializing function, acting out while also in wait to be eliminated. For Harney and Moten, the location and function of antagonism is inverted by comparison to Schmitt's political.

The colonizer antagonizes the space and governing ethos of the common by threatening to enclose what could be distributed with equity and care, and by harming the subjects who inhabit it. This is the ontological condition that spawns resistance, that is, Harney and Moten's undercommons.

The affinities shared between McPherson's polemic and Harney and Moten's introductory comments on the undercommons frame the theoretical work of this chapter. The political diagnoses featured in both contexts make clear that modulation is a territorial operation, resistance to it is characterized by opposition to separation and containment, and that critical histories of race are the access point to such demands for resistance. Concomitantly, the technological connection between vision and knowledge in particular is an invitation to broaden the scope of McPherson's polemic beyond hardware structure and software architecture. This connection opens the door to my analysis of guerrilla cinema in previous chapters, as well as my focus on the production of subjectivity. As in those chapters, my focus here rests on guerrilla histories that reframe the relationship that is shared between vision and knowledge at sites of political contest. This extends to my analysis of archival work and the politics of preservation.

The argument I forward in this chapter is threefold. First, I link Harney and Moten's inverted political to my concerns for the techno-political constitution of the subject. I explore the theoretical underpinnings of Aria Dean's brilliant essay, "Poor Meme, Rich Meme," as a means of realizing this argument, and extrapolate their implications for politically oriented DH work that is specifically focused on the archive. Like chapters 2 and 3, cinema plays an irruptive role in my approach to DH work. It parses the relationship shared between vision and knowledge but also reorients my discussion of preservation. Second, I pair this exploration with a practice of decolonial Dada enacted by Jade E. Davis. I do so to draw out the infrastructural effects of translation in archival production, but also to address debates over access and care that are formative of #femDH—specifically Jacqueline Wernimont's work on feminist digital archives. Third, I return to Harney and Moten's concept of "debt work" at the conclusion of this chapter. This allows me to better articulate differential economic effects that prefigure acts of preservation, and thus the inequities that persist as radical forms of resistance are proclaimed as a remedy. This point highlights the underlying conflicts that undergird collective political formation, but it realizes their productive potential, demonstrating how conflict becomes generative of democratic politics.

Ontology as a Precondition of Epistemology

If DH's contemporary practice is predicated on histories of modularity, socially and technologically oriented, resistance is simultaneously a methodological *and* a political project. How might a concept of preservation predicated on

Harney and Moten's inverted political inform DH's activist aspirations? What might DH gain from such a concept? Harney and Moten's first example of a political response to the colonizer's attack on the common is telling. They invoke guerrilla organization and tactics immediately, claiming that the Black Panther Party (BPP) represented the "first theorists of the revolution of the surround."[7] The BPP's "twinned commitment to revolution and self-defense emerged from the recognition that the preservation of black social life is articulated in and with the violence of innovation."[8] The BPP emerges as a result of the colonizer's antagonism to the common, and its political interventions are coextensive with its ontological status.

This is further corroborated by Robyn C. Spencer's reading of the BPP's affirmation of self-defense via guerrilla organization and tactics in *The Revolution Has Come* (2016). Where the party was "particularly influenced by theories that posited that a small, armed group of dedicated people could lead the revolutionary struggle and that guerrilla warfare could be an effective strategy for progressive social change," Spencer notes, "self-defense was not a means to an end but an organizing tool."[9] It was a collective response to the brutalities of segregation, both intimately and organizationally. What the guerrilla's invocation reveals in its proclamation is thus an ontological priority of violence, what William Haver names as a form of violence that precedes the figure as it prioritizes its extinction, but one that also molds the whole of its political life. What Harney and Moten proclaim, and what Spencer acknowledges, is that racialized violence and its technologies of implementation are the precondition for self-defense. They are operative in our political ideologies, our concepts of space, even our technological infrastructures, calling for radical acts of preservation in their face and in their wake. The colonizer's violent antagonism, as well as the guerrilla's self-defense, is formative of a familiar dispute. What kinds of violence are living, and what kinds of violence are death?

Let's remember that the function of political antagonism, what it accomplishes and where it originates, is a central marker of the guerrilla's ontological status. It undergirds every act of collective self-making generated by guerrilla organization and tactics; it has motivated my critique of the violence that the figure commits against the subjects it interpellates. Yet, the antagonism claimed by Harney and Moten, formative of the BPP, inverted to Schmitt's political, requires a kind of attunement to the ontological conditions of black social life that I have yet to explore, especially as it might pertain to questions of difference and inclusion in DH. Perhaps signaling a departure from previous chapters, the vocabulary and conceptual schema endemic to this discourse are quite different from many of the debates in DH that I have explored thus far. This antagonistic inversion pushes my paleonymy of guerrilla organization and tactics toward new avenues of thought.

In her essay "Poor Meme, Rich Meme" (2016), for example, Aria Dean offers an analysis of mimetic culture that accounts for its economic inequities, rooted in the exploitation of black cultural production, that rearticulates the arguments featured above. Similar to Hannah Giorgis's socioeconomic analysis of "Black Vine," Dean accounts for a kind of mediated selfhood in her essay, arguing that "memes reiterate the inequities between black creators and white appropriators."[10] Memes do so because they concretize creative labor endemic to black social life into a communicable product, but also because they signify different needs and desires. Dean forcefully follows Laur M. Jackson's argument in her essay "The Blackness of Meme Movement" on this point. Jackson argues that a stark difference exists for those for whom cultural transmission is a means of survival as opposed to those whose cultural transmission is simply competition:

> Not only can the origins of many memes be found in Black creators or online Black communities (Black Twitter, Black Tumblr, Black nerd culture at large), memes appear to model the circulatory movement of Black vernacular itself. Black folks are hardly the sole proprietors of internet memes, yet it's undeniable that memes at their liveliest— that is, what allows them to keep living—is in fact indebted to Black processes of cultural survival.[11]

Dean doubles down on this argument.[12] "The meme," she argues, "seems open to appropriation and interpretation by whoever possesses it for a moment, echoing Fred Moten's description of blackness as being only what we hold in our outstretched hands."[13] The meme is the cultural conduit of black social life par excellence in Dean's essay, and is equally ephemeral as blackness itself. The difference between cultural transmission as a form of survival and as a form of competition is therefore located in the play between ephemeral acts of evasion and the desire to grasp. Survival is evasion from the colonizer's brutality, his attack on the common. Competition is appropriation of the indifference to the lives that it affects.

The ontological argument that follows from Dean's analysis intuitively responds to the logic and technologies of modularity. For instance, Dean argues that mimetic culture produces a mode of radical collectivity that is substantively different for black cultural production historically, especially as power moves to separate and contain it:

> Historically, [the collective being of blackness] has always been scattered, stretched across continents and bodies of water. But given how formations like Black Twitter now foster connections and offer opportunities for intense moments of identification, we might say that, at this point in time, the most concrete location we can find for this collective being of blackness is the digital, on social media platforms in the form of viral content—perhaps most importantly, memes.[14]

Mimetic culture links disparate networks of actors together via digital technologies. It offers opportunities for multiple forms of identification within a collective milieu at the same time that it contests the autonomous production of collectivity. Dean's argument might be summarized as such: what is made poor economically is simultaneously rich in cultural production, despite the attack on its collective bonds.

Importantly, the dichotomy that Dean forwards immediately speaks to McPherson's concern for vision and knowledge. This portion of Dean's argument is based on Hito Steyerl's work on "the poor image," specifically by considering how mimetic culture "constructs anonymous global networks just as it creates a shared history."[15] For Steyerl, the poor image is, on the one hand, a question of substandard resolution by contrast to the rich image. Steyerl even goes so far as to say that substandard resolution produces liberatory political potential signified by the poor image, since "poor images are poor because they are not assigned any value within the class society of images—their status as illicit or degraded grants them exemption from its criteria."[16] On the other hand, the poor image reveals the wealth of its communicative possibility as Steyerl likens it to the sociopolitical impact of Third Cinema. "The networks in which poor images circulate," Steyerl writes,

> constitute both a platform for a fragile new common interest and a battleground for commercial and national agendas. They contain experimental and artistic material, but also incredible amounts of porn and paranoia. While the territory of poor images allows access to excluded imagery, it is also permeated by the most advanced commodification techniques. While it enables the users' active participation in the creation and distribution of content, it also drafts them into production. Users become the editors, critics, translators, and (co-)authors of poor images.[17]

Dean's reliance on Steyerl's work is clear in its political motivation and analysis. If mimetic culture forms the technological basis for a collective being of blackness, it does so with the consciousness of that fact that race fundamentally shapes "how we see and know as well as the technologies that underwrite or cement both vision and knowledge."[18] This is the epistemological basis for Dean's digital figuration of blackness.[19] It is the ontological fact through which Harney and Moten's political is rearticulated.

One/Multiple/Nothing

The ontological argument that Dean forwards in "Poor Meme, Rich Meme" is prefigurative of the epistemologies of sight that realize it. The material basis for this argument thus leads her to describe mimetic culture as one that is reliant on digital technology's inherent archival function. The collective being that Dean locates within mimetic culture spans social media platforms, producing a museology of present sociocultural modes of connection that also reflects a language of connection from within a partisan milieu. This is what the digital provides both organizationally and politically. Site specificity concurrent with epiphenomenal time is therefore the subsequent component of Dean's argument—mimetic culture is both generated and generative of this collective figuration of the self *here* and *now*, even as both the labor and culture of African Americans are appropriated within the medium of its articulation. This is what motivates Dean's rearticulation of Moten's ontological argument: "What is nothingness? What is thingliness? What is blackness? What's the relationship between blackness, thingliness, nothingness and the (de/re)generative operations of what Deleuze might call a life in common?"[20] Think back to chapter 3. This series of questions is similar to Fiona Barnett et al.'s "QueerOS: A User's Manual": what does it mean to become one/multiple/nothing through the violence and generativity of our most intimate technologies?

Dean's rearticulation of Harney and Moten's political work is largely medium-specific, but it is also experiential. In Dean's account, the brutalities that undergird vision and knowledge are experienced in the production of one's culture as alienated from oneself, even as one forms collective networks of identification via practices of making. It is the experience of a territorializing impulse—a modular logic that gives way to objectification—even as alternative modes of sociality are made available. The historico-technological condition that Dean describes reiterates Harney and Moten's inversion of political antagonism. The inequities of social media production perfectly describe an attack on the common, an antagonism that sequesters and contains the digital production of the self. And while it also signals a generative horizon upon which this kind of antagonism might be overcome, one I address later in this chapter, it more immediately links to collective iterations of the self that I have explored from a partisan divide. Dean contextualizes her claim to collectivity in explicitly political terms, channeling Moten and Edouard Glissant, to argue that blackness is a continual "consent not to be a single being." She writes:

> For the most part, historically speaking, we could characterize the collective being's attitude toward this consent as begrudging, held in opposition to the desire to constitute ourselves as complex, individual subjects. This "consent not to be a single being" reflects the same fungibility that means that violence against one black body cannot be isolated and understood as being against that body alone, where I am you and you are me, where "we are all [insert #nameofperson-murderedbypolice here]."[21]

The tension between being one and multiple is a complex iteration of one's subjectivity in this discourse. It is posited as a liberatory concept of the self that is radically contingent, but it is also a subjectivity imposed by violence. What is imposed in the movement from being one to being multiple in Dean's view is therefore also an experience of *being nothing*, a violent ontological condition of nothingness that is delimited by the antagonisms that prefigure black social life.[22]

Dean's rhetoric and conceptual path, while heavily reliant on Moten, is perhaps more closely linked to that of the Black Panther Party in this moment; it seems to share the same tactical qualities. When she writes of African American experience as one in which "I am you and you are me," she recalls the violence of innovation that Harney and Moten attribute to BPP praxis. In his 1973 memoir Huey P. Newton, cofounder of the BPP, theorizes a form of violence for which his autobiography is named: revolutionary suicide. In Newton's view, revolutionary suicide is an act of violence focused on the self, an act of destruction that also produces radical collectivity: "There is an old African saying, 'I am we.' If you met an African in ancient times and asked him who he was, he would reply, 'I am we.' This is revolutionary suicide: I, we, all of us are the one and the multitude."[23] The ontological basis for Newton's concept is evident. As a theorist of the surround and activist in opposition to the colonizer's armed incursion, revolutionary suicide provides a kind of anonymity that exists in the open. It provides a communal identity in the face of being made nothing. "I am we" is hiding in plain sight; it is living out the negativity of the ontological totality of blackness while also relying on its collective features to prefigure a mode of subjective formation that is future-oriented *here* and *now*. It prefigures the BPP's organization and tactics. It precedes Dean's generative claim to mimetic culture.

The ontological implications of such a claim—that an experience of one-self as *nothing* exists between the one and the many—are both political and material. They are clearly rooted in histories of colonization and the Middle Passage and their contemporary institutional perpetuation. They are also inherently technological. What Dean's work seeks to answer in the present is therefore a complex question, intimately related to McPherson's challenge above: what material histories and what technologies of the self result in an experience of being one/multiple/nothing? How might this subjective condition reorient fluid techno-political work? While there is not one, clear answer to these questions, the basis for proposing them is perhaps best explored by contrast.

Harney and Moten's inverted political is not a simple conceptual flip. It is coterminous with divergent concepts of the self through which political contest is articulated. The production of blackness stands on the one side, while the preservation of whiteness stands on the other. The radically contingent terms upon which blackness is made stand in direct contrast to the transcendental status presumed by the production of whiteness. Harney and Moten's work acknowledges the dispute between white supremacy and the production of black social life to be formative of the settler's attack on the common. This contrast underlies much of Dean's historico-theoretical work as she draws from this intellectual lineage, and it is mirrored in the analysis of mimetic culture. The keystone for both arguments rests in the equation of white social life with a transcendental subject position and its figuration of vision and knowledge—an ontological status and mode of perception that is thought to be boundless and absolute. In Moten's view, the myth of transcendental subjectivism, perpetrated by German idealists and formative of Enlightenment ideology, imposes a form of social death on black life; it makes blackness into an undifferentiated mass of sociality by comparison to its white counterpart. "This mass," as Moten notes in his essay "Blackness and Nothingness (Mysticism in the Flesh),"

> is understood to be undifferentiated precisely because from the imaginary perspective of the political subject—who is also the transcendental subject of knowledge, grasp, ownership, and selfpossession—difference can only be manifest as the discrete individuality that holds or occupies a standpoint. From that standpoint, from the artificial, officially assumed position, blackness is nothing, that is, the relative nothingness of the impossible, pathological subject and his fellows.[24]

Moten's indictment of the transcendental subject is a further extension of his and Harney's inverted political. It is the foundation of their invocation of self-defense. Like the state, the myth of the transcendental subject delimits the who and the what of knowledge, grasp, ownership, and self-possession. This becomes compounded in the context of Dean's argument. If the digital is the most common location for the collective being of blackness to emerge in the present—a fluid network of interrelationality—then the political axiomatics that mediate self-making are even more powerful and therefore even more suspect. What does the violence of innovation oppose? How does it articulate preservation as a form of self-defense? In the first instance, Moten's work opposes the twin movement in which whiteness is elevated to a transcendental status while blackness is excluded from the production of subjectivity altogether. Dean's work, following Moten, draws out a concept of digitally mediated selfhood that forwards a mode of collective self-making at a future anterior to any form of transcendental subjectivism. Combined, the two directly speak to the politics and contemporary import of McPherson's work.

In sum, the production of black social life within digital milieus is not presumed to be distant from the technologies that manifest it; they are inseparable. There is no such concept of coder as auteur here. Modularity is not given an inch. The violence of innovation endemic to the articulation of black life subsequently opposes the "nothingness" imposed upon it at the same time that exploitation is eluded. The practice of self-defense at work in both

Dean and Moten's work thus forwards a concept of difference that is made to maneuver around its thingliness/nothingness in order to preserve a life in common. This is what the settler's armed incursion both imposes and produces. This is what contours Dean's articulation of collective formation in digital landscapes.

Counter-Memory and Horizontal Archives

The work recounted thus far amounts to two alternatives to McPherson's challenge in the sections that follow, both engaging in speculative responses to it. What Harney and Moten's work and Dean's work makes obvious, respectively, is that critical histories of race are not simply an access point to resistance; they are sites of affinity-making and critical consciousness that realize it. Parallel to McPherson's focus on hardware structure and software architectures, I turn to another site of DH interest: the archive. The struggle for collective self-making plays out in the archives of the present and the archives of the past. The debates staged in chapter 3 lead to this proclamation, as does Dean's argument above. But what of a concept of subjectivity that prioritizes collectivity anterior to the myth of the transcendental subject, reorienting its future? How is this shaped by the archive, and, in turn, how does it transform the archive's status and function?

As Dean notes, Kodwo Eshun's "Further Considerations on Afrofuturism" addresses this precise problem through the production of counter-memory. Eshun writes: "To establish the historical character of black culture, to bring Africa and its subjects into history denied by Hegel et al., it has been necessary to assemble countermemories that contest the colonial archive, thereby situating the collective trauma of slavery as the founding moment of modernity."[25] Eshun rhymes with Moten on this point, even as his site of contestation differs. Where Moten's site of opposition is a highly contentious theoretical landscape, Eshun's is located in the production of blackness via its material culture. Eshun replaces the universal "I" with the collective trauma of slavery in modernity's retelling, fully opposed to the colonial archive. Histories of white supremacy that align with a concept of the transcendental subject are thus defended against in the counter-memory of decolonial archives, undercutting the authority it relies on in order to extend its armed incursion.

Eshun's work is important here not only because it inspires Dean above, but also because it offers a response to the question of self-defense in cultural preservation. Eshun forwards this precise claim, arguing that Afrofuturism is predicated on museological emulation, "laying bare, manipulating, mocking, and critically affirming the contextualizing and historicizing framework of institutional knowledge."[26] One could draw comparisons to the Guerrilla Girls and Black Mask here, and perhaps also to critical DH figures, but neither comparison would capture Eshun's underlying concern, politically or socially. What Eshun proposes cannot be reduced to an act of avant-garde visualization; nor does forwarding a politics of publicity adequately represent it. The museological feature of Eshun's argument appears as a defense of the common, one in which the archive re-creates political imagination *all the way down*. It is a critical practice of inverting the antagonisms confronted by the production of black social life so as to reset the historico-political horizon, generatively and collaboratively, but produced along clear lines of inclusion and exclusion.

The speculative work that Eshun accomplishes with his theorization of archival counter-memory also gives context to Dean's interest in collective self-making in digital landscapes. Where blackness is reduced to a concept of collectivity that finds its conclusion in an undifferentiated mass on the one side, "we are all [insert #nameofpersonmurderedbypolice here]," the archive allows for a concept of collectivized black social life that is future-oriented via histories of self-determination, "I, we, all of us are the one and the multitude." The question of what Eshun's archive might look like beyond a speculative gesture is pressing, especially as it might be imported into a DH context.

Although his concept originates in a different tradition of thought, José Medina's "guerrilla pluralism" helps clarify the political concepts undergirding Eshun's focus on counter-memory in a language that is familiar to DH. In Medina's view, counter-memory formation is insurgent. It thus does not "try to resolve conflicts and overcome struggles, but instead tries to provoke them and to re-energize them"; counter-memories "are not simply the raw materials to be coordinated in a heterogeneous (but nonetheless shared) collective memory; rather, they remain counter-memories that make available multiplicitous pasts for differently constituted and positioned publics and their discursive practices."[27] Guerrilla pluralism describes a condition in which the reduction of one's self and culture to an undifferentiated mass is rejected. Nothingness is refused. Logics of modularity are preempted. Guerrilla pluralism forwards counter-memory formation by "interrogating and contesting any settlement, making the past come undone at the seams, so that it loses its unity, continuity, and naturalness, so that it does not appear any more as a single past that has already been made, but rather, as a heterogeneous array of converging and diverging struggles that are still ongoing and only have the appearance of having been settled."[28] This is certainly aligned with Harney and Moten's inverted political that was discussed earlier. The rhetoric that Medina mobilizes is nearly identical to that of Harney and Moten. The museological question, however, reemerges here. What processes allow such archives to persist?

In her *Physics of Blackness* (2015), Michelle M. Wright forwards a complementary concept to that of Eshun, albeit from a different historical and theoretical orientation: "horizontal archives."[29] For Wright, the production of horizontal archives follows two, related logics. First, horizontal archives refer to the geographical movement of the trans-Atlantic slave trade. Citing

Cassandra Pybus on the formation of the concept, a horizontal archive "draws a connecting line moving horizontally (well, south by southwest) from the moment of the American Revolution in the Middle Passage timeline to other moments in those kingdoms and empires that border the Indian Ocean and, more specifically, to the moment of the British penal colony of Australia."[30] This horizontal line also tracks histories of the present to its past geographical landscapes by acknowledging slavery's position as a founding moment of modernity. As such, the horizontal archive draws a line from present to past and past to present that inherently re-creates the conditions of intellectual formation and self-making. Second, horizontal archives stand opposed to vertical archives. Horizontal archives are defined as "correspondence between peers, diaries, etc.," where vertical archives refer to "state, judicial, colonial, and penal records."[31] Parallel to Eshun's claim to counter-memory as an act of museological protest, horizontal archives oppose the colonial archive as they reanimate historical records which the colonial archive has excluded.

Horizontal archives are thus a dialogue among friends. They mirror Johnson's and Gumbs's black feminist and radical womyn of color politics of citation in chapter 3, but point in alternative directions. Take Moya Bailey's description of her writing process, featured in her article "#transform(ing) DH Writing and Research: An Autoethnography of Digital Humanities and Feminist Ethics," as a potential example of the concept. Bailey writes that her

> research highlights the networks contemporary Black trans women create through the production of digital media and in this article I make the emotional and uncompensated labor of this community visible . . . The networks built through digital media production are significant attempts to redress the lack of care that Black trans women receive from the healthcare community and society. I argue that these processes of digital media production produce more than just redefined representations, but also connections that can be understood as a form of health care praxis themselves.[32]

Bailey's description of her work is certainly an expression of DH's inclusive ethos; it is also a more direct link between the ontological condition that Dean describes above and the production of counter-memory. Bailey wrote a diary to parallel her research as a means of building a digital network similar to those that Dean relies on, but with a difference. Where Dean's focus on mimetic culture is predicated on invisible globalized networks without access or pretension to revealing their origin, Bailey's work publicizes the emotional and uncompensated labor of black trans women as an act of care. Her horizontal archive is to defend against its erasure. It unearths and dialogues with a diffuse history of oppression. As a result, the horizontal archive she constructs not only preserves this work; it manifests the connections that digital media afford an oppressed community. I draw this contrast not to place Dean and

Bailey's work in opposition, but to underscore the original question. What does it mean to be one/multiple/nothing in Dean's view? What is nothingness? What is thingliness? What is blackness? The response to these questions is neither universal nor monolithic.

Each concept and act of preservation already explored here is important for understanding the material basis of their operation. Here, though, I want to focus on the polemics that animate the guerrilla operation of such archival production. I will return to the concept of care via #femDH praxis in the following sections. It is quite complex in its political effect. Eshun's counter-memory and Wright's horizontal archive parallel a line of thought more closely related to guerrilla organization and tactics, one that follows DH literature, but which also augments the response to the questions that frame this chapter. Furthermore, Wright and Eshun's concepts track back to the complex ontological relation forwarded by Moten above, but they also act as a bridge to a third concept that tracks back to the BPP, intentionally limited in its scope.

Seeing (within) Violent Archives

The process of reenergizing a heterogeneous array of converging and diverging struggles in the production of counter-memory is perhaps the closest definition one might link to Harney and Moten's claim to the Black Panther Party's violence of innovation, and thus to self-defense. The linkages that Dean provides are productive for attuning DH to such questions, but they require more exploration. Indeed, if race fundamentally shapes "how we see and know as well as the technologies that underwrite or cement both vision and knowledge," the acts of preservation explored here offer further commentary on its resistances.[33] Where Harney and Moten take a theoretical stance on BPP violence, and Spencer links it more concretely to organization, Jean Genet, a BPP supporter and collaborator, articulates BPP violence as a form of self-defense motivated by ontologies of violence. In his introduction to George Jackson's *Soledad Brother: The Prison Letters of George Jackson*, Genet writes:

> The revolutionary enterprise of the American black, it seems to me, can be born only out of resentment and hatred, that is, by rejecting in disgust and rage, but radically, the values venerated by whites, although this enterprise can continue only on the basis of a common language, at first rejected, finally accepted, whose words will no longer serve the ideas taught by whites, but new ones instead.[34]

Perhaps most clearly, affect, manifesting in the form of political rage, is positioned here as the fundament of BPP politics and the justification for its militancy. Perhaps less clearly, indebtedness to the "values of whites," imposed and incurred on African Americans for over a century in the wake of the slave trade, is the site of abrogation and the scene of inequality that is to be simultaneously rejected and maintained in the struggle for liberation.

Genet's comments parallel Eshun's and Wright's archival concepts above. Although Genet is focused on a specific form of negative affect in his experience of BPP self-defense, the material effects of the BPP's revolutionary enterprise are apparent in the party's acts of preservation through self-defense. In fact, like Eshun's speculative maneuver, and Wright's horizontal maneuver, Genet's comments also begin with a question of perspective. What Genet corroborates in summarizing his experience with the BPP is a violence of innovation that precedes the material culture of revolution. This is to say, where Genet forefronts the BPP's disgust and rage, he forefronts an immanent relation of violence that seems to limit the party's response to its sociopolitical condition. The brutalities that are formative of BPP politics contour the BPP's ability to produce and preserve its revolutionary future. The question of preservation is thus intimately and inextricably linked to the subjects housed in the archive. Perspective delimits the archive.

The violence of innovation attributed to the BPP is perhaps best described by a familiar concept: "guerrilla seeing," "the very experience of non-transcendence, of non-neutrality."[35] Here, the concept does not so much refer to a disjunctive synthesis of decolonial and Dadaist politics, but rather to how the origin of guerrilla organization and tactics stands in opposition to the vertical, transcendental alignment of power, one that William Haver, the theorist of the concept, also ascribes to radical queer subjectivities.[36] The theoretical draw to this work lies precisely in its combination of perspectival immediacy and non-neutrality, formative of a political subject. Guerrilla organization and tactics maximize the violent ontological condition described by so many thinkers cited above, while their partisan character is also delimited by such violence. If the production of counter-memory is typically a speculative enterprise, and if horizontal archives are a dialogue between friends, guerrilla seeing is a site-specific modality of political articulation that preserves itself by caring for a partisan future *here* and *now*, one that is neither universal nor transcendental, but emergent and never fully determined. It is a form of counter-memory that is immanent, but one that also relies on the difficult negotiation of a heterogeneous array of converging and diverging struggles.

This argument can be recast in the language established above: ontologies of violence prefigure the technologies that underwrite epistemologies of perception. What gets made in and through an experience of non-transcendence and non-neutrality? What material artifacts stem from being made one/multiple/nothing form with such a situation, and how might they inform DH praxis? These are difficult questions to answer and, again, there is no universal answer. However, the origin of the concept offers a first step toward considering guerrilla seeing as an immanent archival practice. The BPP's adoption of cinema as a tactic for revolutionary consciousness-raising is perhaps the best example to turn to, given the theoretical lineage explored above. Two films in particular perform this mode of perception at the same time that they capture a record of the BPP's contested political life, *Off the Pig* and *Mayday*.

Filmed with the Newsreel collective in the late 1960s, *Off the Pig* and *Mayday* are examples of both the Black Panther Party's willingness to collaborate with political collectives beyond the scope of their own and a refusal to stand outside of their own context, performing their preservation in a manner comparable to Black Mask in the previous chapter. Cinema is thus situated as a technology of guerrilla seeing while it also doubles as an archival mode.

The opening of both films plays on a similar perceptual trick—each film equates the spectator's field of vision with that of the BPP. Take the opening scene of *Off the Pig* as an example. Here, the camera is situated within a BPP headquarters in Oakland, California, looking out of its main window. The window is riddled with bullet holes. The camera pans between bullet holes, allowing the viewer to observe the street from inside the headquarters as passersby peer through the bullet holes at the viewer's field of vision. The view then switches to the street, detailing bullet holes from the outside as they pierced poster images of the party's leaders, Eldridge Cleaver, Huey Newton, Bobby Hutton, and so on. The film then cuts to flashing text, simply titled The News Reel, along with the sound of continuous gunfire, hitting the spectator like a bullet. The opening to *Mayday* is similar. Like *Off the Pig*, the camera equates its field of vision with its present context; the camera moves through a BPP rally, giving the viewer the feeling that she is a participant among the crowd, part of the collective site of protest.

Quite clearly, the viewer is presented with a substantively different valence of the gun-as-camera debate presented in chapter 2. Like a gun's sight, the camera transposes the viewer from a distant position to one of immediacy. It places the viewer within a site of BPP militancy and the brutalities that animate it. In this way, the camera's placement and movement enact, as much as they are able, the experience of haptic guerrilla seeing. In what is almost an analog precursor to the field of vision offered to someone using a virtual reality headset, the spectator can see what the BPP saw and potentially come to be connected with the feelings of disgust and rage motivating their acts of self-defense. It is a modality of guerrilla seeing that co-opts the viewer, making her a militant within the camera's field of vision. It attempts to situate the viewer within the BPP's field of vision so as to access the affects that motivate BPP action. The camera's ability to situate the viewer within the BPP's field of vision cannot be understated. If the viewer can be made to feel as if she can inhabit BPP positionality, an immanent mode of perception is breached. Each film, but especially *Off the Pig*, offers the viewer a representation of what being made nothing meant for the BPP's organization and tactics. It magnifies the stark contrast between the viewer's shock from suddenly occupying the BPP's field of vision and the everydayness of brutality as experienced by the BPP's members.

The question of the body in this perspectival transposition looms large. On the one hand, the camera connects the viewer's own response to violence (bodily and psychological) with the BPP's situation. The viewer brings her own affective response to police brutality against the party with her. On the other hand, the camera links the viewer to the party's complex gendered politics at a remove from the viewer's gender identity, race, sex, or class. One can read this fact of BPP cinema in two ways. First, the perspectival trick at work in *Off the Pig* and *Mayday* can be read as a form of tactical diversity. Robyn C. Spencer forwards this concept in *The Revolution Has Come*, describing how the party "built on the image of blacks as living in a U.S. internal colony."[37] Here, each film could function as an affinity-making enterprise predicated on diverse experiences of oppression. Second, the perspective offered to the viewer is delimited by the gendered politics of BPP struggle. The modes of violence that the viewer is presented with are limited to a strong, hetero-masculinist, gun-toting figure. The films do not place the viewer within a field of vision that reveals the modes of violence most intimately experienced by Panther women, for example, "the litany of raids and high-profile arrests; . . . the slow erosion of relationships, bouts of incarceration, the heightening of internal hierarchies, and an attack on community-based systems."[38]

What, then, is preserved? What is excluded and what is lost? On the one hand, *Off the Pig* and *Mayday* are a record of BPP collaboration, consciousness-raising, style, and method. Each film is an act of self-defense, an articulation of collectivized experiences of violence that attempts to preserve the situation as it was, all the way down to its field of vision. Perhaps one might say that these films are part horizontal archive, part speculation in counter-memory. They certainly invoke an immanent experience of racialized oppression at an inherently partisan site of being and becoming. When the viewer is placed in the BPP's field of vision, she is located within a position of non-neutrality. The viewer is offered a glimpse of being made one/multiple/nothing. Each film is an artifact that testifies to Moten's argument against the transcendental subject, but is also an example of self-defense at a partisan divide that enacts the generative task of collectivization invoked by Dean in a pre-digital context. *Off the Pig* and *Mayday* preserve the refusal to be neutral or objective while they also attempt to place the viewer in the position of the subjects they maintain, collectivizing the experience. On the other hand, *Off the Pig* and *Mayday* are incomplete archives. There is a limit to their haptic transference of BPP struggle, and a limit to the gendered experience of violence. The perspective that is given to the viewer, melding with that of her own, is liminal and limited, both ephemeral and within the grasp of a hetero-masculinist subjectivity.

Decolonial Dada Revisited

The second alternative I offer to McPherson's argument extends the speculative work of the archive within its DH iterations. Violence is not the focus in this section, but rather archival figurations that are both generative and emergent. The ontological arguments traced above are not ignored or replaced, but rearticulated. Those speculative, horizontal, and immanent maneuvers are the tactical expression of a collaborative ethos from within a partisan milieu. Perhaps they enhance each other in certain moments, and in others, they play on a productive disjunction. At this juncture, however, each archival response leads me back to the discussion of decolonial Dada introduced in chapter 3, and particularly to its digital iterations.

Take Jade E. Davis's website "Historical Glitch" as an alternative example of preservation. Part of a triptych (Vintage Black Beauty and Davis's dissertation), Davis describes "Historical Glitch" as a mode of disarticulation in DH work: "While many Digital Humanities projects are designed to create connections between archives, knowledge, and information, [Historical Glitch] highlights the opposite, as it is a more common digital experience in the platform driven web."[39] She goes on to define the project as a work of decolonial Dada, one that "sees this moment in history as irrational; accepts that language that limited the past but not ideas; is digital; connects across time, space, place, and culture; and attempts to give voice and language to the past even if it fails."[40] There are inherent contradictions to her claim, contradictions that track on to the complex negotiation of the collective being of blackness, but these contradictions do not undermine her project. Rather, the archive she constructs is a digital readymade. It enacts a recursive bricolage in the face of the transcendental subject of knowledge, grasp, ownership, and self-possession. She mobilizes language as a means of connection while understanding that its translation across time and space may fail to communicate. The theoretical framework page on her site auto-generates a "dada poem" by combining portions of Zora Neale Hurston's "How It Feels to Be a Colored Me," an excerpt from chapter 5 of Frantz Fanon's *Black Skin, White Masks*, and Marshall McLuhan's "Playboy Interview." She writes that each poem "*exists only now and just for you. When you come to this page again it will be replaced with something new.*"[41] While the production of her "dada poem" might seem simple, its theoretical ground and political effect are not.

First, Davis forwards a kind of tactical presentism within her decolonial archive by creatively reorganizing the present's already irrational order. The means by which black voices and black lives are erased, homogenized, and atomized is turned on its head via simple lines of code. Texts are archives to be remixed and freely shared. Second, paralleling Wright and Dean, Davis speculates on the "now" "through which all imaginings of Blackness" are mediated, collectivizing an experience of black life via its textual articulation.[42] The Dada poem expands epiphenomenal time to function within a globalized network of text and user interaction, concomitantly expanding its subjective character. One could say that Davis intuitively re-creates Johanna Drucker's definition of the interface: (1) "An interface is a space in which a *subject*, not a *user*, is invoked," and (2) "Interface is an enunciative system."[43] Third, Davis produces a horizontal dialogue in fragments. This upsets the condition in which the colonized are made to speak in the language of the colonizer as new modes of identification are asserted. In so many words, Davis's decolonial archive opposes the subjective condition that coloniality imposes, or what Moten names as "the discrete individuality that holds or occupies a standpoint," by locating speech within a chorus of opposition. Where one text is combined with another, the Dada poem requires the reader to forego rational order. The poem relays a message on the terms that Davis prescribes, rendering a language of resistance that may fail to translate.

The temporal remix that Davis's archive asserts is also important. Where Davis is able to expand the epiphenomenal time of the archive in each iteration of her Dada poem, she cares for the complex negotiation that stands between subjective formation and preservation via textual remix. Her invocation of the glitch aesthetic is what Kim Cascone would call a "post-digital" revelation of control as an illusion, a glitch that upsets a linear flow of history that favors colonial erasure, but one with an alternative site of intervention.[44] The intent of her work can also be likened to Yuk Hui's claim in his "Archivist Manifesto" that care is "the temporal structure by which we can understand our existence, this theme lies at the heart of Heidegger's *Sein und Zeit*. Care is not only, as we say in our daily life 'taking care of something,' but also a temporal structure that create [*sic*] a consistent milieu for ourselves."[45] Davis's archive therefore invokes a collective it also cares for, offering equal attention to the voices it amplifies and the collective it creates. To be sure, this feature of her archive could be pushed toward more radical ends, but it certainly underscores the subjective position articulated by so many thinkers cited above.[46] Care, in this context, is perhaps another form of self-defense as fragmentation and potential failure that operate as liberatory possibilities.

The takeaway from Davis's work is forceful: a decolonial Dada aesthetic can function as a tactic for preservation in which translation structures our acts of care and orients them toward the commons. The criteria guiding Davis's project prioritize the new, the inability to return to a time before, even (and perhaps especially) at the expense of rational thought. Davis's archive is therefore an important example of preservation and counter-memory by comparison to those explored thus far, but it is far more important for how it cares for multiple and overlapping tactics of preservation in the face of the ongoing attack on black social life's common articulation. It is perhaps the exact embodiment of the resistance that McPherson calls for above. The decolonial play on Dadaist aesthetics that Davis enacts at "Historical Glitch" therefore rests on her ability to situate translation *as* the structure of preservation. This is what decolonial Dada might further provoke in DH praxis. It is also a potential link to DH praxis on archival formation and preservation in digital spaces. The politics and tactics that one might attribute to a decolonial Dada aesthetic in acts of preservation, especially within a digital context, rely, to a certain degree, on a willingness to cede control over knowledge production and subjective articulation. Davis's archive is a demand to enact multiplicity and difference. It is at moments speculative, horizontal, and immanent, without homogenizing each tactic. It is a direct expression of survival and competition, as well as the affects that motivate them.

These arguments are further drawn out in DH praxis, specifically that of #femDH. Two of Jacqueline Wernimont's essays on digital archival work, "Feminism in the Age of Digital Archives: The Women Writers Project" with Julia Flanders, and "Whence Feminism? Assessing Feminist Interventions in Digital Literary Archives," draw this point out. In the first article, Wernimont and Flanders give an analysis of the Women Writers Online archive (WWO). They begin by limiting the gap between the archive's use and its theorization. The first pertains to the link between the archive and genre. They argue that the WWO represents more than a recovery project—that of bringing lost women's writing to light—it showcases "the ability of digital technologies to offer information about genre and form, while also enabling the blurring of generic boundaries, and positions such archives as both repositories and sites of translation."[47] Wernimont and Flanders take this claim a step further, writing, "If WWO achieves a feminist intervention by providing a different kind of access, it also makes a literary argument that foregrounds issues of genre and form through its encoding practices."[48] The WWO is thus formative of an archive that makes women's writing more accessible, but its primary intervention lies in the archive's function *as an argument*. The archive is a site of translation in which subjects are invoked via the care taken to preserve feminist histories. One need not create a large-scale platform in order to propose a shift in DH infrastructure. Minimal approaches can have macropolitical effects.

One can see similar potential in "Whence Feminism? Assessing Feminist Interventions in Digital Literary Archives," where Wernimont approaches the question of recovery and access from a different vantage point, arguing that feminist interventions in infrastructure are about "finding ways to enable user engagement in production [that] allow us to more fully consider the operations of the archive and the ways in which it serves as a threshold."[49] The question of what critical infrastructures are for and what they do is of the highest concern in Wernimont's work. A feminist approach to the question of infrastructure as it pertains to archival creation, one that preserves conflict around power relations, demands both a kind of partisan form of care and an ethical reservation concerning the institution in which it is housed. The political imperatives that are formative of DH concerns for care in/of the archive can be extended by the decolonial project, as well as by what it means to care for objects that also produce subjects.

Debt Work

The question of preservation as self-defense at work in this chapter forwards a subjective valence that is distinct from the DH concerns in discussed in chapter 3. Dean's arguments are not focused on the need for individual credit in any institutional instance that academics adhere to, or any subsequent figurations of the self that are focused on the production of a workforce. If a decolonial Dada aesthetic can function as a tactic for preservation in which translation structures our acts of care and orients them toward common futures, then the question of preservation invoked in the production of black social life requires further clarification. These engagements with technology situate it as a generative space, emergent and processual, but what of the figures that produce this kind of technological engagement? How the two cohere rests on the production of subjectivity. To follow both McPherson and Dean, the response is also economic.

When Harney and Moten invert the concept of the political, they reveal the underside of contemporary radical thought, particularly autonomist Marxist iterations of the political, explored in chapter 1, that also speaks to DH's own radical aspirations. In a pointed critique of autonomist Marxist thought, Harney and Moten assert that "the black radical tradition is debt work." Note that, like Wernimont's claim to the archive discussed above, the black radical tradition does not simply demand recovery; it demands that a yet-to-be recognized debt be addressed, a debt that accounts for

> a global politics of blackness emerging out of slavery and colonialism, a black radical politics, a politics of debt without payment, without credit, without limit. This debt was built in a struggle with empire before empire, where power was not with institutions or governments alone, where any owner or colonizer had the violent power of a ubiquitous state. This debt attached to those who through dumb insolence or nocturnal plans ran away without leaving, left without getting out. This debt got shared with anyone whose soul was sought for labor power, whose spirit was borne with a price marking it. And it is still shared, never credited and never abiding credit, a debt you play, a debt you walk, and debt you love. And without credit this debt is infinitely complex.[50]

Harney and Moten target autonomist Marxist thought in particular for the distance it keeps from the black radical tradition even as it appropriates its central concerns and concepts. Following the quote above, the question of credit is invoked, but again, this is not a claim to individual credit connected to institutional processes like tenure or promotion. This is a question of meeting the debt that results from appropriating or refusing to recognize the complexities of modular thinking. It foregrounds the questions consistently invoked in this chapter: What is nothingness? What is thingliness? What is blackness?

The archival strategies that I have explored address the debt to which Harney and Moten refer, but they invoke a double burden. This is to say, the work of Dean, Eshun, and Wright, respectively, can be compared to that of Johnson and Gumbs. In order to have their labor preserved with respect to its context and modes of production, those formative of the black radical tradition must also take on the labor of preserving it in the face of contest. There is perhaps a triple burden here. Once components of the tradition are preserved, they must also be defended against modular forces that would separate and contain them. There are thus also two potentially distinct subject positions in archival formation. There are subjects who embody the burden of preservation and defense, on the one hand, and there are those who might appropriate the language and culture of those they archive, on the other. The decolonial turn therefore leads to more immediate questions. How is radical difference preserved in the defense of the common? When the archive invokes a subject, which side of the political is represented? It is not enough to remix and translate one textual archive through another; this would simply be a poor appropriation of the Dada aesthetic. Nor is it permissible to massify the ontological conditions of black social life. Difference in subjectivity cannot be equated, but perhaps a common understanding of the ontological conditions through which preservation becomes an imperative is possible.

The ontological conditions that establish a debt owed to the black radical tradition are the very same ones that animate the difference between preservation as self-defense and the acts of its appropriation. Their economic and structural effects run deep. Consider the following excerpt from an 1864 letter attributed to Karl Marx and sent to Abraham Lincoln:

> While the workingmen, the true political powers of the North, allowed slavery to defile their own republic, while before the Negro, mastered and sold without his concurrence, they boasted it the highest prerogative of the white-skinned laborer to sell himself and choose his own master, they were unable to attain the true freedom of labor, or to support their European brethren in their struggle for emancipation; but this barrier to progress has been swept off by the red sea of civil war.[51]

Here, Marx identifies the root of inequality and the emancipatory potential of the slave's tactical complicity with capital as a question of free labor. This is to say, where emancipation from slavery might rest on a universal proclamation to life, liberty, and the pursuit of happiness, it certainly rests, in Marx's view, on the ability to sell one's labor—the first step toward actualizing the communist ideal. What Marx could not foresee is that the lasting effects of slavery, that is, structural inequality, racism, and so on, do not and have not resulted in a position of socioeconomic freedom. The ability to sell one's free labor does not compel one toward freedom, politically or economically. Recall Dean: "memes reiterate the inequities between black creators and white appropriators."[52] Recall McPherson: "if the first half of the twentieth century laid bare its racial logics, from 'Whites Only' signage to the brutalities of lynching, the second half increasingly hides its racial 'kernel,' burying it below a shell of neoliberal pluralism."[53] In contemporary terms, one could say that the ability to sell one's free labor, even as particular features of the slave trade were abolished, only ever produces an indebted subject, one still subordinate to the original conditions of inequality that animated the slave trade. Recall again Patricia Hill Collins's characterization of the *outsider within*," cited in chapter 3: black women "were economically exploited workers and thus would remain outsiders. The result was being placed in a curious outsider within social location."[54]

In *The Making of the Indebted Man* (2012), Maurizio Lazzarato links the material conditions of living in a debt society with the affects that undergird its hegemony explicitly. He frames the relation of debt to affect as a question of biopolitical production and control, arguing that with the birth of neoliberalism, practices of self-making emerge from a biopolitical force that is almost fully aligned with the capitalist mode of production. In this argument, Lazzarato claims that as the state form and financial capital merge under neoliberal regimes, biopolitical control becomes fully saturated with a market logic that is founded on debt.[55] The subject as entrepreneur of the self is limited spatially, temporally, and relationally by the debts it acquires, but also by those that precede it, infiltrating our practices of self-making at every step of their articulation. This could be stated in an Althusserian language as well. The "Absolute Subject," who is interpellated as "free" and compelled to be "free," emerges as both an entrepreneur of the self and an "Indebted Man" who is produced and delimited by the debts he acquires, but also of those that precede him, simply by living under the imperatives of a free market.

This leads Lazzarato to articulate how neoliberalism "forces us to be free," giving a better picture of McPherson's neoliberal invocation above, as he theorizes a "memnotechnics of subjectivation," or an "ethico-political work on the self, an individualization involving a mix of responsibility, guilt, hypocrisy, and distrust."[56] This so-called memnotechnics is precisely the co-articulation of capital and affect as a mechanism of control. It is both ontologically constitutive and functions in such a way that feelings and desires are cultivated in order to make oppressed subjects feel a responsibility for their oppression. Moreover, it is a modular force. The necessity to compete, to accumulate social capital, and to internalize the demands of the market destroys any experience of communal self-provision or complex coalition. The co-articulation of capital and affect as a memnotechnics of subjectivation is a fairly new and emerging feature of neoliberalism, although feelings of responsibility, guilt, hypocrisy, and distrust are historically common under the long history of capitalist accumulation and exploitation. In Lazzarato's view, the effects that result from and maintain one's indebtedness to capital do not substantively figure into one's resistance to it. In fact, Lazzarato seems to ignore the material specificity of contemporary political struggle altogether in favor of a kind of ontological abstraction at the level of resistance, proving Harney and Moten's reading.

Following this line of thought, the common understanding that could be drawn between black creators and white appropriators is the material effects of neoliberal regimes. The negative affects that Genet attributes to the Black Panthers' organization and tactics perhaps find a generalized correlate in Lazzarato's memnotechnics. However, the debt that Harney and Moten invoke is of a different order. They name a debt between friends, or, at the very least, between histories and figures of resistance who seem to be in solidarity. The burden of preservation and defense is thus also magnified under neoliberalism's differential modes of exploitation. This is to say, Harney and Moten provide clarification to the question of preservation and defense by inverting the double burden. We are all indebted to capital, but we are indebted differentially. When the defense and preservation of black social life takes place, inequity permeates its context. Any act of translation bearing liberatory potential, digital or otherwise, passes through the fact of this inequity. Any liberatory engagement with technology must address it.

Undercommoning DH

Having attuned the arguments and political tactics I have explored throughout this book to the ontological conditions of black social life that Harney, Moten, Dean, and others articulate, especially as it might pertain to questions of difference and inclusion in DH, I will conclude by gesturing in two directions. On the one hand, the theoretical framework in this chapter leads back to intersectional approaches to diversity and inclusion, which are particularly oriented toward the preservation of radical difference. On the other hand, my conclusion marks a return to guerrilla organization and tactics.

The intersectional argument is necessary here for two reasons. First, let's recall Patricia Hill Collins's definition of intersectionality: "Intersectional paradigms remind us that oppression cannot be reduced to one fundamental type, and that oppressions work together in producing injustice."[57] Where intersectionality becomes an imperative for DH work, it underscores problems related to epistemological access, resource allocation, and cooperative labor, but it is also a potentially irreconcilable approach to the problem of inclusion. This is to say, intersectionality demands processes of inclusion that belie modulation. Intersectionality marks the proliferation of difference in the face of overt forms of oppression. Second, intersectionality can also provide further criteria for conceptualizing translation as an act of preservation. For example, if Davis's decolonial Dada "sees this moment in history as irrational; accepts that language that limited the past but not ideas; is digital; connects across time, space, place, and culture; and attempts to give voice and language to the past even if it fails," intersectionality can offer further criteria for enacting this process in the face of multiple and overlapping oppressions. Decolonial Dada does not erase difference as it intermingles fragments from larger corpora; it maximizes difference to a potentially irrational order. Intersectionality provides further criteria for enacting multiple and overlapping solidarities as difference is recognized and magnified. This is perhaps a direct response to the BPP iterations of guerrilla seeing.

By contrast, the guerrilla concept is necessary at the conclusion of this chapter because it speaks to the institutional demand that this kind of work manifests. In Jack Halberstam's introduction to Harney and Moten's *Undercommons*, he argues that what results from the authors' analysis of collectivity is an alternative institutional principle—an alternative mode of connection and self-determination. It is, in Halberstam's view, in stark refusal of reparative work predicated on recognition:

> If you want to know what the undercommons wants, what Moten and Harney want, what black people, indigenous peoples, queers and poor people want, what we (the "we" who cohabit in the space of the undercommons) want, it is this—we cannot be satisfied with the recognition and acknowledgement generated by the very system that denies a) that anything was ever broken and b) that we deserved to be the broken part; so we refuse to ask for recognition and instead we want to take apart, dismantle, tear down the structure that, right now, limits our ability to find each other, to see beyond it and to access the places that we know lie outside its walls.[58]

What is interesting about Halberstam's figuration of the undercommons is precisely its insurgent stance. Where Harney and Moten claim that "the only possible relationship to the university today is a criminal one," they inhabit the position of the insurgent, abusing the university's hospitality, as they say, much like the guerrilla does with the state.[59] The question of labor reappears here. The fugitive work of the undercommons is necessary for the university to function, but it does not contribute to its reformation in the polite company of "rational men."[60] Antagonism also reappears here. Still inverted, Harney and Moten prefer to stand in the break, in the ruptural moment when antagonism is turned on its head: "To enter this space is to inhabit the ruptural and enraptured disclosure of the commons that fugitive enlightenment enacts, the criminal, matricidal, queer, in the cistern, on the stroll of the stolen life, the life stolen by enlightenment and stolen back, where the commons give refuge, where the refuge gives commons."[61]

The commons functions as a mode of connection across multiple and overlapping solidarities, across a multiplicity of subject positions, and across radically different experiences of oppression. To rephrase this, acts of preservation and self-defense are not simply aimless expressions of the negative; they define a practice of differential articulation that refuses to be separated and contained, refuses to be subsumed within a homogenizing and neutralizing body. Acts of preservation in this lineage of thought refuse to be modulated; refuse to feign objectivity; and upend the presumed consent that is formative of transcendental subjectivity.

Conclusion

Practice is a set of relays from one theoretical point to another, and theory is a relay from one practice to another. No theory can develop without eventually encountering a wall, and practice is necessary for piercing this wall.

— Gilles Deleuze, "Intellectuals and Power"

The intellectual's role is no longer to place himself "somewhat ahead and to the side" in order to express the stifled truth of the collectivity; rather, it is to struggle against the forms of power that transform him into its object and instrument in the sphere of "knowledge," "truth," "consciousness," and "discourse."

— Michel Foucault, "Intellectuals and Power"

Guerrilla Theory approaches digital humanities on its own methodological turf. It looks beyond the scope of DH's disciplinary formation and points of impact. It tracks back, well before DH became a popular academic practice, to a set of political concerns and aesthetic acts that prioritize partisan intervention and collective becoming. To think in the guerrilla's wake is to recall these concerns in the present, but also to situate them within the continued development of critical DH work. *Guerrilla Theory* excludes as much as it includes. It is an insurgent reading of DH praxis that is mobilized toward unforeseen ends.

I conclude this text not by looking forward or backward, but by exploring the subjective valences of present DH-related methods that amplify autonomy, collectivity, and political intervention. I explore arguments that propose minimal computing as a DH method, hacking as a form of transformative critique, and finally pairing political DH method with that of Critical University Studies (CUS). Minimal computing provokes DH. It calls for our work to address our needs at scale. It is firmly situated within radical democratic lineages that acknowledge their non-digital heritage. Hacking asks that we upend political economies that would privatize knowledge's free dissemination. It challenges us to rethink our subjectivity as networked interrelationality mediates the conflict between personal autonomy and institutional power. Thinking DH as CUS demands that DH direct its critical attention to the infrastructures that make our intellectual work possible. It forefronts economic inequity so as to reveal the asymmetries and potential affinities of our disciplinary standing.

Each method I embrace below embodies contested political configurations. Each method enacts a good-faith attempt at producing liberatory horizons. This is what *Guerrilla Theory* aims to produce: relays of political praxis that actualize radical potential in the present, indifferent to their name, and wary and weary of their instrumentalization. Its collective will augments DH's critical insurgencies. Its partisan stance maintains the democratic desire to nurture common communities of understanding and further politically oppositional goals.

Minimal Computing

In two short pieces on minimal computing, Alex Gil and Jentery Sayers frame the practice as a needs-based political economy. "Minimal computing is the application of minimalist principles to computing," Gil writes, but how and to what end minimalist principles are adopted is left to the maker.[1] Outfitting a Raspberry Pi, making a Jekyll website, or producing a lo-fi prototype of a digitally assisted project all fall under the practices' methodological umbrella. Minimal computing's political spirit is articulated by analog. It compels DH to think outside of its own methodological circumstances in order to consider the limitations its work might overcome.

Gil introduces minimal computing's politics by asking an enigmatic question: "What's a finished stairway?"[2] The question originates from Ernesto Oroza's *For an Architecture of Necessity and Disobedience* (2006), where Oroza recounts the story of a man who is renovating a house and must build an exterior stairway to finish it. The problem the man confronts is that his stairway does not cohere with the law—the appearance of an exterior stairway is not permitted until the house is finished. He builds the stairway anyway, waiting to be fined, or worse, to lose his property rights altogether. The man's attitude and commitment to meeting his needs is precisely what Gil's question is meant to duplicate. Gil follows Oroza's story by posing several questions of his own: "When I ask 'what do we need?' I'm asking scholars around the world—librarians, professors, students, cultural workers, independents: What is enough? What's your finished stairway?"[3]

A finished stairway is a provocation. It is a decision to stretch the limits of the law. It conceives of necessity in at least two ways. What do the constraints of the man's situation demand of him? Can he disregard his constraints in order to meet his needs? Gil's description of minimal computing follows in the same vein:

> My own posing of the question "what do we need?" comes from an acknowledgement of the hybrid and global future we see being shaped for the scholarly record: parts digital, parts analog. In this new mediatic environment we continue to protect, study and renew the analog, as we attempt to harness the new media in smart, ethical and sustainable ways. For several reasons, this implies learning how to produce, disseminate and preserve digital scholarship ourselves, *without the help we can't get*, even as we fight to build the infra-structures we need at the intersection of and beyond our libraries and schools. This means that my minimal computing does not stand in as a universal call, but rather as a space for new questions and practices, an injunction to constantly repeat the question, "what do we need?"[4]

While there are many noteworthy moments in this paragraph, its tactical ethos jumps out. Gil's practice of minimal computing is situational, both digital and analog, and stands at the intersection of institutional and personal need. He refuses the lure of dictation—the command of a universal need—while adopting an attitude of immanent critique. What do we need *now*? How can we organize to change our present circumstances and alter the course of our action?

The tactical features of Gil's work underscore the fact that what one might need to participate in DH praxis is not always large-scale tools for large-scale projects. Minimal computing's scale, and the importance of preserving a concept of scale based on what one needs, oppose a one-size-fits-all model along a spectrum of possible outcomes. Each act of minimal computing is as important as the deficiency it addresses. It may require one to sidestep or even ignore best practice. It underscores the fact that ethics are contingent upon the conditions of one's work.

Alongside Gil, Sayers furthers the tactical ethos ascribed to minimal computing within an equally pragmatic frame. He asks three questions: What do we need? What don't we need? What do we want? Where Sayers's practice of minimal computing is focused more heavily on acts of design, the ends to which he orients it are also expressly political. Minimal computing is a sustainable enterprise in Sayers's view (he frames the practice as a form of minimal consumption), as he mobilizes it to oppose the fetishization of con-sumer products. Perhaps most provocatively, Sayers connects the contingent and processual features of minimal computing to Marx's figuration of the "general intellect," writing:

> *How might minimal computing increase our shared capacities to think or imagine, and not just our individual capacities to work or produce?* Such shared capacities are what Marx (1857–58), Nick Dyer-Witheford (1999), and Christian Fuchs (2016) call the "general intellect." Minimal computing suggests we can engage shared capacities to think or imagine without resorting to theory/practice or yack/hack binaries (e.g., internalized life of the mind vs. externalized products of work).[5]

Sayers tacitly relies on a Marxist conception of cooperation to frame his practice, establishing it as a collective act that fundamentally alters the context of its use. Minimal computing manifests in and through our shared capacities to think and produce in common. It asks that we maintain a diversity of tactics for producing these shared capacities. Acts of cooperation further point to a kind of intersubjective mode of relation that works to surpass dichotomous thinking (theory/practice, hack/yack, virtual/real). Perhaps this extends to the friend-enemy relation as well, contingently and cautiously, in the agonistic play of collective labor.

The subjective element of Sayers's Marxist invocation is a familiar one:

> As a way to engage the discourse and practice of minimal design, we might consider what we can marginalize, reify, or appropriate through minimal design techniques and minimalist aesthetics, in addition to how we define "we" in relation to necessity and simplicity. How are we to interpret the renaissance of simple sites or flat interfaces? What's the link between simplicity and trust? Who or what does simplicity ignore?[6]

The "we" that Sayers invokes here recalls the militant concerns of the autonomist Marxist tradition alongside intersectional claims to radical difference. The agonistic work of this discourse is realized by the task of meeting needs, collectively articulated and collectively made. *We* produce what we need, at the scale that meets our needs, and with the political will to maintain it. How we accomplish these tasks may reignite ideological conflicts. How we maintain our commitments could produce new adversarial relations. The care with which collectivity is formed could allow the diversity of its practitioners to further politically oppositional goals.

Above all, minimal computing poses difficult questions. What must I give up and what must I ignore in the effort to meet my needs? How do I meet my needs without reproducing the antinomies I oppose? If the master's tools are the only tools available, am I willing to wield them against the contemporary political economy of their use? Any response to these questions is radically contingent—dependent on the context of minimal computing's employ—and extend to feminist, decolonial, and Marxist iterations of the task.

Hacking

In their coauthored article "Can Digital Humanities Mean Transformative Critique?" Alexis Lothian and Amanda Phillips aim to upend DH's political commitments as they turn toward a radical transformational logic. The pair aim to "rattle the poles of big tent politics rather than slip seamlessly into it."[7] They do so most explicitly by appropriating an inhuman metaphor that was first offered by Matthew K. Gold. In his 2012 Modern Language Association presentation, "Whose Revolution? Towards a More Equitable Digital Humanities," Gold claims that "any software engineer can tell you, the more eyes you have on a problem, the more likely you are to find and fix bugs in the system."[8] For Lothian and Phillips, bugs are not something to be fixed or eliminated. Rather, they argue, "we should inhabit, rather than eradicate, the status of bugs—even of viruses—in the system. Perhaps there are different systems and anti-systems to be found: DIY projects, projects that don't only belong to the academy, projects that still matter even if they aren't funded, even if they fail."[9]

Where Lothian and Phillips attempt to broaden DH's methodological scope by reclaiming inhuman figures, they also open the door to more subversive tendencies. To be a bug is to upset a system's seamless flow. To be a virus is to infiltrate a system from without, infect it, and use it to one's advantage. Its ontological implications are simultaneously subjective and descriptive of one's actions. Consider Paola Antonelli and Jamer Hunt's definition of hacking here. To hack is "to utilize the structure or code of an object or system against itself," they write. Hacking is accomplished "either through subversive reconfiguration or by the introduction of an active foreign agent."[10] Why hack? To do so is to push the dialectic between system and anti-system to a productive confrontation. It is to be a functional bug. If DH is to mean transformative critique, the call demands more than augmenting its archive of subversive figures and expanding its impact. The guerrilla, the bug, the virus, the hacker—these are access points for DH to address problems of political economy in the interplay of decentralized institutional powers.

The hacker's alignment with transformative critique extends DH's critical insurgencies. Perhaps most importantly, it gives DH an opportunity to oppose neoliberal logics wherever information acts as the twin currency of freedom and oppression. McKenzie Wark's "A Hacker Manifesto" better contextualizes these claims. There, hackers and vectoralists (read contemporary capitalists) battle over our capacity to produce and disseminate information. In her fifteenth axiom, Wark offers a definition of our present postcapitalist condition, arguing that the need to hack is contextualized by capital's evolution from owning the means of production to owning the circulation of knowledge. Wark writes:

> Vectoralists try to break capital's monopoly on the production process, and subordinate the production of goods to the circulation of

information. The leading corporations divest themselves of their productive capacity, as this is no longer a source of power. Their power
lies in monopolising intellectual property—patents and brands—and
the means of reproducing their value—the vectors of communication.
The privatisation of information becomes the dominant, rather than
a subsidiary, aspect of commodified life. As private property advances
from land to capital to information, property itself becomes more
abstract. As capital frees land from its spatial fixity, information as
property frees capital from its fixity in a particular object.[11]

The condition that Wark describes is one also identified in the presumptions,
methods, and outcomes of much DH praxis. DH understands that the privatization of information is a dominant aspect of commodification. It often
works to redirect it. The political task that Wark proposes—one difficult to
even imagine in our contemporary moment—is how information might be
freed from the commodity form entirely. Lothian and Phillips arguably gesture
in this direction, but it is something that DH has not proposed or seen the
need to actualize.

Following from these examples, the hacker emerges as a figure of knowledge's free dissemination that embodies the abstract character of its environment. The hacker produces abstractions—the hacker produces herself as an
abstraction—and these abstractions preserve our capacity to make across
differential planes of exchange. These differential planes of exchange encom-
pass subjectivity and organization, potentially forming concepts of knowledge
as commons, and extend those concepts to the social reproduction of the
commons. Again, Wark argues:

> Production produces all things, and all producers of things. Produc-
> tion produces not only the object of the production process, but also
> the producer as subject. Hacking is the production of production.
> The hack produces a production of a new kind, which has as its result
> a singular and unique product, and a singular and unique producer.
> Every hacker is at one and the same time producer and product of
> the hack, and emerges in its singularity as the memory of the hack as
> process.[12]

The subjective turn that Wark takes is an interesting one. The hacker is
both the producer and product of abstraction. She is a figure who preserves
her skill set by embodying its process. Wark understands this subjective feature to be a tactical advantage when the hacker acts—freedom from the commodity form is bound up in the productive potential of hacker subjectivity
even as capital establishes vectors of communication that delimit the subjects
of their making. Though perhaps inhuman in scope, the gendered and racial
contours of this claim are perhaps the most generative for DH.

Consider SSL Nagbot's definition of hacker subjectivity, stemming from feminist and queer iterations of the practice.[13] Hacker subjectivity is "largely shaped by notions of trickery," SSL Nagbot argues, and is

> grounded not only in technological acumen but, more importantly, in technological subversion (Coleman 2008). Hacking is guided by an ethics that attempts to eschew categories such as academic degrees, age, race, or position (Levy 1984). Instead, technological skill attempts to transcend these socially binding markers, and hacker communities trade in technological trickery as the currency of status and recognition.[14]

Hacking is guided by an anti-institutional ethos while it operates within para-institutional sites of social organization. Skill (hacking) is not reduced to its function as wage labor, but rather refers to our capacity to produce, to what Marx would identify as our capacity for labor power beyond its capture by work and wage. Production upsets social reproduction, orienting what is made toward the formation of the new. The collective parallels Wark here, but also draws a direct connection to practices of making.

SSL Nagbot continues by combining hacking with acts of making via their gendered discourses. Concepts of production require this combination and distinction, especially when they are not oriented toward social reproduction. The collective better contextualizes concepts of technological skill oriented toward trickery by drawing out gendered difference. SSL Nagbot writes:

> While hacking and making exist as distinct technocultural discourses, we see that they are very much in dialogue with one another, especially from an activist and feminist point of view. These more recent efforts around notions of making signal a broader feminist turn within technoculture more generally. Therefore, taken together, hacking and making might represent a gendered spectrum of technoculture, with transgression and masculinity on one side and care and femininity on the other. Rather than assert the differences within these discourses and practices, we prefer to underscore their continuity, given that hacking and making practices often coincide and therefore bring together gender considerations in idiosyncratic and unsuspecting ways.[15]

SSL Nagbot clearly understands the genealogy that Angela Nagle constructs without the need to invoke it. The collective seems to situate hetero-masculine cultures propped up by transgressive politics within a dialectical relation to feminist acts of care and preservation. What is made via our modes of production bears out political difference, given their gendered order in contemporary culture. If the hack results in a singular and unique product, it is contingent and partisan, wading through forces of freedom and oppression that would determine the subjects of its making.

I want to conclude this section with a consideration of race, falling under the moniker of "Black Code Studies," that complicates this discourse. Let's consider the following provocations from Jessica Marie Johnson and Mark Anthony Neal's introduction to their special issue of *Black Scholar*, "Introduction: Wild Seed in the Machine." First, "Black Code Studies is queer, femme, fugitive, and radical. As praxis and methodology, it waxes insurgent. It refutes conceptions of the digital that remove black diasporic people from engagement with technology, modernity, or the future."[16] Second, "Black Code Studies roots itself in the challenge of living in the wake of black people rendered inhuman, non-existent, and disposable by the slave ship, the plantation, the colonial state, the prison, the border."[17] Third, "Black Code Studies rejects formulations of Black Studies that tie intellectual production only to institutional structures or digital humanities only to grant-seeking projects with university affiliations. Black thought, art, and activist work manifests in many forms."[18]

Johnson and Anthony's provocations exist within the same techno-cultural spheres as Wark and SSL Nagbot's considerations of hacking, and echo Lothian and Phillips's work discussed above. However, Johnson and Neal mark an interesting rhetorical distinction to DH's nascent archive of subversive figures. To be an insurgent is to situate the discourse of inhumanity within its racialized histories and operate on the basis of need. It is to situate one's skill as a kind of guerrilla technological force so as to express a multiplicity of tactics in the face of racialized oppression. Any liberatory potential that Black Code Studies elicits acknowledges the brutalities that precede its making. This is not so much the production of a singular unique product, but the articulation of communal self-provision where inhumanity does not necessarily signify liberation. The interplay between freedom and oppression in this discourse emerges from the situation in which information acts as its currency, but the abstraction it produces is contoured by the particularities that set black life apart, complicating the hack as a transformative process.

Johnson and Neal's third provocation is especially poignant where hacking and transformative critique coincide. If Black Code Studies were to realize something like Lothian and Phillips's do-it-yourself culture, Wark's singular and unique product, or SSL Nagbot's combination of hacking and making, it, too, does so from within para-institutional sites of social organization. Black Code Studies is queer, femme, fugitive, and radical, small-scale, needs-based, and acutely aware of its subjectivity. Perhaps not guerrilla in name, this concept recasts the focus and intent of technological trickery, insurgency, and production, complicating the spectrum that moves from transgression to care in our present political circumstances. It bears out many of the political ambiguities explored in this text from the underside. It is perhaps best situated to address the oppressions of our postcapitalist present.

DH as Critical University Studies

In her book *Feminism without Borders* (2003), Chandra Talpade Mohanty argues that "the moment we tie university-based research to economic development—and describe this research as fundamentally driven by market forces—it becomes possible to locate the university as an important player in capitalist rule."[19] This claim is couched in a decolonial method committed to developing "the urgent political necessity of forming strategic coalitions across class, race, and national boundaries," but it is also motivated by a commitment to feminist struggle.[20] The university is a site of struggle in particular because it is a "contradictory place where knowledges are colonized but also contested . . . It is one of the few remaining spaces in a rapidly privatized world that offers some semblance of a public arena for dialogue, engagement, and visioning of democracy and justice."[21] What follows is a simple claim, but one that is difficult to realize in a contemporary context: "Feminist literacy necessitates learning to see (and theorize) differently—to identify and challenge the politics of knowledge that naturalizes global capitalism and business-as-usual in North American higher education."[22]

With the rise of the for-profit university and the precaritization of intellectual labor that results in fewer tenure-track jobs, low adjunct wages, and a glut of applicants on the job market, the neoliberal reformation of the university is undeniable. It is also undeniable that DH emerged as a contemporary force of disciplinary transformation during this precise socioeconomic shift. Matthew K. Gold states this matter-of-factly in "The Digital Humanities Moment," his introduction to the 2012 *Debates in the Digital Humanities* anthology:

> At a time when many academic institutions are facing austerity budgets, department closings, and staffing shortages, the digital humanities experienced a banner year that saw cluster hires at multiple universities, the establishment of new digital humanities centers and initiatives across the globe, and multimillion-dollar grants distributed by federal agencies and charitable foundations. . . . Clearly, this is a significant moment of growth and opportunity for the field, but it has arrived amid larger questions concerning the nature and purpose of the university system.[23]

The financial boon that DH received in the wake of 2008 has led many to equate it with the wholesale neoliberalization of the university, transforming critically focused humanistic inquiry into a skills-based mercantile regime. This is not news to anyone in DH, but it does bear repeating. There is a necessary but vacant link between DH's critical insurgencies and its institutional position as the humanities continue their decline. The issue that remains—the issue with which DH must contend—is precisely how DH praxis paradoxically commands institutional support at the same time that it disavows institutional austerity.

Incorporating work like Mohanty's into DH praxis is a first step toward addressing this fundamental issue. Co-articulating the rhetoric and method of both DH and Critical University Studies more generally would broaden the awareness and need to refuse the university's continued neoliberalization. In many ways, the connection is in-built to activist DH method. Consider Moya Bailey's argument in her 2011 article "All the Digital Humanists Are White, All the Nerds Are Men, but Some of Us Are Brave." There, Bailey unearths a political line of thought that broadens DH's disciplinary horizon and valorizes its politically situated work:

> In blog posts, Miriam Posner and Bethany Nowviskie have both addressed the structures that impede women from connecting to digital humanities. The increase of women in higher level positions within universities has led to changes in the infrastructure, with child care and nursing nests cropping up on campuses across the country. Similarly, people of color have been engaging in critical university studies long before the 1990s when the field is said to have emerged. By demanding space as students and faculty, in addition to advocating for rights as the laborers that built and maintain these institutions, people of color have organized through concerted effort to bring about changes in institutional culture and structure.[24]

Bailey's comments point to a more fundamental problem connected to DH's institutional rise. How might DH's own methods for supporting diversity and inclusion interface with economic logics that undermine the university's democratic vision? Facts like those that Gold lists above have been and continue to be a primary source of hostility toward DH at the same time that DH scholar-practitioners have staged their most significant debates concerning diversity and inclusion. The radical potential that is inherent to DH's intense focus on diversity and inclusion often gets lost when DH is situated as neoliberalization's disciplinary equivalent.[25] But the issue remains: what transformations must take place for DH to realize its radical potential in the face of austere logics? With whom must we align ourselves if we are to realize our collective vision of the university?

Of the work in Critical University Studies that forwards this sentiment, the conclusion to Christopher Newfield's *Unmaking the Public University* (2011) is perhaps the most accessible. After a sustained exegesis of the University of California system's acquiescence to austerity and conservative cultural politics over the 1980s, 1990s, and 2000s, Newfield positions CUS as a transformative methodological operation at the infrastructural level, advocating for numerous institutional remedies to the cultural and economic interests that undermine higher education. Newfield's intervention is vital because of the concrete rallying points it provides from which to act. Akin to Mohanty's argument, Newfield pairs the managerial demand placed on humanistic disciplines in particular with a liberatory politics that refuses the university's continuous contour toward corporate directives. His political imperatives speak directly to Bailey's concerns above. The most pertinent imperatives of the five that Newfield proposes are listed here: "First, racial equality needs to be reaffirmed as a value and as a goal." "Third, the university needs to be understood as an engagement in forms of individual and collective development that cannot be captured in economic terms." "Fifth, public universities need to insist on the value of understanding societies beyond their status as commercial markets."[26] It is perhaps undeniable that DH and CUS's political cohesion would better ground egalitarian visions of the university's future, but the theoretical linkages necessary for doing so are only just emerging. CUS work acts as a bridge between the critical attitude that conceptualizes diversity and inclusion as an economic issue and the infrastructural stance that would realize it.

It is perhaps not a surprise that "infrastructure" has become a buzzword in critical DH praxis. Austerity demands that we create the conditions for our work to exist at the same time that we perform it. DH's recent infrastructural turn is best summarized by Alan Liu: critical infrastructure studies is a "call for digital humanities research and development informed by, and able to influence, the way scholarship, teaching, administration, support services, labor practices, and even development and investment strategies in higher education intersect with society."[27] The rhetorical shift from "critical university" to "critical infrastructure" is interesting here. Where Liu goes so far as to say that most, *if not the whole of our lives*, are organized through institutional mechanisms formative of a "social-cum-technological milieu," "the word 'infrastructure' give[s] us the same kind of general purchase on social complexity that Stuart Hall, Raymond Williams, and others sought when they reached for their all-purpose word, 'culture.'"[28]

This claim is motivated by three logical moments in Liu's view, and proceeds as follows: (1) "critique recognizes that the 'real,' 'true,' or 'lawful' groundwork (i.e., infrastructure) for anything, especially the things that matter most to people, such as the allocation of goods or the assignation of identity, is ungrounded";[29] (2) "critique then goes antifoundationalist to the second degree by criticizing its own standing in the political-economic system—a recursion effect attested in now familiar, post-May-1968 worries that critics themselves are complicit in elitism, 'embourgeoisment,' 'recuperation,' 'containment,' and majoritarian identity, not to mention tenure";[30] and (3) "critique seeks to turn its complicity to advantage—for example, by positioning critics as what Foucault called embedded or 'specific intellectuals' acting on a particular institutional scene to steer social forces."[31]

Liu's logic clearly presumes a politics. It is not the simple recognition of technocratic regimes or the acceptance of cybernetic culture, nor is it a naive attempt to capitalize on our current socioeconomic condition. It offers a mode of inquiry that preserves the radical possibilities inherent to leftist critique while placing them within DH praxis. His argument culminates in a potentially critical DH method because it signifies our "ability to treat infrastructure not as a foundation, a given, but instead as a tactical medium that opens the possibility of critical infrastructure studies as a mode of cultural studies."[32]

A similar stance is also apparent in Roopika Risam's essay "Navigating the Global Digital Humanities: Insights from Black Feminism." There, Risam argues that

> as the field of digital humanities has grown in size and scope, the question of how to navigate a scholarly community that is diverse in geography, language, and participant demographics has become pressing. An increasing number of initiatives have sought to address these concerns, both in scholarship—as in work on postcolonial digital humanities or #transformDH—and through new organizational structures like the Alliance of Digital Humanities Organizations (ADHO) Multi-Lingualism and Multi-Culturalism Committee and Global Outlook::Digital Humanities (GO::DH), a special interest group of ADHO. From the work of GO::DH in particular, an important perspective has emerged: digital humanities, as a field, can only be inclusive and its diversity can only thrive in an environment in which local specificity—the unique concerns that influence and define digital humanities at regional and national levels—is positioned at its center and its global dimensions are outlined through an assemblage of the local.[33]

Paired with Liu's work discussed above, Risam draws us closer to a critique that would mirror Mohanty's critique. Two features of Liu and Risam's arguments, respectively, draw this point out. First, Liu's argument offers a strategic intervention in DH's complicity with neoliberal educational imperatives. His anti-foundationalism makes space for self-critique as DH extends into new arenas of influence. Liu's invocation of figures like Stuart Hall and Raymond Williams does indicate a claim to a radical, unrealized potential for diversity and inclusion in DH. Second, Risam's work pairs a global/local concept within DH praxis at the same time that she considers questions of diversity from a socioeconomic standpoint. This feature of Risam's work speaks directly to Mohanty's concern for a transformative concept of feminist literacy. The global/local focus in Risam's work is thus a tactical opening to rework Liu's remarks on thinking critical infrastructure as a form of cultural studies, problematizing the kinds of partnerships we make with noneducational entities.

The final step in thinking DH as CUS lies in developing common organizational models that would better oppose institutionally imposed inequities. Risam's work is a deft articulation of this desire in DH praxis, but its economic difficulties are a constant barrier. Bethany Nowviskie is clear on this point. "Class divisions among faculty and staff in the academy are profound," she writes, and alt-ac (alternative academic) labor serves as a coalitional site of collectivized labor:

> Among us are: administrators with varied levels of responsibility for supporting the academic enterprise; instructional technologists and software developers who collaborate on scholarly projects; journalists, editors, and publishers; cultural heritage workers in a variety of institutional roles and institutions; librarians, archivists, and other information professionals; entrepreneurs who partner on projects of value to scholars; program officers for funding agencies and humanities centers, and many more.[34]

Nowviskie's entrepreneurial inclusion complicates her coalitional stance. Does the invitation limit the individualizing effects of capital—its modular division that underlies collectivity? Or does it reinscribe them? Nevertheless, her point is profound: what would a collective body of academic labor look like if class division was viewed as a cooperative relation, an opportunity to redistribute the division of labor and protect all included, rather than a relation of prestige meant to parse and magnify inequity?

This is perhaps the most direct challenge to DH's infrastructural incursions, but it is also the most direct opportunity to align ourselves with critical traditions like CUS that make the university their object of analysis in addition to the material basis of their thought. To echo Harney and Moten's *Undercommons*, the task of thinking DH as CUS may rely on thinking in opposition to our own critical vocabulary if we are to realize more equitable horizons. Coalitional sites of collectivized labor are to be oriented beyond institutional goals as they currently exist—even those of an anti-foundational nature:

> The mode of professionalization that is the American university is precisely dedicated to promoting this consensual choice: an antifoundational critique of the University or a foundational critique of the university. Taken as choices, or hedged as bets, one tempered with the other, they are nonetheless always negligent. Professionalization is built on this choice. It rolls out into ethics and efficiency, responsibility and science, and numerous other choices, all built upon the theft, the conquest, the negligence of the outcast mass intellectuality of the undercommons.[35]

Under this conception of university organization and critique, thinking DH as CUS is only a first step toward making critical insurgency and tactical subversion truly transformative praxes. The autonomy such a project promises is revolutionary. The agonims and antagonisms that follow are constitutive.

Political Concepts Critical of DH

A definitive conclusion to my project would ultimately be self-defeating. The political work this text proposes does not conclude. It only mutates, awaiting its time to manifest and act. *Guerrilla Theory* is a provocation. *Guerrilla Theory* is an attempt to meet needs, even if those with influence do not recognize those needs, and to orient restless negativities toward their broader articulation within present intellectual discourse. DH praxis pierces walls. *Guerrilla Theory* is a relay point. If the two intersect beyond the political work of this text, their intersection will undoubtedly manifest as something new, different, and challenging to our present political order, perhaps a political situation where democracy and justice find a more equitable realignment.

The whole of this text amounts to a theory-focused engagement with DH praxis. *Guerrilla Theory*'s priority rests on thinking situationally, embracing partisan politics, and acting beyond a narrow set of political dyads. Its actualization lies in the process of realizing these outcomes, rather than in the outcomes themselves. This text is ultimately a speculative enterprise, but its provocations are not intangible. The political concepts explored here are critical of DH, but they are also indicative of a generative horizon in which contemporary criticism might be transformed into actually existing radicalisms of the discipline's future.

Preface

The first epigraph is from p. 16 of the Invisible Committee, *Now*, trans. Robert Hurley (Los Angeles: Semiotext(e), 2017). The second epigraph is from pp. 11–12 of George Orwell, *Animal Farm* (New York: Signet, 1946).

1. "Doctoral Programs by the Numbers," Philosophy, *Chronicle of Higher Education*, last modified September 30, 2010, https://www.chronicle.com/article /NRC-Rankings-Overview-/124753.

Introduction

The first epigraph is from p. 170 of Chandra Talpade Mohanty, *Feminism without Borders: Decolonizing Theory, Practicing Solidarity* (Durham, N.C.: Duke University Press, 2003). The second epigraph is from p. 121 of Amy Earhart, *Traces of the Old, Uses of the New: The Emergence of Digital Literary Studies* (Ann Arbor: University of Michigan Press, 2015).

1. Brian Greenspan, "The Scandal of Digital Humanities," *Hyperlab: Hyperbolic* (blog), May 4, 2016, https://carleton.ca/hyperlab/2018/the-scandal-of -digital-humanities/.

2. Jacques Derrida, *Dissemination* (Chicago: University of Chicago Press, 1983), 4.

3. "About #transformDH," #transformDH, http://transformdh.org/about -transformdh/.

4. Claire Fontaine, "Matthew K. Gold Presents on Guerrilla Pedagogy @ Information 2.0 Lecture Series," HASTAC, last modified October 5, 2009, https:// www.hastac.org/opportunities/matthew-k-gold-presents-guerrilla-pedagogy -information-20-lecture-series.

5. Simon Rowberry, "A Guerrilla Digital Humanities," *Simon Rowberry* (blog), August 14, 2014, https://www.sprowberry.com/a-guerrilla-digital-humanities/.

6. "The Digital Humanities Manifesto 2.0," Humanities Blast, http://www .humanitiesblast.com/manifesto/Manifesto_V2.pdf.

7. Jacques Derrida, *Of Hospitality* (Stanford, Calif.: Stanford University Press, 2000), 5.

8. Elizabeth Grosz, "Menstruation Machine," in *Design and Violence*, ed. Paola Antonelli and Jamer Hunt (New York: Museum of Modern Art, 2017), 53–54.

9. Roger Whitson, "Does DH Really Need to Be Transformed? My Reflections on #mla12," *Roger Whitson* (blog), January 8, 2012, http://www.rogerwhitson .net/?p=1358.

10. William Panapacker, "Pannapacker at MLA: Digital Humanities Triumphant?" *Brainstorm: The Chronicle of Higher Education* (blog), January 8,

2011, https://www.chronicle.com/blogs/brainstorm/pannapacker-at-mla-digital
-humanities-triumphant/30915.

11. Whitson has more recently recanted his opposition to #transformDH in a blog post titled "Mea Culpa for #transformdh," recognizing that in his criticism of the guerrilla's invocation, he "theorized the digital humanities as an already-formed field that gradually expanded its boarders [*sic*] to make its discipline accessible to marginalized voices, rather than envisioning a grassroots process in which various communities construct heterogeneous forms of association that . . . create the disciplinary space for the digital humanities."

12. "Digital Humanities Manifesto 2.0."

13. Natalia Cecire, "In Defense of Transforming DH," *Works Cited: Natalia Cecire's Blog* (blog), January 8, 2012, http://nataliacecire.blogspot.com/2012/01/in-defense-of-transforming-dh.html.

14. Tara McPherson, "Why Are the Digital Humanities So White? or Thinking the Histories of Race and Computation," in *Debates in the Digital Humanities: 2012*, ed. Matthew K. Gold (Minneapolis: University of Minnesota Press, 2012), 139.

15. "Digital Humanities Manifesto 2.0."

16. Stanley Fish, "The Digital Humanities and the Transcending of Morality," *New York Times*, January 9, 2012, http://opinionator.blogs.nytimes.com/2012/01/09/the-digital-humanities-and-the-transcending-of-mortality/?_r=0.

17. "Digital Humanities Manifesto 2.0."

18. On two occasions, the authors of *Digital_Humanities* argue that the phrase "digital humanities" "describes not just a collective singular but also the humanities in the plural, able to address and engage disparate subject matters across media, language, location, and history" (24). The combination of the digital with the humanities is both an extension of humanistic inquiry and a break with narrower methods.

19. In her article "Marked Bodies, Transformative Scholarship, and the Question of Theory in Digital Humanities," Alexis Lothian discusses a panel that she co-organized for the American Studies Association. There, questioning the hegemonic work that "theory" has perpetrated in the humanities in recent history, she articulates theory in a generative style, writing: "This was not 'Theory' as a vague revolutionary concept all too easily written off by the image of turtlenecked graduate students sitting around talking about Foucault that it conjures. We were talking about theory as making, about making objects that critique, that *are* critique, that are transformative reimaginings of the world." Although she is interested in distancing herself from the stigma of abstraction that follows where theory reigns, her articulation of theory as making dovetails well with Foucault's later work, specifically his essay "What Is Enlightenment?"

20. Karl Marx and Friedrich Engels, *The Communist Manifesto*, ed. David McLellan (Oxford: Oxford University Press, 1998), 6.

21. bell hooks, *Talking Back: Thinking Feminist, Thinking Black* (New York: Routledge, 2014), 22.

22. hooks, *Talking Back*, 21.

23. Alan Liu, "Where Is Cultural Criticism in the Digital Humanities?" in *Debates in the Digital Humanities: 2012*, ed. Matthew K. Gold (Minneapolis: University of Minnesota Press, 2012), 491.

24. Wendy Hui Kong Chun, Richard Grusin, Patrick Jagoda, and Rita Raley, "The Dark Side of the Digital Humanities," in *Debates in the Digital Humanities: 2016*, ed. Matthew K. Gold and Lauren F. Klein (Minneapolis: University of Minnesota Press, 2016), 506.

25. Todd Presner, "Critical Theory and the Mangle of Digital Humanities," in *Between Humanities and the Digital*, ed. Patrik Svensson and David Theo Goldberg (Cambridge, Mass.: MIT Press, 2015), 56.

26. Adeline Koh, "More Hack, Less Yack? Modularity, Theory and Habitus in the Digital Humanities," *Adeline Koh* (blog), May 21, 2012, https://web .archive.org/web/20120721195443/http://www.adelinekoh.org/blog/2012 /05/21/more-hack-less-yack-modularity-theory-and-habitus-in-the-digital -humanities/.

27. Earhart, *Traces of the Old, Uses of the New*, 123.

28. McKenzie Wark (@mckenziewark), "To only see friends versus enemies is to misunderstand the whole art of politics," June 22, 2015, 11:25 p.m., https:// twitter.com/mckenziewark/status/613186203823775744.

29. Elizabeth Losh, Jacqueline Wernimont, Laura Wexler, and Hong-An Wu, "Putting the Human Back into the Digital Humanities: Feminism, Generosity, and Mess," in *Debates in the Digital Humanities: 2016*, ed. Matthew K. Gold and Lauren F. Klein (Minneapolis: University of Minnesota Press, 2016), 98.

30. Roopika Risam, "Beyond the Margins: Intersectionality and the Digital Humanities," *Digital Humanities Quarterly* 9, no. 2 (2015).

31. Risam, "Beyond the Margins."

32. Consider the "Textures" section of Risam's co-developed DH project "Torn Apart / Separados." There, the team's work shows how "the crisis for immigrants in the United States is not only happening at the Mexico-United States border or other ports of entry. Rather, 'the border is everywhere.'"

33. Maria Lugones, "Toward a Decolonial Feminism," *Hypatia* 25, no. 4 (2010): 742.

34. Louis Althusser, "Ideology and the State," in *Lenin and Philosophy and Other Essays* (New York: Monthly Review, 1971), 56.

35. Steven Shaviro, "The Bitter Necessity of Debt," *Steven Shaviro* (blog), May 1, 2010, http://www.shaviro.com/Othertexts/Debt.pdf.

36. Jason Read, *The Micro-Politics of Capital: Marx and the Prehistory of the Present* (New York: State University of New York Press, 2003), 136.

37. Chela Sandoval, *Methodology of the Oppressed* (Minneapolis: University of Minnesota Press, 2000), 43.

38. Sandoval, *Methodology of the Oppressed*, 44.

39. Dorothy Kim and Jesse Stommel, "Introduction: Disrupting the Digital Humanities," in *Disrupting the Digital Humanities*, ed. Dorothy Kim and Jesse Stommel, http://www.disruptingdh.com/.

40. Rita Raley, "Digital Humanities for the Next Five Minutes," *Differences: A Journal of Feminist Cultural Studies* 1, no. 25 (2014): 40.

41. Raley, "Digital Humanities," 40.

42. Alan Liu, "Drafts for *Against the Cultural Singularity* (book in progress)," *Alan Liu* (blog), May 2, 2016, http://liu.english.ucsb.edu/drafts-for-against-the -cultural-singularity/.

43. Cathy N. Davidson, "Collaboration by Difference, Yet Again," *HASTAC*

(blog), November 23, 2008, https://www.hastac.org/blogs/cathy-davidson/2008/11/23/collaboration-difference-yet-again.

44. Jesse Stommel, "Critical Digital Pedagogy: A Definition," *Hybrid Pedagogy* (blog), August 8, 2016, http://hybridpedagogy.org/critical-digital-pedagogy-definition/.

45. Roopika Risam, "As Che says. . . . 'At the risk of sounding ridiculous, the true revolutionary is guided by a feeling of great love,' #guerrilladh #keydh," June 23, 2016, 10:19 a.m., https://twitter.com/roopikarisam/status/745984535544889344.

46. Raley, "Digital Humanities," 37.

47. Raley, "Digital Humanities," 37.

48. Matthew Kirschenbaum, "Digital Humanities As/Is a Tactical Term," in *Debates in the Digital Humanities: 2012*, ed. Matthew K. Gold (Minneapolis: University of Minnesota Press, 2012), 427.

49. Moya Bailey, Anne Cong-Huyen, Alexis Lothian, and Amanda Phillips, "Reflections on a Movement: #transformDH, Growing Up," in *Debates in the Digital Humanities: 2016*, ed. Matthew K. Gold and Lauren F. Klein (Minneapolis: University of Minnesota Press, 2016), 72.

50. Geert Lovink, *Dark Fiber: Tracking Critical Internet Culture* (Cambridge, Mass.: MIT Press, 2003), 271.

51. Invisible Committee, *Now*, 199.

52. Paolo Virno, "On Armed Struggle," in *Autonomia: Post-Political Politics*, ed. Sylvere Lotringer and Christian Marazzi (Los Angeles: Semiotext(e), 2007), 238.

53. Virno, "On Armed Struggle," 239.

54. Karl Marx, *Capital: A Critique of Political Economy, Vol. 1*, trans. Ben Fowkes (London: Penguin in association with New Left Review, 1990), 443.

55. Jason Read, "The Production of Subjectivity: From Transindividuality to the Commons," *New Formations* no. 70 (2010): 118.

56. Read, "Production of Subjectivity," 118.

57. Jason Read, "Transindividuality, Equaliberty, Short-Circuit: Notes on the Recent Thought of Etienne Balibar," *Unemployed Negativity* (blog), August 11, 2010, http://www.unemployednegativity.com/2010/08/transindividuality-equaliberty-short.html.

58. Judith Butler, *Giving an Account of Oneself* (New York: Fordham University Press, 2005), 7.

59. Cathy N. Davidson, "Why Yack Needs Hack (and Vice Versa): From Digital Humanities to Digital Literacy," in *Between Humanities and the Digital*, ed. Patrik Svensson and David Theo Goldberg (Cambridge, Mass.: MIT Press, 2015), 138.

60. This reading of politicized cinematic work perhaps offers a response to David M. Berry and Anders Fagerjord's call for a "post-screenic" understanding of DH in their coauthored *Digital Humanities: Knowledge and Critique in the Digital Age* (Cambridge: Polity, 2017). They argue that "the digital humanities must be able to offer theoretical interventions and digital methods for a historical moment when the computational has become both hegemonic and post-screenic," a "move away from the computer screen or visual interface as the key site of interaction" (2). My focus on guerrilla cinema prioritizes collective acts of making that either precede the screen or demand its de-prioritization via collective modes of becoming. While not focused on computation, guerrilla theory operates

within a compatible site of intervention, even as the screen figures into its political interventions.

61. Jussi Parikka, *What Is Media Archaeology?* (Malden, Mass.: Polity, 2012), 20.

62. Domenico Fiormonte, "Toward a Cultural Critique of Digital Humanities," in *Debates in the Digital Humanities: 2016*, ed. Matthew K. Gold and Lauren F. Klein (Minneapolis: University of Minnesota Press, 2016), 451.

63. Michael Hardt, "Reclaim the Common in Communism." *The Guardian*, February 3, 2011, https://www.theguardian.com/commentisfree/2011/feb/03/communism-capitalism-socialism-property.

64. Carl DiSalvo, *Adversarial Design* (Cambridge, Mass.: MIT Press, 2015), 16.

65. Jeffrey J. Williams. "The Need for Critical University Studies," in *A New Deal for the Humanities: Liberal Arts and the Future of Public Higher Education*, ed. Gordon Hunter and Feisal G. Mohamed (New Brunswick, N.J.: Rutgers University Press, 2015), 149.

66. Williams, "The Need for Critical University Studies," 149.

67. Black Mask, "UAW/MF: The Free Press Report," in *Black Mask & Up Against the Wall Motherfucker: The Incomplete Works of Ron Hahne, Ben Morea, and the Black Mask Group* (Oakland, Calif.: PM, 2011), 95.

68. Jean Genet, "Violence & Brutality," in *The Declared Enemy: Texts and Interviews*, ed. Albert Dichey, trans. Jeff Fort (Palo Alto, Calif.: Stanford University Press, 2004), 171.

69. Genet, "Violence & Brutality," 171.

70. Huey P. Newton, *Revolutionary Suicide* (New York: Penguin, 2009), 359.

71. Neera Chandhoke, *Democracy and Revolutionary Politics* (New York: Bloomsbury Academic. 2015), 10.

72. Chandhoke, *Democracy*, 30.

73. Mark Bray, *Antifa: The Anti-Fascist Handbook* (New York: Melville House, 2017), 144.

Chapter 1

The first epigraph is from p. 216 of Jacques Derrida, *The Politics of Friendship*, trans. George Collins (New York: Verso, 2005). The second epigraph is from p. 103 of Anne Burdick, Johanna Drucker, Peter Lunenfeld, Todd Presner, and Jeffrey Schnapp, *Digital_Humanities* (Cambridge, Mass.: MIT Press, 2016).

1. Chun, Grusin, Jagoda, and Raley, "The Dark Side of the Digital Humanities," 493–509.

2. Tavia Nyong'o and Kyla Wazana Tompkins, "Eleven Theses on Civility," *Social Text Online*, https://socialtextjournal.org/eleven-theses-on-civility/.

3. Nyong'o and Wazana Tompkins, "Eleven Theses."

4. Michael Hardt, "The Militancy of Theory," *South Atlantic Quarterly* 110, no. 1 (2011): 19.

5. Earhart, *Traces of the Old, Uses of the New*, 126.

6. Hardt, "Militancy of Theory," 23.

7. Robin D. G. Kelley and Fred Moten, "Fred Moten and Robin D.G. Kelley in Conversation: 'Do Black Lives Matter?'" *E-flux Conversations* (blog), January 20, 2015, https://conversations.e-flux.com/t/fred-moten-and-robin-d-g-kelley-in-conversation-do-black-lives-matter-video/945.

8. Stefano Harney and Fred Moten, *The Undercommons: Fugitive Planning & Black Study* (Brooklyn, N.Y.: Minor Compositions, 2013), 38.

9. Jack Halberstam, "The Wild Beyond: With and for the Undercommons," in *The Undercommons: Fugitive Planning and Black Study* (Brooklyn, N.Y.: Minor Compositions, 2013), 9–10.

10. Stefano Harney, "Hapitcality in the Undercommons," in *The Routledge Companion to Art and Politics*, ed. Randy Martin (New York: Routledge, 2015), 178.

11. Fish, "The Digital Humanities and the Transcending of Morality."

12. Rita Raley, *Tactical Media* (Minneapolis: University of Minnesota Press, 2009), 7.

13. Raley, *Tactical Media*, 8.

14. Raley, *Tactical Media*, 3.

15. Raley, *Tactical Media*, 151.

16. See p. 18 of Harney and Motens, *Undercommons*.

17. There are a few key moments featured in Raley's *Tactical Media* that highlight the processual quality of guerrilla organization and tactics. The most important reference is articulated as follows: "Absolute victory is neither a desirable nor a truly attainable object for tactical media, which is why it will be possible for me to trace parallels between guerrilla warfare and systems disruption" (10).

18. See p. 327 of Schmitt's *The Nomos of the Earth: In the International Law of the Jus Publicum Europaeum*, trans. G. L. Ulmen (New York: Telos, 2006).

19. Chantal Mouffe, *Agonistics: Thinking the World Politically* (New York: Verso, 2013), xii.

20. Mouffe, *Agonistics*, 5.

21. Carl Schmitt, *The Concept of the Political*, trans. George Schwab (Chicago: University of Chicago Press, 2007), 27.

22. Carl Schmitt, *The Theory of the Partisan*, trans. G. L. Ulmen (New York: Telos, 2007), 4.

23. Schmitt, *Theory of the Partisan*, 4–5.

24. G. L. Ulmen, "Translator's Introduction," in *The Theory of the Partisan*, by Carl Schmitt, trans. G. L. Ulmen (New York: Telos, 2007), ix–xii.

25. Schmitt, *Theory of the Partisan*, 14.

26. Alexander Galloway, "Love of the Middle," in *Excommunication: Three Inquiries in Media and Mediation* (Chicago: University of Chicago Press, 2014), 60.

27. Simon Critchley, *Infinitely Demanding: Ethics of Commitment, Politics of Resistance* (London: Verso, 2008), 5.

28. Michael Hardt and Antonio Negri, *Multitude: War and Democracy in the Age of Empire* (New York: Penguin, 2005), 56.

29. Virno, "On Armed Struggle," 238–39.

30. Hardt and Negri, *Multitude*, 77.

31. Michael Hardt and Antonio Negri, *Empire* (Cambridge, Mass.: Harvard University Press, 2000), 25.

32. See Hardt and Negri, *Empire*, 160–82.

33. See Hardt and Negri, *Empire*, 295.

34. Hardt and Negri, *Empire*, 161.

35. Hardt and Negri, *Empire*, 161.

36. Hardt and Negri, *Multitude*, 78.

37. Hardt and Negri, *Multitude*, 78.

38. Michael Hardt and Antonio Negri, *Commonwealth* (Cambridge, Mass.: Belknap of Harvard University Press, 2011), 61.

39. Hardt and Negri, *Empire*, 23–24.

40. Hardt and Negri, *Empire*, 25.

41. Hardt and Negri, *Empire*, 211, 289.

42. Alexander R. Galloway and Eugene Thacker, *The Exploit: A Theory of Networks* (Minneapolis: University of Minnesota Press, 2007), 19.

43. Galloway and Thacker, *The Exploit*, 5.

44. Galloway and Thacker, *The Exploit*, 14.

45. Galloway and Thacker, *The Exploit*, 27.

46. See Galloway and Thacker, *The Exploit*, 28.

47. Galloway and Thacker, *The Exploit*, 68.

48. Galloway and Thacker, *The Exploit*, 68.

49. Although Schmitt does claim that recognizing the face of one's enemy is necessary for political conflict, Galloway and Thacker rely on a Levinasian ethic of faciality in political division in order to undermine Schmitt's political. Schmitt does rely on a concept of mutual recognition, which Galloway and Thacker use to their advantage. If the swarm cannot be recognized in common terms (i.e., through the recognition of one's face), the swarm manifests an ontological condition of defacement, rendering the friend-enemy relation inoperative. See Galloway and Thacker, *The Exploit*, 64–67.

50. Galloway and Thacker, *The Exploit*, 66.

51. Galloway and Thacker, *The Exploit*, 68.

52. Galloway and Thacker, *The Exploit*, 65.

53. Galloway and Thacker, *The Exploit*, 66.

54. Galloway and Thacker, *The Exploit*, 69.

55. Galloway and Thacker, *The Exploit*, 78.

56. Harney and Moten, *The Undercommons*, 64.

57. Alexander G. Weheliye, *Habeas Viscus: Racializing Assemblages, Biopolitics, and Black Feminist Theories of the Human* (Durham, N.C.: Duke University Press, 2014), 4.

58. Byung-Chul Han, *In the Swarm: Digital Prospects*, trans. Erik Butler (Boston: MIT Press. 2017), 10.

59. Han, *In the Swarm*, 22.

60. Shaka McGlotten, "Black Data," in *Traversing Technologies*, ed. Patrick Keilty and Leslie Regan Shade, http://sfonline.barnard.edu/traversing-technologies/shaka-mcglotten-black-data/.

61. McGlotten, "Black Data."

62. McGlotten, "Black Data."

63. Galloway and Thacker, *The Exploit*, 98.

64. Cecire, "In Defense of Transforming DH."

65. Mouffe, *Agonistics*, 7.

66. Alexander R. Galloway, "A Network Is a Network Is a Network: Reflections on the Computational and the Societies of Control," interview by David M. Berry, *Theory, Culture, and Society* 0, no. 0 (2015): 12.

67. Chun, Grusin, Jagoda, and Raley, "The Dark Side of the Digital Humanities," 493.

68. Rosi Braidotti, "A Theoretical Framework for the Critical Posthumanities," *Theory, Culture, and Society* 0, no. 0 (2018): 14.

69. Braidotti, "A Theoretical Framework," 15.

70. Braidotti, "A Theoretical Framework," 20.

71. Miriam Posner, "What's Next: The Radical, Unrealized Potential of Digital Humanities," in *Debates in the Digital Humanities: 2016*, ed. Matthew K. Gold and Lauren F. Klein (Minneapolis: University of Minnesota Press. 2016), 32.

72. Posner, "What's Next," 39.

73. Sara B. Pritchard, Adeline Koh, and Michelle Moravec, "We Look like Professors, Too," *Inside Higher Ed*, August 10, 2015, https://www.insidehighered.com/views/2015/08/10/essay-explains-new-hashtag-campaign-draw-attention-diversity-professors-and-their.

74. Adeline Koh, "Who Gets to Say #ILookLikeAProfessor? And Who Would Want To?" The Synapse, August 9, 2015, https://medium.com/synapse/who-gets-to-say-ilooklikeaprofessor-and-who-would-want-to-568fbe698198#.oschk3s1a.

75. Consider Kristen Monroe, Saba Ozyurt, Ted Wrigley, and Amy Alexander's study and subsequent 2008 article "Gender Equality in Academia: Bad News from the Trenches, and Some Possible Solutions," *Perspectives on Politics* 6, no. 2 (2008): 215–33. There, Monroe et al. interviewed eighty women faculty at the University of California–Irvine between 2002 and 2006, finding that "in part, discrimination occurs through a process of gender devaluation, whereby the status and power of an authoritative position is downplayed when that position is held by a woman. The UCI women find legal mechanisms and overt, direct political action to be of limited utility. As a result, they increasingly turn to more understated forms of incremental collective action, revealing an adaptive response to discrimination and a keen sense of the power dynamics within the university" (216). The narrative reporting that the authors provide from their study demonstrates that women don't feel that the institution or its policies respects their needs, especially during and leading up to evaluation processes.

76. Bailey, Cong-Huyen, Lothian, and Phillips, "Reflections on a Movement," 76.

77. Jessica M. Johnson, "The Digital in the Humanities: An Interview with Jessica Marie Johnson," interview by Melissa Dinsman, *Los Angeles Review of Books*, July 23, 2016, https://lareviewofbooks.org/article/digital-humanities-interview-jessica-marie-johnson/.

78. Anne Balsamo, *Technologies of the Gendered Body: Reading Cyborg Women* (Durham, N.C.: Duke University Press, 1996), 3.

79. Balsamo, *Technologies of the Gendered Body*, 9.

80. Karl Marx, *Grundrisse: Foundations of the Critique of Political Economy*, trans. Martin Nicolaus (New York: Penguin Books, 1993), 92.

81. Fiona Barnet, "The Brave Side of Digital Humanities," *differences: A Journal of Feminist Cultural Criticism* 25, no. 1 (2014): 68.

82. As a self-proclaimed extension of Donna Haraway's "A Cyborg Manifesto: Science, Technology, and Socialist Feminism in the Late Twentieth Century," Balsamo's work acts as an access point to a much broader literature set that is focused on process and the body. Indeed, where Haraway argues that "a cyborg is a cybernetic organism, a hybrid of machine and organism, a creature of social reality as well as a creature of fiction," she is not primarily concerned with questions of

inclusion. Haraway is concerned with the production of radical difference. In her manifesto, Haraway argues that as both a real and a figurative body, the cyborg is the quintessental assemblage of contemporary human-being, demonstrating what bodies have the capacity to do as they are affected by a multiplicity of other bodies, technologies, and prosthetics. The Deleuzean adage, found in his *Expressionism in Philosophy: Spinoza*, rings true here: "What a body can do corresponds to the nature and limits of its capacity to be affected" (218). Brian Massumi furthers this position. In his *Parables for the Virtual: Movement, Affect, Sensation* (Durham, N.C.: Duke University Press, 2002), Massumi claims that the body is always in transition, always in movement, always "in process." Applying a broad range of technological apparatuses and prosthetics to the construction of the body and the formation of the self is unavoidable; human beings are techno-logical beings. But the use and effect of the apparatus puts the body in motion, so to speak. The technological apparatus overtly alters the body's composition and function across a spectrum of possible uses and outcomes. The processual work of the body is thus one of self-making and self-perception—when prosthetic alterations are made to the body, the knowledge of what a body can do reaches a novel plane: "body and thing are extensions of each other" (95).

83. Balsamo, *Technologies of the Gendered Body*, 160.

84. Roger Whitson, "Steampunk Anachronisms: Queer Histories of the Digital Humanities," *Rhizomes: Cultural Studies in Emerging Knowledge*, no. 28 (2015), http://rhizomes.net/issue28/whitson/.

85. Whitson, "Steampunk Anachronisms."

86. See Emerson's course website, "Theory & Practice of 'Doing' // From Digital Humanities to Posthumanities," https://dhtoph.wordpress.com/.

87. David M. Berry, "Tactical Infrastructures," *STUNLAW* (blog), http://stunlaw.blogspot.co.uk/2016/09/tactical-infrastructures_94.html?m=1.

88. Helen Hester, *Xenofeminism* (Medford, Mass.: Polity, 2018), 64.

89. Laboria Cuboniks, "Xenofeminism: A Politics for Alienation," http://www.laboriacuboniks.net/.

90. In Hester's subsequent book, *Xenofeminism*, she argues that "Xenofemi-nism, or XF, can to some extent be viewed as a labour or bricolage, synthesizing cyberfeminism, posthumanism, accelerationism, neorationalism, materialist feminism, and so on, in an attempt to forge a project suited to contemporary political conditions. From this litany of influences xenofeminism assembles, not a hybrid politics—which would suggest the prior existence of some impossible, un-hybridized state—but a politics without 'the infection of purity.' In collecting, discarding, and revising influences for parts—xenofeminism positions itself as a project for which the future remains open as a site of radical recomposition" (1).

91. Steven Shaviro, *No Speed Limit: Three Essays on Accelerationism* (Minne-apolis: University of Minnesota Press, 2015), 7.

92. Shaviro, *No Speed Limit*, 20.

93. Laboria Cuboniks, "Xenofeminism."

94. Hester defines "xeno-hospitality" as follows: "the opening up of cur-rently curtailed choices, and the creation of the ideological and material infrastructures required to synthesize new desires as accessible, feasible choices" (*Xenofeminism*, 64).

95. Adrienne Shaw, "The Trouble with Communities," in *Queer Game Studies*, ed. Bonnie Ruberg and Adrienne Shaw (Minneapolis: University of Minnesota Press, 2017), 158.

96. Shaw, "The Trouble with Communities," 159.

Chapter 2

The first epigraph is from Elizabeth Losh, "What Can the Digital Humanities Learn from Feminist Game Studies?" *Digital Humanities Quarterly* 9, no. 2 (2015), http://www.digitalhumanities.org/dhq/vol/9/2/000200/000200.html. The second epigraph is from Daniel Charny, "Power of Making," in *Critical Making: Manifestos*, ed. Garnet Hertz (Hollywood, Calif.: Telharmonium, 2012), http://conceptlab.com/criticalmaking/PDFs/CriticalMaking2012Hertz-Manifestos-pp01to06-Charny-PowerOfMaking.pdf

1. Sandoval, *Methodology of the Oppressed*, 79.

2. Sandoval, *Methodology of the Oppressed*, 70.

3. Sandoval, *Methodology of the Oppressed*, 71.

4. Sandoval, *Methodology of the Oppressed*, 72.

5. Bethany Nowviskie, "On the Origin of 'Hack' and 'Yack,'" in *Debates in the Digital Humanities: 2016*, ed. Matthew K. Gold and Lauren F. Klein (Minneapolis: University of Minnesota Press, 2016), 69.

6. Matt Ratto and Stephen Hockema, "FLWR PWR—Tending the Walled Garden," CriticalMaking.com, http://criticalmaking.com/wpcontent/uploads/2009/10/2448_alledgarden_ch06_ratto_hockema.pdf.

7. To see an alternative figuration of this debate, see the "Xenofeminist Technologies" section of Helen Hester's *Xenofeminism*.

8. Marx, *Grundrisse*, 92.

9. Moira Weigel, "Silicon Valley's Sixty-Year Love Affair with the Word 'Tool,'" *The New Yorker*, April 12, 2018, http://www.newyorker.com/tech/elements/silicon-valleys-sixty-year-love-affair-with-the-word-tool.

10. Weigel, "Silicon Valley's Sixty-Year Love Affair," http://www.newyorker.com/tech/elements/silicon-valleys-sixty-year-love-affair-with-the-word-tool.

11. Ian Bogost, *Alien Phenomenology, or, What It's Like to Be a Thing* (Minneapolis: University of Minnesota Press, 2012), 110.

12. Bogost, *Alien Phenomenology*, 110.

13. Hardt, "The Militancy of Theory," 21.

14. Rachel Rose Ulgado and Sarah Fox, "Critical Design in Feminist Hacker Spaces," OpenLab, https://openlab.ncl.ac.uk/socially-engaged-art/files/2014/03/Critical-Design-in-Feminist-Hackerspaces.pdf.

15. Ulgado and Fox, "Critical Design."

16. Michael Dieter and Geert Lovink, "Theses on Making in the Digital Age," in *Critical Making: Manifestos*, ed. Garnet Hertz (Hollywood, Calif.: Telharmonium, 2012), http://conceptlab.com/criticalmaking/PDFs/CriticalMaking2012Hertz-Manifestos-pp23to32-Csikszentmihalyi-SixteenReflectiveBits.pdf.

17. Dieter and Lovink, "Theses on Making."

18. Alexander R. Galloway, *Protocol: How Control Exists after Decentralization* (Cambridge, Mass.: MIT Press, 2004), 7.

19. Dieter and Lovink, "Theses on Making."

20. Chris Csikszentmihalyi, "Sixteen Reflective Bits," in *Critical Making:*

Manifestos, ed. Garnet Hertz (Hollywood, Calif.: Telharmonium, 2012), http://conceptlab.com/criticalmaking/PDFs/CriticalMaking2012Hertz-Manifestos-pp23to32-Csikszentmihalyi-SixteenReflectiveBits.pdf.

21. Liu, "Where Is Cultural Criticism," 491.

22. Koh, "More Hack, Less Yack?"

23. Jentery Sayers, "I Don't Know All the Circuitry," in *Making Things and Drawing Boundaries: Experiments in the Digital Humanities*, ed. Jentery Sayers (Minneapolis: University of Minnesota Press, 2017), 7.

24. Carl DiSalvo, "Introduction to Adversarial Design," in *Critical Making: Manifestos*, ed. Garnet Hertz (Hollywood, Calif.: Telharmonium, 2012), http://conceptlab.com/criticalmaking/PDFs/CriticalMaking2012Hertz-Manifestos-pp21to22-DiSalvo-IntroducingAdversarialDesign.pdf.

25. Carl DiSalvo, *Adversarial Design* (Cambridge, Mass.: MIT Press, 2015), 111.

26. Garnet Hertz and Jussi Parikka, "Zombie Media: Circuit Bending Media Archaeology into an Art Method," *Leonardo* 45, no. 5 (2012): 427.

27. See "MoMALearning Tools and Tips," Museum of Modern Art, https://www.moma.org/learn/moma_learning/tools_tips.

28. Steve F. Anderson. "Aporias of the Avant-Garde," *Digital Humanities Quarterly* 1, no. 2 (2007), http://www.digitalhumanities.org/dhq/vol/1/2/000011/000011.html.

29. Roger Whitson, "Genealogies of the Digital Humanities: The Avant-Garde and the University of Florida," *RogerWhitson* (blog), March 5, 2016, http://www.rogerwhitson.net/?p=3439.

30. Bill Enders, "A Literacy of Building: Making in the Digital Humanities," in *Making Things and Drawing Boundaries: Experiments in the Digital Humanities*, ed. Jentery Sayers (Minneapolis: University of Minnesota Press, 2017), 52.

31. Holly Willis, "Writing Images and the Cinematic Humanities," *Visible Language* 49, no. 3 (2015), http://visiblelanguagejournal.com/issue/172.

32. Suzanne W. Churchill, Linda Kinnahan, and Susan Rosenbaum, Mina Loy: Navigating the Avant-Garde, http://dev.gplord.com/.

33. Suzanne W. Churchill, Linda Kinnahan, and Susan Rosenbaum, "The En Dehors Garde," Mina Loy: Navigating the Avant-Garde, http://dev.gplord.com/the-en-dehors-garde/.

34. Kevin L. Ferguson, "To Cite or to Steal? When a Scholarly Project Turns Up in a Gallery," Hyperallergic, June 30, 2016, https://hyperallergic.com/308436/to-cite-or-to-steal-when-a-scholarly-project-turns-up-in-a-gallery/.

35. Filippo Tommaso Marinetti, "The Founding and Manifesto of Futurism," *Niuean Pop Cultural Archive* (blog), https://www.unknown.nu/futurism/manifesto.html.

36. Tristan Tzara, "Dada Manifesto 1918," in *Modernism: An Anthology*, ed. Lawrence S. Rainey (Malden, Mass.: Blackwell, 2005), 481.

37. André Breton, "Manifesto of Surrealism 1924," in *Manifestoes of Surrealism*, ed. Helen R. Lane, trans. Richard Seaver (Ann Arbor: University of Michigan Press. 1969), 26.

38. Guy Debord, *The Society of the Spectacle*, trans. Donald Nicholson-Smith (New York: Zone Books. 1994), 23.

39. In his book *European Film Theory and Cinema: A Critical Introduction*, Ian Aitken notes that Cinéma Pur "attempted to isolate the fundamental formal

properties of shape, form, rhythm and movement of the medium of film" (80). This led to the "anarchic" and "disorganized" films of the Dada movement, in his view, but also to a "highly composed aesthetic indeterminacy" characterized by impressionism (80). The Dadaist approach to Cinéma Pur coheres with the revolutionary aesthetic championed by the avant-garde.

40. Walter Benjamin, "The Work of Art in the Age of Mechanical Reproduction," in *Illuminations*, ed. Hannah Arendt, trans. Harry Zohn (New York: Schocken Books), 238.

41. Benjamin contextualizes his criticism of Dadaism by arguing that Dadaism disallows contemplation, further separating the spectator from any form of authentic experience inspired by an art object. He concludes by generalizing this position: "By means of its technical structure, the film has taken the physical shock effect out of the wrappers in which Dadaism had, as it were, kept inside the moral shock effect" ("Work of Art," 238).

42. Walter Benjamin, "The Last Snapshot of the European Intelligentsia," in *Walter Benjamin: Selected Writings, 1927–1930*, ed. Michael W. Jennings, Howard Eiland, and Gary Smith (New York: Belknap, 2005), 210.

43. Susan Sontag, *On Photography* (New York: Picador USA, 2001), 55.

44. Sontag, *On Photography*, 54.

45. Paul Virilio, *War and Cinema: The Logistics of Perception* (London: Verso, 1989), 1.

46. Virilio, *War and Cinema*, 15.

47. Paul Virilio, *Art and Fear* (New York: Bloomsbury Academic, 2006), 17.

48. Losh, "What Can the Digital Humanities Learn."

49. Losh, "What Can the Digital Humanities Learn."

50. Losh, What Can the Digital Humanities Learn."

51. See pp. 28, 35, and 38 of Angela Nagle's *Kill All Normies*.

52. Angela Nagle, *Kill All Normies: Online Culture Wars from 4Chan and Tumblr to Trump and the Alt-Right* (Winchester, U.K.: Zero Books. 2017), 38.

53. Nagle, *Kill All Normies*, 35–38.

54. Nagle, *Kill All Normies*, 24.

55. Nagle, *Kill All Normies*, 37.

56. Guy Stevenson offers a similarly framed argument in a Facebook Live lecture given on February 19, 2018. There, he explores how the alt-right "use the language and methods of previous countercultures to present themselves as a new counterculture," further connecting Nagle's criticism of the avant-garde ethos to Situationist politics and aesthetics.

57. Maria Lugones, "Indigenous Movements and Decolonial Feminism," Department of Women's, Gender and Sexuality Studies at Ohio State University, https://wgss.osu.edu/sites/wgss.osu.edu/files/LugonesSeminarReadings.pdf. 3.

58. Lugones, "Indigenous Movements," 12–13.

59. Lugones, "Indigenous Movements," 13.

60. Sandoval, *Methodology of the Oppressed*, 58.

61. Sandoval, *Methodology of the Oppressed*, 58.

62. Sandoval, *Methodology of the Oppressed*, 59.

63. Sandoval, *Methodology of the Oppressed*, 59.

64. Sandoval, *Methodology of the Oppressed*, 59.

65. Sandoval, *Methodology of the Oppressed*, 59.

66. Sandoval, *Methodology of the Oppressed*, 44.

67. Emily Apter, "Weaponized Thought: Ethical Militance and the Group Subject," *Grey Room* no. 14 (2004): 13.

68. *La Hora de los Hornos / Hour of Furnaces*, dir. Fernando Solanas and Octavio Getino (Argentina: Grupo Cine Liberacion, 1968).

69. Fernando Solanas and Octavio Getino, "Towards a Third Cinema," in *Documentary Is Never Neutral | Towards a Third Cinema by Fernando Solanas and Octavio Getino*, http://www.marginalutility.org/wp-content/uploads/2017/03/Towards-a-Third-Cinema-by-Fernando-Solanas-and-Octavio-Getino.pdf.

70. Solanas and Getino, "Towards a Third Cinema."

71. Solanas and Getino, "Towards a Third Cinema."

72. Frantz Fanon, *The Wretched of the Earth*, trans. Richard Philcox (New York: Grove, 2004), 23.

73. Solanas and Getino, "Towards a Third Cinema."

74. Aníbal Quijano, "Coloniality of Power, Eurocentrism, and Latin America," *Nepantla: Views from the South* 1, no. 3 (2000): 534.

75. Quijano, "Coloniality of Power," 540.

76. Solanas and Getino, "Towards a Third Cinema."

77. Jacqueline Wernimont, "Remediation, Activation, and Entanglement in Performative (Digital) Archives—MLA2017," *Jacqueline Wernimont* (blog), January 7, 2017, https://jwernimont.com/2017/01/07/remediation-activation-and-entanglement-in-performative-digital-archives-mla2017/.

78. Gimena del Río, Alex Gil, Daniel O'Donnell, and Élika Ortega, "About," The Translation Toolkit, http://go-dh.github.io/translation-toolkit/about/.

79. Río, Gil, O'Donnell, and Ortega, "About."

80. Solanas and Getino, "Towards a Third Cinema."

81. Michael Chanan, "The Changing Geography of Third Cinema," *Screen* 38, no. 4 (1997): 376.

82. Hito Steyerl, "Is a Museum a Factory?" *e-flux* (blog), June 7, 2009, http://www.e-flux.com/journal/07/61390/is-a-museum-a-factory/.

83. Chanan, "Changing Geography," 373.

84. Solanas and Getino, "Towards a Third Cinema."

85. Although Foucault offers these concepts in the discussion of a Judeo-Christian self-making and technologies of the self, the example stands. As Cynthia R. Nielsen describes it, "First, in exomologesis ('recognition of fact'), a believer recognizes his or her condition as both a Christian and a sinner. In the latter expression—recognition as a sinner—exomologesis becomes increasingly connected with one's status in the Church as a penitent which involved various obligations, abstinences, self-punishment, and public ceremonial gestures such as prostration and wearing ashes as a sign of mourning one's spiritual condition."

86. See pp. 73 and 90 of Mao Tse-tung's *On Guerrilla Warfare*, trans. Samuel B. Griffith (Thousand Oaks, Calif.: BN Publishing, 2007).

87. Carlos Marighella, *Mini-Manual of the Urban Guerrilla* (Montreal: Abraham Guillen, 2002), 35.

88. Solanas and Getino, "Towards a Third Cinema."

89. Nelson Maldonado-Torres, "On the Coloniality of Being: Contributions to the Development of a Concept," *Cultural Studies* 21, no. 2 (2007): 248.

90. Maria Lugones, "The Coloniality of Gender," https://globalstudies.trinity .duke.edu/wp-content/themes/cgsh/materials/WKO/v2d2_Lugones.pdf.

91. Sandoval, *Methodology of the Oppressed*, 79.

92. Sayers, "I Don't Know All the Circuitry," 7.

93. Judith Butler, *Gender Trouble: Feminism and the Subversion of Identity* (New York: Routledge, 2006), 20.

94. Butler, *Gender Trouble*, 20.

Chapter 3

The first epigraph comes from p. 56 of Theodor W. Adorno, *Minima Moralia*, trans. E. F. N. Jephcott (New York: Verso, 2016). The second epigraph comes from bell hooks, "Postmodern Blackness," *Postmodern Culture* 1, no. 10 (1990).

1. Black Mask, "Black Mask No. 1—November 1966: Let the Struggle Begin," in *Black Mask & Up Against the Wall Motherfucker: The Incomplete Works of Ron Hahne, Ben Morea, and the Black Mask Group* (Oakland, Calif.: PM, 2011), 5.

2. Black Mask explicitly aligns itself with Dadaism in "Black Mask No. 10," including a piece titled *Berlin Dada* by David Stuart Wise. This piece outlines Dadaist intervention in Western art, homing in on its call for absolute refusal, automation, and global revolution.

3. Hardt and Negri, *Commonwealth*, viii.

4. Cathy N. Davidson, "Humanities 2.0," in *Debates in the Digital Humanities: 2012*, ed. Matthew K. Gold (Minneapolis: University of Minnesota Press, 2012), 486.

5. Silvia Federici and George Caffentzis, "Commons Against and Beyond Capitalism," *Upping the Anti: A Journal of Theory and Action*, no. 15 (2013): 91.

6. Osha Neumann, *Up Against the Wall Motherf**ker: A Memoir of the '60s, with Notes for Next Time* (New York: Seven Stories, 2008), 7.

7. Gavin Grindon, "Poetry Written in Gasoline: Black Mask and Up Against the Wall Motherfucker," *Art History*, 38 (2015): 6–7.

8. Grindon, "Poetry Written in Gasoline," 187.

9. Black Mask, "Let the Struggle Begin," 6–7.

10. Black Mask, "Black Mask No. 2—December 1966: The Total Revolution," in *Black Mask & Up Against the Wall Motherfucker: The Incomplete Works of Ron Hahne, Ben Morea, and the Black Mask Group* (Oakland, Calif.: PM, 2011), 13.

11. See chapter 10 of *Capital, Vol. 1,* by Karl Marx.

12. Jason Read, *The Micro-Politics of Capital: Marx and the Prehistory of the Present* (New York: State University of New York Press, 2003), 62.

13. In *The Problem with Work*, Weeks is clear to claim that in the autonomist Marxist tradition, work takes priority in the act of refusal: "The crucial point and the essential link to the refusal of work is that work—not private property, the market, the factory, or the alienation of our creative capacities—is understood as the primary basis of capitalist relations, the glue that holds the system together" (97). Black Mask holds a liminal position here. While focused on creative capacity, the collective's acts of refusal take work for granted, so to speak—the creative capacities that Black Mask valorizes already take place outside of a system of

wage labor. In so many words, work has already been refused—the refusal of work is doubled in their focus on living culture.

14. Kathi Weeks, *The Problem with Work: Feminism, Marxism, Antiwork Politics, and Postwork Imaginaries* (Durham, N.C.: Duke University Press, 2011), 100.

15. Black Mask, "Black Mask No. 3—January 1967: Art and Revolution," in *Black Mask & Up Against the Wall Motherfucker: The Incomplete Works of Ron Hahne, Ben Morea, and the Black Mask Group* (Oakland, Calif.: PM, 2011), 23.

16. Guerrilla Girls, *The Guerrilla Girls' Bedside Companion to the History of Western Art* (New York: Penguin Books, 1998), 7.

17. Guerrilla Girls, *Bedside Companion*, 91.

18. Guerrilla Girls, *Confessions of the Guerrilla Girls* (New York: Harper-Perennial, 1995), 26.

19. Guerrilla Girls, *Confessions*, 32.

20. Dorothy Kim and Eunsong Kim, "The #TwitterEthics Manifesto: You Don't Need to Speak for Us—We Are Talking," Model View Culture: A Magazine about Technology, Culture and Diversity, April 7, 2014, https://modelviewculture.com/pieces/the-twitterethics-manifesto.

21. Kim and Kim, "#Twitter Ethics Manifesto."

22. Kevin L. Ferguson, "To Cite or to Steal? When a Scholarly Project Turns Up in a Gallery," Hyperallergic, June 30, 2016, https://hyperallergic.com/308436/to-cite-or-to-steal-when-a-scholarly-project-turns-up-in-a-gallery/.

23. Bethany Nowviskie, "On Capacity and Care," *nowviskie.org* (blog), October 4, 2015, http://nowviskie.org/2015/on-capacity-and-care/.

24. Jeffrey T. Schnapp and Matthew Battles, *The Library beyond the Book* (Cambridge, Mass.: Harvard University Press, 2014), 29.

25. Mia Bay, Farah J. Griffin, Martha S. Jones, and Barbara Dianne Savage, "Introduction," in *Toward an Intellectual History of Black Women*, ed. Mia Bay, Farah J. Griffin, Martha S. Jones, and Barbara Dianne Savage (Chapel Hill: University of North Carolina Press, 2015), 2.

26. Alexis Pauline Gumbs, "Seeking the Roots: An Immersive and Interactive Archive of Black Feminist Practice," *Feminist Collectives* 32, no. 1 (2012): 19.

27. Gumbs, "Seeking the Roots," 17.

28. I refer to Kim Brillante Knight's "Making Space: Feminist DH and a Room of One's Own" in particular here. Her argument motivates a feminist critique of minimal computing, a practice I take up in this book's conclusion, that rests on the need for "maker space" in the absence of grant funding, recognition by elite GLAM spaces, and more. Her comments mirror parts of Johnson's argument above, for example, when describing her own minimal DH project, Fashioning Circuits: "I do almost everything. I have a group of enthusiastic and dedicated volunteers for community events, whom I will return to in a moment. But the infrastructure, the planning and administration all comes down to me."

29. Jessica M. Johnson, "Doing and Being Intellectual History: #Formation as Curated by Black Women," *Black Perspective* (blog), February 12, 2016, https://www.aaihs.org/doing-and-being-intellectual/.

30. Black Mask, "UAW/MF: The Free Press Report," in *Black Mask & Up Against the Wall Motherfucker: The Incomplete Works of Ron Hahne, Ben Morea, and the Black Mask Group* (Oakland, Calif.: PM, 2011), 95.

31. Garnet Hertz and Jussi Parikka, "Zombie Media: Circuit Bending Media Archaeology into an Art Method," *Leonardo* 45, no. 5 (2012): 429.

32. Hertz and Parikka, "Zombie Media," 430.

33. Fiona Barnett, Zach Blas, Micha Cárdenas, Jacob Gaboury, Jessica Marie Johnson, and Margaret Rhee, "QueerOS: A User's Manual," in *Debates in the Digital Humanities: 2016*, ed. Matthew K. Gold and Lauren F. Klein (Minneapolis: University of Minnesota Press, 2016), 54.

34. Barnett et al., "QueerOS," 54.

35. Jacob Gaboury, "Critical Unmaking: Toward a Queer Computation," in *The Routledge Companion to Media Studies and Digital Humanities*, ed. Jentery Sayers (New York: Routledge, 2018), https://escholarship.org/uc/item/0cq870wh. 490.

36. Nadja Millner-Larsen, "Black Mask: Revolution as Being," in *If I Can't Dance to It, It's Not My Revolution*, curated by Natalie Musteata, http://exhibits .haverford.edu/ificantdancetoit/essays/black-mask-revolution-as-being/#_ftn14.

37. Millner-Larsen, "Black Mask."

38. Aldo Tambellini, "Biography," AldoTambellini.com, http://www .aldotambellini.com/bio4.html.

39. Tambellini, "Biography."

40. Losh, "What Can the Digital Humanities Learn."

41. Aldo Tambellini and Cecil Taylor, "Black," *artscanada* no. 113 (1967): 5.

42. Tambellini and Taylor, "Black," 5.

43. Tambellini and Taylor, "Black," 9.

44. Tambellini famously invokes the first Soviet cosmonaut to reinforce human being's continued reemergence from a state of primitiveness to a state of knowledge and enlightenment. See p. 12 of *artscanada*.

45. Tambellini and Taylor, "Black," 12.

46. Tambellini and Taylor, "Black," 15.

47. Fred Moten, *The Universal Machine: Consent Not to Be a Single Being* (Durham, N.C.: Duke University Press, 2018), 162.

48. Millner-Larsen, "Black Mask."

49. Black Mask, "Black Mask No. 10—April/May 1968: The New Proletariat: Nigger as Class," in *Black Mask & Up Against the Wall Motherfucker: The Incomplete Works of Ron Hahne, Ben Morea, and the Black Mask Group* (Oakland, Calif.: PM, 2011), 76.

50. Nadja Millner-Larsen, "The Subject of Black: Abstraction and the Politics of Race in the Expanded Cinema Environment," *Grey Room*, no. 67 (2017): 70.

51. Millner-Larsen, "The Subject of Black," 86.

52. Patricia Hill Collins, *Black Feminist Thought: Knowledge, Consciousness, and the Politics of Empowerment* (New York: Routledge, 2000), 10.

53. Collins, *Black Feminist Thought*, 10–11.

54. Collins, *Black Feminist Thought*, 18.

55. TreaAndrea M. Russworm's articulation of "critical racial dystopias" in her coedited volume *Gaming Representation* offers perhaps the most pointed critique of this misapprehension in contemporary terms. In Russworm's view, "black and brown bodies have historically functioned as signs of abjection and exclusion, on the one hand, and as catalysts for tolerance and radical change, on the other" (117). These tropes are attributable to slavery and colonization's post-apocalyptic character, and directly correlate to Tambellini's site-specific art practice and Black

Mask's turn toward erasure. Tambellini's invocation of black power via aesthetic intervention in particular is the precise step taken to make black bodies function as both signs of abjection and catalysts for radical social change. What follows from Russworm's analysis of games like *The Last of Us* and *The Walking Dead* is a consideration of how racial empathy is limited by its instrumentalization within a larger socioeconomic regime, similar in concept to Collins's outside within. If *BLACK PLUS X* utilizes the black body to cultivate empathy in its white viewer, allowing him to identify with black children by altering the color of their skin, it follows Russworm's characterization of racial empathy's limit as the performance of abjection and radical change which draws on, spectacularizes, and then dissolves black intersubjectivity (123–26).

56. Millner-Larsen, "Black Mask."

57. William Haver, "The Ontological Priority of Violence: On Several Really Smart Things about Violence in Jean Genet's Work," Polylog, http://www.polylog.org/index-en.htm.

58. Millner-Larsen, "Black Mask."

59. Tzara, "Dada Manifesto 1918," 484.

60. Black Mask, "Black Mask No. 10—April/May 1968: Revolution as Being," in *Black Mask & Up Against the Wall Motherfucker: The Incomplete Works of Ron Hahne, Ben Morea, and the Black Mask Group* (Oakland, Calif.: PM, 2011), 77–78.

61. Black Mask, "Revolution as Being," 78.

62. Black Mask, "UAW/MF Magazine: Affinity Groups," in *Black Mask & Up Against the Wall Motherfucker: The Incomplete Works of Ron Hahne, Ben Morea, and the Black Mask Group* (Oakland, Calif.: PM, 2011), 112.

63. Black Mask, "Affinity Groups," 112.

64. Black Mask, "Affinity Groups," 112.

65. Black Mask, "Affinity Groups," 112.

66. Black Mask, "Let the Struggle Begin," 7.

67. Black Mask, "UAW/MF: Another Carnival of Leftist Politics," in *Black Mask & Up Against the Wall Motherfucker: The Incomplete Works of Ron Hahne, Ben Morea, and the Black Mask Group* (Oakland, Calif.: PM, 2011), 131.

68. Grindon, "Poetry Written in Gasoline," 175.

69. Rowberry, "A Guerrilla Digital Humanities."

70. Rowberry, "A Guerrilla Digital Humanities."

71. Alex Gil, "#guerrilladh," *@elotroalex* (blog), July 27, 2015, http://www.elotroalex.com/guerrilladh/.

72. Gil, "#guerrilladh."

73. "Digital Humanities Manifesto 2.0."

74. Geoff Cox and Alex McLean, *Speaking Code: Coding as Aesthetic and Political Expression* (Cambridge, Mass.: MIT Press, 2012), 53.

75. McKenzie Wark, "The RetroDada Manifesto," *Public Seminar* (blog), February 8, 2016, http://www.publicseminar.org/2016/02/retrodada-manifesto/.

76. Sarah Ahmed, "Selfcare as Warfare," *feministkilljoys* (blog), August 25, 2014, https://feministkilljoys.com/2014/08/25/selfcare-as-warfare/.

77. Ahmed, "Selfcare as Warfare."

78. Ahmed, "Selfcare as Warfare."

79. Ahmed, "Selfcare as Warfare."

80. Sarah Ahmed, "White Men," *feministkilljoys* (blog), November 4, 2014, https://feministkilljoys.com/2014/11/04/white-men/.

Chapter 4

The first epigraph comes from Abdul Alkalimat, Ronald W. Bailey, Adam J. Banks, Jonathan B. Fenderson, Dawn-Elissa T. I. Fischer, Kayla D. Hayles, Jill M. Humphries, DeReef F. Jamison, Carmen Mitchell, Jamila Moore-Pewu, Angel David Nieves, Charles G. Ransom, Reginold A. Royston, Debra Smith, and Allison M. Sutton, "The Next Movement in Black Studies: 'eBlack Studies,'" http://eblackstudies.org/workshop/manifesto.html. The second epigraph comes from Michel Foucault, "Of Other Spaces: Utopias and Heterotopias," trans. Jay Miskowiec, *Architecture / Mouvement / Continuité* (1967): 1–9.

1. Tara McPherson, "Why Are the Digital Humanities So White? or Thinking the Histories of Race and Computation," in *Debates in the Digital Humanities: 2012*, ed. Matthew K. Gold (Minneapolis: University of Minnesota Press, 2012), 155.

2. McPherson, "Why Are the Digital Humanities So White?" 145.

3. McPherson, "Why Are the Digital Humanities So White?" 148.

4. McPherson, "Why Are the Digital Humanities So White?" 143.

5. Harney and Moten, *The Undercommons*, 17.

6. Harney and Moten, *The Undercommons*, 17.

7. Harney and Moten, *The Undercommons*, 17.

8. Harney and Moten, *The Undercommons*, 18.

9. See pp. 30 and 37 of Robyn C. Spencer's *The Revolution Has Come: Black Power, Gender, and the Black Panther Party in Oakland* (Durham, N.C.: Duke University Press, 2016).

10. Aria Dean, "Poor Meme, Rich Meme," Real Life, July 25, 2016, http://reallifemag.com/poor-meme-rich-meme/

11. Laur M. Jackson, "The Blackness of Meme Movement," Model View Culture: A Magazine about Technology, Culture and Diversity, March 28, 2016, https://modelviewculture.com/pieces/the-blackness-of-meme-movement.

12. Jackson extends related work in her *Teen Vogue* article, "We Need to Talk about Digital Blackface in Reaction GIFs." There she reminds us that when black culture is appropriated online, it often appears as "digital blackface," or the use of "relative anonymity of online identity to embody blackness . . . Digital minstrels often operate under stolen profile pictures and butchered AAVE [African American Vernacular English]. Quite often it comes in the form of an excessive use of reaction GIFs with images of black people."

13. Dean, "Poor Meme, Rich Meme."

14. Dean, "Poor Meme, Rich Meme."

15. Hito Steyerl, "In Defense of the Poor Image," *e-flux* (blog), November 10, 2009, http://www.e-flux.com/journal/in-defense-of-the-poor-image/.

16. Steyerl, "In Defense."

17. Steyerl, "In Defense."

18. McPherson, "Why Are the Digital Humanities So White?" 143.

19. As a result, Dean asserts that her work also offers a broad techno-historical basis from which to think collectivity beyond the political limits that the "white avant-garde" places on concepts of alienation and mediated selfhood. Where Dean charges the white avant-garde in particular with exercising a kind of political

myopia with regard to surveillance and state control, she is clear to point out that the surveillance of black social life is also the source of new modes of subjective formation.

20. Fred Moten, "Blackness and Nothingness (Mysticism in the Flesh)," *South Atlantic Quarterly* 112, no. 4 (2013): 742

21. Dean, "Poor Meme, Rich Meme."

22. Although rooted in negativity, Moten claims a celebratory dimension of this kind of thought, especially when it is featured in contemporary iterations of Afro-pessimism, since it "allows and compels one to move past that contradictory impulse to affirm in the interest of negation and to begin to consider *what nothing is*, not from its own standpoint or from any standpoint, but from the absoluteness of its generative dispersion of a general antagonism that blackness holds and protects in as critical celebration and degenerative and regenerative preservation" ("Blackness and Nothingness," 741–42).

23. Newton, *Revolutionary Suicide*, 359.

24. Moten, "Blackness and Nothingness," 741.

25. Kodwo Eshun, "Further Considerations on Afrofuturism," *CR: The New Centennial Review* 3, no. 2 (2003): 288.

26. Eshun, "Further Considerations," 292.

27. José Medina, "Toward a Foucaultian Epistemology of Resistance: Counter-Memory, Epistemic Friction, and Guerrilla Pluralism," *Foucault Studies*, no. 12 (2011): 24.

28. Medina, "Toward a Foucaultian Epistemology," 27.

29. Michelle M. Wright, *Physics of Blackness: Beyond the Middle Passage Epistemology* (Minneapolis: University of Minnesota Press, 2015), 150.

30. Wright, *Physics of Blackness*, 149.

31. Wright, *Physics of Blackness*, 149–50.

32. Moya Bailey, "#transform(ing)DH Writing and Research: An Autoethnography of Digital Humanities and Feminist Ethics," *Digital Humanities Quarterly* 9, no. 2 (2015), http://www.digitalhumanities.org/dhq/vol/9/2/000209/000209 .html.

33. McPherson "Why Are the Digital Humanities So White?" 143.

34. Jean Genet, "Introduction to *Soledad Brother*," in *The Declared Enemy*, trans. Jeff Fort (Stanford, Calif.: Stanford University Press, 2004), 54.

35. Haver, "Ontological Priority of Violence."

36. Haver develops this concept in his "Several Really Smart Things" essay, focused on Genet's work with the Palestine Liberation Army and the Black Panthers, but also from Genet's essays on Rembrandt. Haver also applies it as a mode of queer theory, though, particularly the concept of "queer honour." See Haver's article "Really Bad Infinities: Queer's Honour and the Pornographic Life," in *Parallax* 5, no. 4 (1999), specifically pp. 11–12: "Queer's honour is a comportment, an attention, that is something quite other than interpretation; it is a seeing irreducible to looking, a hearing irreducible to listening; it is the perversity of the singularity at stake when, in Jean-Luc Nancy's phrase, 'touch touches touching,' when the word withdraws from signification—or when body fluids no longer bear the glad tidings of intersubjective recognition."

37. Spencer, *The Revolution Has Come*, 204.

38. Spencer, *The Revolution Has Come*, 89.

39. Jade E. Davis, "Historical Glitch: Understanding Media through the Photographic Lens," Ph.D. diss., University of North Carolina at Chapel Hill, 2015, p. 121.

40. Davis, "Historical Glitch," 124.

41. Jade E. Davis, "Decolonial Dada," Historical Glitch // Jade E. Davis: A Dissertation Playground, http://historicalglitch.com.

42. Wright, *Physics of Blackness*, 14.

43. Johanna Drucker, *Graphesis: Visual Forms of Knowledge Production* (Cambridge, Mass.: Harvard University Press, 2014), 177.

44. Kim Casone, "The Aesthetics of Failure: 'Post-Digital' Tendencies in Contemporary Computer Music," *Computer Music Journal* 24, no. 4 (winter 2000): 13.

45. Yuk Hui, "Archivist Manifesto," Mute Magazine, May 22, 2013, http://www.metamute.org/editorial/lab/archivist-manifesto.

46. In June 2017, Jade Davis authored "A Cyborg Manifesto of Black People in Theory," an introduction to a 2011 GoogleDoc project in which she replaced each reference to the "cyborg" in Donna Haraway's "A Cyborg Manifesto" with "black slave." At the opening of the piece, she writes: "There is not a theoretical absence of blackness and the black body (both male and female) because they are used as political frame or experience (blackness) or object of study (the black body) by academics who strive to subvert or chip at the hegemonic force known as the canon (which does occasionally release its heavy blows on people who attempt to go against it). No, blackness and the black body are not missing. Black people are missing." This project is a political analogue to her "Historical Glitch" project in both concept and application.

47. Jacqueline Wernimont and Julia Flanders, "Feminism in the Age of Digital Archives: The Women Writers Project," *Tulsa Studies in Women's Literature* 29, no. 2 (fall 2010): 427.

48. Wernimont and Flanders, "Feminism in the Age of Digital Archives," 429.

49. Jacqueline Wernimont, "Whence Feminism? Assessing Feminist Interventions in Digital Literary Archives," *Digital Humanities Quarterly* 7, no. 1 (2007), http://www.digitalhumanities.org/dhq/vol/7/1/000156/000156.html.

50. Harney and Moten, *The Undercommons*, 64.

51. "Address of the International Working Men's Association," Marxists .org, https://www.marxists.org/archive/marx/iwma/documents/1864/lincoln -letter.htm.

52. Dean, "Poor Meme, Rich Meme."

53. McPherson, "Why Are the Digital Humanities So White?" 148.

54. Collins, *Black Feminist Thought*, 11.

55. Maurizio Lazzarato, *The Making of the Indebted Man*, trans. Joshua David Jordan (Los Angeles: Semiotext(e), 2012), 226.

56. Lazzarato, *The Making of the Indebted Man*, 130.

57. Collins, *Black Feminist Thought*, 18.

58. Halberstam, "The Wild Beyond: With and for the Undercommons," 6.

59. Harney and Moten, *The Undercommons*, 26.

60. Harney and Moten, *The Undercommons*, 26.

61. Harney and Moten, *The Undercommons*, 28.

Conclusion

Both epigraphs come from an exchange between Gilles Deleuze and Michel Foucault on pp. 206–8 of "Intellectuals and Power: A Conversation between Michel Foucault and Gilles Deleuze," in *Language, Counter-Memory, and Practice*, ed. Donald F. Bouchard, trans. Donald F. Bouchard and Sherry Simon (Ithaca, N.Y.: Cornell University Press, 1977), 205–17.

1. Alex Gil, "Minimal Computing," *Minimal Computing* (blog), May 21, 2015, http://go-dh.github.io/mincomp/thoughts/2015/05/21/user-vs-learner/.

2. Gil, "Minimal Computing."

3. Gil, "Minimal Computing."

4. Gil, "Minimal Computing."

5. Jentery Sayers, "Minimal Definitions," *Minimal Computing* (blog), October 2, 2016, http://go-dh.github.io/mincomp/.

6. Sayers, "Minimal Definitions."

7. Alexis Lothian and Amanda Phillips, "Can Digital Humanities Mean Transformative Critique?" *e-Media Studies* 3, no. 1 (2013).

8. Matthew K. Gold, "Whose Revolution? Towards a More Equitable Digital Humanities," *The Lapland Chronicles* (blog), January 10, 2012, http://mkgold.net/blog/2012/01/10/whose-revolution-toward-a-more-equitable-digital-humanities/.

9. Lothian and Phillips, "Can Digital Humanities Mean Transformative Critique?"

10. Paola Antonelli and Jamer Hunt, "Hack," in *Design and Violence* (New York: Museum of Modern Art, 2015), 18.

11. McKenzie Wark, "A Hacker Manifesto [version 4.0]," subsol, http://subsol .c3.hu/subsol_2/contributors0/warktext.html.

12. Wark, "A Hacker Manifesto."

13. An explanation of "who" SSL Nagbot is from the "Research" section of feministhacktivism.com: "SSL Nagbot is a moniker that is composed of three editors namely and in alphabetical order: Shaowen BarDzell, Lily Nguyen and Sophie Toupin. With the moniker, we decided to experiment with feminist trickstery ourselves by hacking the academic authorship system in merging our three names and creating the pseudonym, SSL Nagbot, a practice reminiscent of the feminist geographers J.K. Gibson-Graham."

14. SSL Nagbot, "Feminist Hacking/Making: Exploring New Gender Horizons of Possibility," *Journal of Peer Production* no. 8 (2016), http://peerproduction.net /issues/issue-8-feminism-and-unhacking/.

15. SSL Nagbot, "Feminist Hacking/Making."

16. Jessica Marie Johnson and Mark Anthony Neal, "Introduction: Wild Seed in the Machine," *Black Scholar* 47, no. 3 (2017): 1.

17. Johnson and Neal, "Introduction," 1.

18. Johnson and Neal, "Introduction," 2.

19. Mohanty, *Feminism without Borders*, 173.

20. Mohanty, *Feminism without Borders*, 9.

21. Mohanty, *Feminism without Borders*, 170.

22. Mohanty, *Feminism without Borders*, 171.

23. Matthew K. Gold, "The Digital Humanities Moment," in *Debates in the*

Digital Humanities: 2012, ed. Matthew K. Gold (Minneapolis: University of Minnesota Press. 2012), ix.

24. Moya Z. Bailey, "All the Digital Humanists Are White, All the Nerds Are Men, but Some of Us Are Brave," *Journal of Digital Humanities* 1, no. 1 (2011), http://journalofdigitalhumanities.org/1-1/all-the-digital-humanists-are-white-all-the-nerds-are-men-but-some-of-us-are-brave-by-moya-z-bailey/.

25. Think of "Neoliberal Tools (and Archives): A Political History of Digital Humanities" by Daniel Allington, Sarah Brouillette, and David Golumbia. Where the authors claim that "Digital Humanities has played a leading role in the corporatist restructuring of the humanities," they do not address recent movements like postcolonial DH or feminist DH in any detail.

26. Christopher Newfield, *Unmaking the Public University: The Forty-Year Assault on the Middle Class* (Cambridge, Mass.: Harvard University Press, 2011), 272–74.

27. Alan Liu, "Drafts for *Against the Cultural Singularity* (book in progress)," *Alan Liu* (blog), May 2, 2016, http://liu.english.ucsb.edu/drafts-for-against-the-cultural-singularity/.

28. Liu, "Drafts for *Against the Cultural Singularity*."

29. Liu, "Drafts for *Against the Cultural Singularity*."

30. Liu, "Drafts for *Against the Cultural Singularity*."

31. Liu, "Drafts for *Against the Cultural Singularity*."

32. Liu, "Drafts for *Against the Cultural Singularity*."

33. Roopika Risam, "Navigating the Global Digital Humanities: Insights from Black Feminism," in *Debates in the Digital Humanities: 2016*, ed. Matthew K. Gold and Lauren F. Klein (Minneapolis: University of Minnesota Press, 2016), 359.

34. BethanyNowviskie, "#alt-ac: Alternate Academic Careers for Humanities Scholars," *Bethany Nowviskie* (blog), January 2, 2010, http://nowviskie.org/2010/alt-ac/.

35. Harney and Moten, *The Undercommons*, 33.

BIBLIOGRAPHY

"Address of the International Working Men's Association." Marxists.org. https://www.marxists.org/archive/marx/iwma/documents/1864/lincoln-letter.htm.

Adorno, Theodor W. *Minima Moralia: Reflections from Damaged Life.* Translated by E. F. N. Jephcott. New York: Verso, 2016.

Ahmed, Manan, Maira E. Álvarez, Sylvia A. Fernández, Alex Gil, Merisa Martinez, Moacir P. de Sá Pereira, Linda Rodriguez, and Roopika Risam. "Torn Apart / Separados." http://xpmethod.plaintext.in/torn-apart/.

Ahmed, Sarah. "Selfcare as Warfare." *feministkilljoys* (blog), August 25, 2014. https://feministkilljoys.com/2014/08/25/selfcare-as-warfare/.

———. "White Men." *feministkilljoys* (blog), November 4, 2014. https://feministkilljoys.com/2014/11/04/white-men/.

Aitken, Ian. *European Film Theory and Cinema: A Critical Introduction.* Bloomington: Indiana University Press, 2001.

Alkalimat, Abdul, Ronald W. Bailey, Adam J. Banks, Jonathan B. Fenderson, Dawn-Elissa T. I. Fischer, Kayla D. Hayles, Jill M. Humphries, DeReef F. Jamison, Carmen Mitchell, Jamila Moore-Pewu, Angel David Nieves, Charles G. Ransom, Reginold A. Royston, Debra Smith, and Allison M. Sutton. "The Next Movement in Black Studies: 'eBlack Studies.'" http://eblackstudies.org/workshop/manifesto.html.

Allington, Daniel, Sarah Brouilette, and David Goumbia. "Neoliberal Tools (and Archives): Political History of Digital Humanities." *Los Angeles Review of Books*, May 1, 2016. https://lareviewofbooks.org/article/neoliberal-tools-archives-political-history-digital-humanities/.

Althusser, Louis. "Ideology and the State." In *Lenin and Philosophy and Other Essays.* New York: Monthly Review, 1971.

Anderson, Steve F. "Aporias of the Avant-Garde." *Digital Humanities Quarterly* 1, no. 2 (2007). http://www.digitalhumanities.org/dhq/vol/1/2/000011/000011.html.

Antonelli, Paola, and Jamer Hunt. "Hack." In *Design and Violence*, edited by Paola Antonelli and Jamer Hunt, 17–18. New York: Museum of Modern Art, 2015.

Apter, Emily. "Weaponized Thought: Ethical Militance and the Group Subject." *Grey Room* no. 14 (2004): 6–25.

Bailey, Moya Z. "All the Digital Humanists Are White, All the Nerds Are Men, but Some of Us Are Brave." *Journal of Digital Humanities* 1, no. 1 (2011). http://journalofdigitalhumanities.org/1-1/all-the-digital-humanists-are-white-all-the-nerds-are-men-but-some-of-us-are-brave-by-moya-z-bailey/.

———. "#transform(ing)DH Writing and Research: An Autoethnography of

Digital Humanities and Feminist Ethics." *Digital Humanities Quarterly* 9, no. 2 (2015). http://www.digitalhumanities.org/dhq/vol/9/2/000209/000209.html.

Bailey, Moya, Anne Cong-Huyen, Alexis Lothian, and Amanda Phillips. "Reflections on a Movement: #transformDH, Growing Up." In *Debates in the Digital Humanities: 2016*, edited by Matthew K. Gold and Lauren F. Klein, 71–82. Minneapolis: University of Minnesota Press, 2016.

Balsamo, Anne. *Technologies of the Gendered Body: Reading Cyborg Women.* Durham, N.C.: Duke University Press, 1996.

BarDzell, Shaowen, et al. "Research." *Feminist Hackers* (blog). feministhacktivism .noblogs.org/research/.

Barnett, Fiona. "The Brave Side of Digital Humanities." *differences: A Journal of Feminist Cultural Criticism* 25, no. 1 (2014): 64–78.

Barnett, Fiona, Zach Blas, Micha Cárdenas, Jacob Gaboury, Jessica Marie Johnson, and Margaret Rhee. "QueerOS: A User's Manual." In *Debates in the Digital Humanities: 2016*, edited by Matthew K. Gold and Laura F. Klein, 50–59. Minneapolis: University of Minnesota Press, 2016.

Bay, Mia, Farah J. Griffin, Martha S. Jones, and Barbara Dianne Savage. "Introduction." In *Toward an Intellectual History of Black Women*, edited by Mia Bay, Farah J. Griffin, Martha S. Jones, and Barbara Dianne Savage, 1–16. Chapel Hill: University of North Carolina Press, 2015.

Benjamin, Walter. "The Last Snapshot of the European Intelligentsia." In *Walter Benjamin: Selected Writings, 1927–1930*, edited by Michael W. Jennings, Howard Eiland, and Gary Smith, 207–21. New York: Belknap, 2005.

———. "The Work of Art in the Age of Mechanical Reproduction." In *Illuminations*, edited by Hannah Arendt, translated by Harry Zohn, 217–52. New York: Schocken Books.

Berry, David M. "Tactical Infrastructures." *STUNLAW* (blog). http://stunlaw .blogspot.co.uk/2016/09/tactical-infrastructures_94.html?m=1.

Berry, David M., and Anders Fagerjord. *Digital Humanities: Knowledge and Critique in a Digital Age.* Cambridge: Polity, 2017.

Black Mask. "Black Mask No. 1—November 1966: Let the Struggle Begin." In *Black Mask & Up Against the Wall Motherfucker: The Incomplete Works of Ron Hahne, Ben Morea, and the Black Mask Group*, 4–10. Oakland, Calif.: PM, 2011.

———. "Black Mask No. 2—December 1966: The Total Revolution." In *Black Mask & Up Against the Wall Motherfucker: The Incomplete Works of Ron Hahne, Ben Morea, and the Black Mask Group*, 12–13. Oakland, Calif.: PM, 2011.

———. "Black Mask No. 3—January 1967: Art and Revolution." In *Black Mask & Up Against the Wall Motherfucker: The Incomplete Works of Ron Hahne, Ben Morea, and the Black Mask Group*, 22–23. Oakland, Calif.: PM, 2011.

———. "Black Mask No. 10—April/May 1968: The New Proletariat: Nigger as Class." In *Black Mask & Up Against the Wall Motherfucker: The Incomplete Works of Ron Hahne, Ben Morea, and the Black Mask Group*, 75–77. Oakland, Calif.: PM, 2011.

———. "Black Mask No. 10—April/May 1968: Revolution as Being." In *Black Mask & Up Against the Wall Motherfucker: The Incomplete Works of Ron*

Hahne, Ben Morea, and the Black Mask Group, 77–78. Oakland, Calif.: PM, 2011.

———. "UAW/MF: Affinity Groups." In *Black Mask & Up Against the Wall Motherfucker: The Incomplete Works of Ron Hahne, Ben Morea, and the Black Mask Group*, 111–12. Oakland, Calif.: PM, 2011.

———. "UAW/MF: Another Carnival of Leftist Politics." In *Black Mask & Up Against the Wall Motherfucker: The Incomplete Works of Ron Hahne, Ben Morea, and the Black Mask Group*, 130–31. Oakland, Calif.: PM, 2011.

———. "UAW/MF: The Free Press Report." In *Black Mask & Up Against the Wall Motherfucker: The Incomplete Works of Ron Hahne, Ben Morea, and the Black Mask Group*, 88–104. Oakland, Calif.: PM, 2011.

Bogost, Ian. *Alien Phenomenology, or, What It's Like to Be a Thing*. Minneapolis: University of Minnesota Press, 2012.

Breton, André. "Manifesto of Surrealism 1924." In *Manifestoes of Surrealism*, edited by Helen R. Lane, translated by Richard Seaver, 1–30. Ann Arbor: University of Michigan Press, 1969.

Braidotti, Rosi. "A Theoretical Framework for the Critical Posthumanities." *Theory, Culture, and Society* 0, no. 0 (2018): 1–31.

Bray, Mark. *Antifa: The Anti-Fascist Handbook*. New York: Melville House, 2017.

Burdick, Anne, Johanna Drucker, Peter Lunenfeld, Todd Presner, and Jeffrey Schnapp. *Digital_Humanities*. Cambridge, Mass.: MIT Press, 2016.

Butler, Judith. *Gender Trouble: Feminism and the Subversion of Identity*. New York: Routledge, 2006.

———. *Giving an Account of Oneself*. New York: Fordham University Press, 2005.

Caffentzis, George, and Silvia Federici. "Notes on the Edu-factory and Cognitive Capitalism." In *Toward a Global Autonomous University*, edited by the Edu-factory Collective, 125–31. New York: Autonomedia, 2009.

Casone, Kim. "The Aesthetics of Failure: 'Post-Digital' Tendencies in Contemporary Computer Music." *Computer Music Journal* 24, no. 4 (winter 2000): 12–18.

Cecire, Natalia. "In Defense of Transforming DH." *Works Cited: Natalia Cecire's Blog* (blog), January 8, 2012. http://nataliacecire.blogspot.com/2012/01/in -defense-of-transforming-dh.html.

Chanan, Michael. "The Changing Geography of Third Cinema." *Screen* 38, no. 4 (1997): 372–88.

Chandhoke, Neera. *Democracy and Revolutionary Politics*. New York: Bloomsbury Academic, 2015.

Charny, Daniel. "Power of Making." In *Critical Making: Manifestos*, edited by Garnet Hertz. Hollywood, Calif.: Telharmonium, 2012. http://conceptlab .com/criticalmaking/PDFs/CriticalMaking2012Hertz-Manifestos-pp01to06 -Charny-PowerOfMaking.pdf.

Chun, Wendy Hui Kong, Richard Grusin, Patrick Jagoda, and Rita Raley. "The Dark Side of the Digital Humanities." In *Debates in the Digital Humanities: 2016*, edited by Matthew K. Gold and Lauren F. Klein, 493–509. Minneapolis: University of Minnesota Press, 2016.

Churchill, Suzanne W., Linda Kinnahan, and Susan Rosenbaum. "The En Dehors

Garde." Mina Loy: Navigating the Avant-Garde. http://dev.gplord.com/the-en
-dehors-garde/.

———. Mina Loy: Navigating the Avant-Garde. http://dev.gplord.com/.

Collins, Patricia Hill. *Black Feminist Thought: Knowledge, Consciousness, and the Politics of Empowerment*. New York: Routledge, 2000.

———. "Intersectionality's Definitional Dilemmas." *Annual Review of Sociology* 41, no. 1 (2015): 1–20.

Cox, Geoff, and Alex McLean. *Speaking Code: Coding as Aesthetic and Political Expression*. Cambridge, Mass.: MIT Press, 2012.

Critchley, Simon. *Infinitely Demanding: Ethics of Commitment, Politics of Resistance*. London: Verso, 2008.

Csikszentmihalyi, Chris. "Sixteen Reflective Bits." In *Critical Making: Manifestos*, edited by Garnet Hertz. Hollywood, Calif.: Telharmonium, 2012. http://conceptlab.com/criticalmaking/PDFs/CriticalMaking2012Hertz-Manifestos-pp23to32-Csikszentmihalyi-SixteenReflectiveBits.pdf.

Cuboniks, Laboria. *Xenofeminism: A Politics for Alienation*. http://www.laboriacuboniks.net/.

Davidson, Cathy N. "Collaboration by Difference, Yet Again." *HASTAC* (blog), November 23, 2008. https://www.hastac.org/blogs/cathy-davidson/2008/11/23/collaboration-difference-yet-again.

———. "Humanities 2.0: Promise, Perils, Predictions." In *Debates in the Digital Humanities: 2012*, edited by Matthew K. Gold, 476–89. Minneapolis: University of Minnesota Press, 2012.

———. "Why Yack Needs Hack (and Vice Versa): From Digital Humanities to Digital Literacy." In *Between Humanities and the Digital*, edited by Patrik Svensson and David Theo Goldberg, 131–43. Cambridge, Mass.: MIT Press, 2015.

Davis, Jade E. "A Cyborg Manifesto of Black People in Theory." *Performing the Digital → Blog* (blog), June 9, 2017. http://jadedid.com/performingthedigital/2017/06/09/a-cyborg-manifesto-of-black-people-in-theory/.

———. "Decolonial Dada." Historical Glitch // Jade E. Davis: A Dissertation Playground. http://historicalglitch.com

———. "Historical Glitch: Understanding Media through the Photographic Lens." Ph.D. dissertation, University of North Carolina at Chapel Hill, 2015.

Dean, Aria. "Poor Meme, Rich Meme." Real Life, July 25, 2016. http://reallifemag.com/poor-meme-rich-meme/

Debord, Guy. *The Society of the Spectacle*. Translated by Donald Nicholson-Smith. New York: Zone Books, 1994.

Deleuze, Gilles. *Expressionism in Philosophy: Spinoza*. Translated by Martin Joughin. New York: Zone, 1990.

———. "Intellectuals and Power: A Conversation between Michel Foucault and Gilles Deleuze." In *Language, Counter-Memory, and Practice*, edited by Donald F. Bouchard, translated by Donald F. Bouchard and Sherry Simon, 205–17. Ithaca, N.Y.: Cornell University Press, 1977.

del Río, Gimena, Alex Gil, Daniel O'Donnell, and Élika Ortega. "About." The Translation Toolkit. http://go-dh.github.io/translation-toolkit/about/.

Derrida, Jacques. *Dissemination*. Translated by Barbara Johnson. Chicago: University of Chicago Press, 1983.

———. *Of Hospitality*. Translated by Rachel Bowlby. Stanford, Calif.: Stanford University Press, 2000.

———. *The Politics of Friendship*. Translated by George Collins. New York: Verso, 2005.

Dieter, Michael and Geert Lovink. "Theses on Making in the Digital Age." In *Critical Making: Manifestos*, edited by Garnet Hertz. Hollywood, Calif.: Telharmonium, 2012. http://conceptlab.com/criticalmaking/PDFs/CriticalMaking2012Hertz-Manifestos-pp23to32-Csikszentmihalyi-SixteenReflectiveBits.pdf.

"The Digital Humanities Manifesto 2.0." *Humanities Blast* (blog). http://www.humanitiesblast.com/manifesto/Manifesto_V2.pdf.

DiSalvo, Carl. *Adversarial Design*. Cambridge, Mass.: MIT Press, 2015.

———. "Introduction to Adversarial Design." In *Critical Making: Manifestos*, edited by Garnet Hertz. Hollywood, Calif.: Telharmonium, 2012. http://conceptlab.com/criticalmaking/PDFs/CriticalMaking2012Hertz-Manifestos-pp21to22-DiSalvo-IntroducingAdversarialDesign.pdf.

"Doctoral Programs by the Numbers." *Chronicle of Higher Education*. https://www.chronicle.com/article/NRC-Rankings-Overview-/124753.

Drucker, Johanna. *Graphesis: Visual Forms of Knowledge Production*. Cambridge, Mass.: Harvard University Press, 2014.

Earhart, Amy. *Traces of the Old, Uses of the New: The Emergence of Digital Literary Studies*. Ann Arbor: University of Michigan Press, 2015.

Enders, Bill. "A Literacy of Building: Making in the Digital Humanities." In *Making Things and Drawing Boundaries: Experiments in the Digital Humanities*, edited by Jentery Sayers, 44–54. Minneapolis: University of Minnesota Press, 2017.

Eshun, Kodwo. "Further Considerations on Afrofuturusm." *CR: The New Centennial Review* 3, no. 2 (2003): 287–302.

Fanon, Frantz. *The Wretched of the Earth*. Translated by Richard Philcox. New York: Grove, 2004.

Federici, Silvia and George Caffentzis. "Commons Against and Beyond Capitalism." *Upping the Anti: A Journal of Theory and Action* no. 15 (2013): 83–91.

Ferguson, Kevin. L. "To Cite or to Steal? When a Scholarly Project Turns Up in a Gallery." Hyperallergic, June 30, 2016. https://hyperallergic.com/308436/to-cite-or-to-steal-when-a-scholarly-project-turns-up-in-a-gallery/.

Fiormonte, Domenico. "Toward a Cultural Critique of Digital Humanities." In *Debates in the Digital Humanities: 2016*, edited by Matthew K. Gold and Lauren F. Klein, 438–58. Minneapolis: University of Minnesota Press, 2016.

Fish, Stanley. "The Digital Humanities and the Transcending of Morality." *New York Times*, January 9, 2012. http://opinionator.blogs.nytimes.com/2012/01/09/the-digital-humanities-and-the-transcending-of-mortality/?_r=0.

Fontaine, Claire. "Matthew K. Gold Presents on Guerrilla Pedagogy @ Information 2.0 Lecture Series." *HASTAC* (blog), October 5, 2009. https://www.hastac.org/opportunities/matthew-k-gold-presents-guerrilla-pedagogy-information-20-lecture-series.

Foucault, Michel. *The Birth of Biopolitics: Lectures at the Collège de France, 1978–1979*. Edited by Michel Senellart, translated by Graham Burchell. New York: Picador, 2008.

———. "Intellectuals and Power: A Conversation between Michel Foucault and

Gilles Deleuze." In *Language, Counter-Memory, and Practice*, edited by Donald F. Bouchard, translated by Donald F. Bouchard and Sherry Simon, 205–17. Ithaca, N.Y.: Cornell University Press, 1977.

———. "Of Other Spaces: Utopias and Heterotopias." Translated by Jay Miskowiec. *Architecture / Mouvement / Continuité* (1967): 1–9.

———. "Truth and Power." In *Power/Knowledge: Selected Writings and Other Interviews 1972–1977*, edited by Colin Gordon, translated by Colin Gordon, Leo Marshall, John Mepham, and Kate Soper, 109–33. New York: Pantheon Books, 1980.

Gaboury, Jacob. "Critical Unmaking: Toward a Queer Computation." In *The Routledge Companion to Media Studies and Digital Humanities*, edited by Jentery Sayers. New York: Routledge, 2018. https://escholarship.org/uc/item /0cq870wh.

Galloway, Alexander R. "A Network Is a Network Is a Network: Reflections on the Computational and the Societies of Control." Interview by David M. Berry. *Theory, Culture, and Society* 0, no. 0 (2015): 1–22.

———. "Love of the Middle." In *Excommunication: Three Inquiries in Media and Mediation*, 25–76. Chicago: University of Chicago Press, 2014.

———. *Protocol: How Control Exists after Decentralization*. Cambridge, Mass.: MIT Press, 2004.

Galloway, Alexander R., and Eugene Thacker. *The Exploit: A Theory of Networks*. Minneapolis: University of Minnesota Press, 2007.

Genet, Jean. "Introduction to *Soledad Brother*." In *The Declared Enemy: Texts and Interviews*, edited by Albert Dichey, translated by Jeff Fort, 49–55. Stanford, Calif.: Stanford University Press, 2004.

———. "Violence & Brutality." In *The Declared Enemy: Texts and Interviews*, edited by Albert Dichey, translated by Jeff Fort, 199–206. Stanford, Calif.: Stanford University Press, 2004.

Gil, Alex. "#guerrilladh." *@elotroalex* (blog), July 27, 2015. http://www.elotroalex .com/guerrilladh/.

———. "Minimal Computing," *Minimal Computing* (blog), May 21, 2015. http:// go-dh.github.io/mincomp/thoughts/2015/05/21/user-vs-learner/.

Giorgis, Hannah. "Black Users on Vine: Celebrating Blackness 6 Seconds at a Time." *The Guardian*, May 17, 2015. https://www.theguardian.com/commentisfree /2015/may/17/black-users-on-vine-celebrating-blackness-6-seconds-at-a-time.

Gold, Matthew K. "The Digital Humanities Moment." In *Debates in the Digital Humanities: 2012*, edited by Matthew K. Gold, ix–xvi. Minneapolis: University of Minnesota Press, 2012.

———. "Whose Revolution? Towards a More Equitable Digital Humanities." *The Lapland Chronicles* (blog), January 10, 2012. http://mkgold.net/blog/2012/01 /10/whose-revolution-toward-a-more-equitable-digital-humanities/.

Greenspan, Brian. "The Scandal of Digital Humanities." *Hyperlab: Hyperbolic* (blog), May 4, 2016. https://carleton.ca/hyperlab/2018/the-scandal-of-digital -humanities/.

Grindon, Gavin. "Poetry Written in Gasoline: Black Mask and Up Against the Wall Motherfucker." *Art History* 38 (2015): 170–209.

Grosz, Elizabeth. "Menstruation Machine." In *Design and Violence*, edited by

Paola Antonelli and Jamer Hunt, 52–54. New York: Museum of Modern Art, 2017.

Grusin, Richard. Interview by Melissa Dinsman. "The Digital in the Humanities: An Interview with Richard Grusin." *Los Angeles Review of Books*, August 18, 2016. https://lareviewofbooks.org/article/digital-humanities-interview-richard-grusin/.

Guerrilla Girls. *Confessions of the Guerrilla Girls*. New York: HarperPerennial, 1995.

———. *The Guerrilla Girls' Bedside Companion to the History of Western Art.* New York: Penguin Books, 1998.

Gumbs, Alexis Pauline. "Seeking the Roots: An Immersive and Interactive Archive of Black Feminist Practice." *Feminist Collectives* 32, no. 1 (2012): 17–20.

Halberstam, Jack. "The Wild Beyond: With and for the Undercommons." In *The Undercommons: Fugitive Planning & Black Study*, 9–10. Brooklyn, N.Y.: Minor Compositions, 2013.

Han, Byung-Chul. *In the Swarm: Digital Prospects*. Translated by Erik Butler. Boston: MIT Press, 2017.

Haraway, Donna. *Simians, Cyborgs, and Women: The Reinvention of Nature.* New York: Routledge, 1990.

Hardt, Michael. "The Militancy of Theory." *South Atlantic Quarterly* 110, no. 1 (2011): 19–35.

———. "Reclaim the Common in Communism." *The Guardian*, February 3, 2011. https://www.theguardian.com/commentisfree/2011/feb/03/communism-capitalism-socialism-property.

Hardt, Michael, and Antonio Negri. *Commonwealth*. Cambridge, Mass.: Belknap of Harvard University Press, 2011.

———. *Empire*. Cambridge, Mass.: Harvard University Press, 2000.

———. *Multitude: War and Democracy in the Age of Empire*. New York: Penguin, 2005.

Harney, Stefano. "Hapitcality in the Undercommons." In *The Routledge Companion to Art and Politics*, edited by Randy Martin, 173–79. New York: Routledge, 2015.

Harney, Stefano, and Fred Moten. *The Undercommons: Fugitive Planning & Black Study*. Brooklyn, N.Y.: Minor Compositions, 2013.

Haver, William. "The Ontological Priority of Violence: On Several Really Smart Things about Violence in Jean Genet's Work." Polylog. http://www.polylog.org/index-en.htm

———. "Really Bad Infinities: Queer's Honour and the Pornographic Life." *Parallax* 5, no. 4 (1999): 9–21.

Hertz, Garnet, and Jussi Parikka. "Zombie Media: Circuit Bending Media Archaeology into an Art Method." *Leonardo* 45, no. 5 (2012): 424–30.

Hester, Helen. *Xenofeminism*. Medford, Eng.: Polity, 2018.

hooks, bell. "Postmodern Blackness." *Postmodern Culture* 1, no. 10 (1990).

———. *Talking Back: Thinking Feminist, Thinking Black*. New York: Routledge, 2014.

Hui, Yuk. "Archivist Manifesto." Mute Magazine, May 22, 2013. http://www.metamute.org/editorial/lab/archivist-manifesto.

Invisible Committee. *Now*. Translated by Robert Hurley. Los Angeles: Semiotext(e), 2017.

Jackson, Lauren M. "The Blackness of Meme Movement." Model View Culture: A Magazine about Technology, Culture and Diversity, March 28, 2016. https://modelviewculture.com/pieces/the-blackness-of-meme-movement.

———. "We Need to Talk about Digital Blackface in Reaction GIFs." *Teen Vogue*, August 3, 2017. www.teenvogue.com/story/digital-blackface-reaction-gifs.

Johnson, Jessica M. "The Digital in the Humanities: An Interview with Jessica Marie Johnson." Interview by Melissa Dinsman. *Los Angeles Review of Books*, July 23, 2016. https://lareviewofbooks.org/article/digital-humanities-interview-jessica-marie-johnson/.

———. "Doing and Being Intellectual History: #Formation as Curated by Black Women." *Black Perspective* (blog), February 12, 2016. https://www.aaihs.org/doing-and-being-intellectual/.

Johnson, Jessica Marie, and Mark Anthony Neal. "Introduction: Wild Seed in the Machine." *Black Scholar* 47, no. 3 (2017): 1–2.

Kelley, Robin D. G., and Fred Moten. "Fred Moten and Robin D.G. Kelley in Conversation: 'Do Black Lives Matter?'" *E-flux Conversations* (blog), January 20, 2015. https://conversations.e-flux.com/t/fred-moten-and-robin-d-g-kelley-in-conversation-do-black-lives-matter-video/945.

Kim, Dorothy, and Eunsong Kim. "The #TwitterEthics Manifesto: You Don't Need to Speak for Us—We Are Talking." Model View Culture: A Magazine about Technology, Culture and Diversity, April 7, 2014. https://modelviewculture.com/pieces/the-twitterethics-manifesto.

Kim, Dorothy, and Jesse Stommel. "Introduction: Disrupting the Digital Humanities." In *Disrupting the Digital Humanities*, edited by Dorothy Kim and Jesse Stommel. http://www.disruptingdh.com/.

Kirschenbaum, Matthew. "Digital Humanities As/Is a Tactical Term." In *Debates in the Digital Humanities: 2012*, edited by Matthew K. Gold, 415–28. Minneapolis: University of Minnesota Press, 2012.

Knight, Kim Brillante. "Making Space: Feminist DH and a Room of One's Own." https://jentery.github.io/.

Koh, Adeline. "More Hack, Less Yack? Modularity, Theory and Habitus in the Digital Humanities." *Adeline Koh* (blog), May 21, 2012. https://web.archive.org/web/20120721195443/http://www.adelinekoh.org/blog/2012/05/21/more-hack-less-yack-modularity-theory-and-habitus-in-the-digital-humanities/.

———. "Who Gets to Say #ILookLikeAProfessor? And Who Would Want To?" The Synapse, August 9, 2015. https://medium.com/synapse/who-gets-to-say-ilooklikeaprofessor-and-who-would-want-to-568fbe698198#.oschk3s1a.

La Hora de los Hornos / Hour of Furnaces. Directed by Fernando Solanas and Octavio Getino. Argentina: Grupo Cine Liberacion, 1968.

Lazzarato, Maurizio. *The Making of the Indebted Man*. Translated by Joshua David Jordan. Los Angeles: Semiotext(e), 2012.

Liu, Alan. "Drafts for *Against the Cultural Singularity* (book in progress)." *Alan Liu* (blog), May 2, 2016. http://liu.english.ucsb.edu/drafts-for-against-the-cultural-singularity/.

———. "Where Is Cultural Criticism in the Digital Humanities?" In *Debates in the Digital Humanities: 2012*, edited by Matthew K. Gold, 490–510. Minneapolis: University of Minnesota Press, 2012.

Losh, Elizabeth. "What Can the Digital Humanities Learn from Feminist Game Studies?" *Digital Humanities Quarterly* 9, no. 2 (2015). http://www.digitalhumanities.org/dhq/vol/9/2/000200/000200.html.

Losh, Elizabeth, Jacqueline Wernimont, Laura Wexler, and Hong-An Wu. "Putting the Human Back into the Digital Humanities: Feminism, Generosity, and Mess." In *Debates in the Digital Humanities: 2016*, edited by Matthew K. Gold and Lauren F. Klein, 92–103. Minneapolis: University of Minnesota Press, 2016.

Lothian, Alexis. "Marked Bodies, Transformative Scholarship, and the Question of Theory in Digital Humanities." *Journal of Digital Humanities* 1, no. 1 (2011).

Lothian, Alexis, and Amanda Phillips. "Can Digital Humanities Mean Transformative Critique?" *e-Media Studies* 3, no. 1 (2013).

Lovink, Geert. *Dark Fiber: Tracking Critical Internet Culture*. Cambridge, Mass.: MIT Press, 2003.

Lugones, Maria. "The Coloniality of Gender." https://globalstudies.trinity.duke.edu/wp-content/themes/cgsh/materials/WKO/v2d2_Lugones.pdf.

———. "Indigenous Movements and Decolonial Feminism." Department of Women's, Gender, and Sexuality Studies at Ohio State University. https://wgss.osu.edu/sites/wgss.osu.edu/files/LugonesSeminarReadings.pdf, 1–20.

———. "Toward a Decolonial Feminism." *Hypatia* 25, no. 4 (2010): 742–59.

Maldonado-Torres, Nelson. "On the Coloniality of Being: Contributions to the Development of a Concept." *Cultural Studies* 21, no. 2 (2007): 240–70.

Mao Tse-tung. *On Guerrilla Warfare*. Translated by Samuel B. Griffith. Thousand Oaks, Calif.: BN Publishing, 2007.

Marighella, Carlos. *Mini-Manual of the Urban Guerrilla*. Montreal: Abraham Guillen, 2002.

Marinetti, Fillippo Tommaso. "The Founding and Manifesto of Futurism." *Niuean Pop Cultural Archive* (blog). https://www.unknown.nu/futurism/manifesto.html.

Marx, Karl. *Capital: A Critique of Political Economy, Vol. 1*. Translated by Ben Fowkes. London: Penguin in association with New Left Review, 1990.

———. *Grundrisse: Foundations of the Critique of Political Economy*. Translated by Martin Nicolaus. New York: Penguin Books in association with New Left Review, 1993.

Marx, Karl, and Friedrich Engels. *The Communist Manifesto*. Edited by David McLellan. Oxford: Oxford University Press, 1998.

Massumi, Brian. *Parables for the Virtual: Movement, Affect, Sensation*. Durham, N.C.: Duke University Press, 2002.

McGlotten, Shaka. "Black Data." In *Traversing Technologies*, edited by Patrick Keilty and Leslie Regan Shade. http://sfonline.barnard.edu/traversing-technologies/shaka-mcglotten-black-data/.

McPherson, Tara. "Why Are the Digital Humanities So White? or Thinking the Histories of Race and Computation." In *Debates in the Digital Humanities: 2012*, edited by Matthew K. Gold, 139–60. Minneapolis: University of Minnesota Press. 2012.

Medina, José. "Toward a Foucaultian Epistemology of Resistance: Counter-

Memory, Epistemic Friction, and Guerrilla Pluralism." *Foucault Studies* no. 12 (2011): 9–35.

Millner-Larsen, Nadja. "Black Mask: Revolution as Being." In *If I Can't Dance to It, It's Not My Revolution*, curated by Natalie Musteata. http://exhibits .haverford.edu/ificantdancetoit/essays/black-mask-revolution-as-being/#_ftn14.

———. "The Subject of Black: Abstraction and the Politics of Race in the Expanded Cinema Environment." *Grey Room* no. 67 (2017): 64–99.

Mohanty, Chandra Talpade. *Feminism without Borders: Decolonizing Theory, Practicing Solidarity*. Durham, N.C.: Duke University Press, 2003.

Monroe, Kristen, Saba Ozyurt, Ted Wrigley, and Amy Alexander. "Gender Equality in Academia: Bad News from the Trenches, and Some Possible Solutions." *Perspectives on Politics* 6, no. 2 (2008): 215–33.

Moten, Fred. "Blackness and Nothingness (Mysticism in the Flesh)." *South Atlantic Quarterly* 112, no. 4 (2013): 737–80.

———. *The Universal Machine: Consent Not to Be a Single Being*. Durham, N.C.: Duke University Press, 2018.

Mouffe, Chantal. *Agonistics: Thinking the World Politically*. New York: Verso, 2013.

Nagbot, SSL. "Feminist Hacking/Making: Exploring New Gender Horizons of Possibility." *Journal of Peer Production* no. 8 (2016). http://peerproduction.net /issues/issue-8-feminism-and-unhacking/.

Nagle, Angela. *Kill All Normies: Online Culture Wars from 4Chan and Tumblr to Trump and the Alt-Right*. Winchester, U.K.: Zero Books, 2017.

Neumann, Osha. *Up Against the Wall Motherf**ker: A Memoir of the '60s, with Notes for Next Time*. New York: Seven Stories, 2008.

Newfield, Christopher. *Unmaking the Public University: The Forty-Year Assault on the Middle Class*. Cambridge, Mass.: Harvard University Press, 2011.

Newton, Huey P. *Revolutionary Suicide*. New York: Penguin, 2009.

Nielsen, Cynthia N. "Foucault on Christian Technologies of the Self: Toward the Non-Identity of Christian Subjectivity." *Per Caritatem* (blog), November 21, 2010. http://percaritatem.com/2010/11/21/foucault-on-christian-technologies -of-the-self-toward-the-non-identity-of-christianity-subjectivity/.

Nowviskie, Bethany. "#alt-ac: Alternate Academic Careers for Humanities Scholars." *Bethany Nowviskie* (blog), January 2, 2010. http://nowviskie.org/2010 /alt-ac/.

———. "On Capacity and Care." *nowviskie.org* (blog), October 4, 2015. http:// nowviskie.org/2015/on-capacity-and-care/.

———. "On the Origin of 'Hack' and 'Yack.'" In *Debates in the Digital Humanities: 2016*, edited by Matthew K. Gold and Lauren F. Klein, 66–70. Minneapolis: University of Minnesota Press, 2016.

Nyong'o, Tavia, and Kyla Wazana Tompkins. "Eleven Theses on Civility." *Social Text Online*. https://socialtextjournal.org/eleven-theses-on-civility/.

Orwell, George. *Animal Farm*. New York: Signet, 1946.

Pannapacker, William. "Pannapacker at MLA: Digital Humanities Triumphant?" *Brainstorm: The Chronicle of Higher Education* (blog), January 8, 2011. https:// www.chronicle.com/blogs/brainstorm/pannapacker-at-mla-digital-humanities -triumphant/30915.

Parikka, Jussi. *What Is Media Archaeology?* Malden, Mass.: Polity, 2012.

Posner, Miriam. "What's Next: The Radical, Unrealized Potential of Digital Humanities." In *Debates in the Digital Humanities: 2016*, edited by Matthew K. Gold and Lauren F. Klein, 32–41. Minneapolis: University of Minnesota Press, 2016.

Presner, Todd. "Critical Theory and the Mangle of Digital Humanities." In *Between Humanities and the Digital*, edited by Patrik Svensson and David Theo Goldberg, 55–67. Cambridge, Mass.: MIT Press, 2015.

Pritchard, Sara B., Adeline Koh, and Michelle Moravec. "We Look like Professors, Too." *Inside Higher Ed*, August 10, 2015. https://www.insidehighered.com/views/2015/08/10/essay-explains-new-hashtag-campaign-draw-attention-diversity-professors-and-their.

Quijano, Anibal. "Coloniality of Power, Eurocentrism, and Latin America." *Nepantla: Views from the South* 1, no. 3 (2000): 533–80.

Raley, Rita. "Digital Humanities for the Next Five Minutes." *Differences: A Journal of Feminist Cultural Studies* 1, no. 25 (2014): 26–45.

———. *Tactical Media*. Minneapolis: University of Minnesota Press, 2009.

Ratto, Matt, and Stephen Hockema. "FLWR PWR—Tending the Walled Garden." CriticalMaking.com. http://criticalmaking.com/wp-content/uploads/2009/10/2448_alledgarden_ch06_ratto_hockema.pdf.

Read, Jason. *The Micro-Politics of Capital: Marx and the Prehistory of the Present*. New York: State University of New York Press, 2003.

———. "The Production of Subjectivity: From Transindividuality to the Commons." *New Formations* no. 70 (2010): 113–31.

———. "Transindividuality, Equaliberty, Short-Circuit: Notes on the Recent Thought of Etienne Balibar." *Unemployed Negativity* (blog), August 11, 2010. http://www.unemployednegativity.com/2010/08/transindividuality-equaliberty-short.html.

Risam, Roopika. "As Che says. . . . 'At the risk of sounding ridiculous, the true revolutionary is guided by a feeling of great love.' #guerrilladh #keydh." June 23, 2016, 10:19 a.m. https://twitter.com/roopikarisam/status/745984535544889344.

———. "Beyond the Margins: Intersectionality and the Digital Humanities." *Digital Humanities Quarterly* 9, no. 2 (2015).

———. "Navigating the Global Digital Humanities: Insights from Black Feminism." In *Debates in the Digital Humanities: 2016*, edited by Matthew K. Gold and Lauren F. Klein, 359–67. Minneapolis: University of Minnesota Press, 2016.

Rowberry, Simon. "A Guerrilla Digital Humanities." *Simon Rowberry* (blog), August 14, 2014. https://www.sprowberry.com/a-guerrilla-digital-humanities/.

Russworm, TreaAndrea M. "Dystopian Blackness and the Limits of Racial Empathy in *The Walking Dead* and *The Last of Us*." In *Gaming Representation*, edited by Jennifer Malkowski and TreaAndrea M. Russworm, 109–28. Bloomington: Indiana University Press, 2017.

Sandoval, Chela. *Methodology of the Oppressed*. Minneapolis: University of Minnesota Press, 2000.

Sayers, Jentery. "I Don't Know All the Circuitry." In *Making Things and Drawing Boundaries: Experiments in the Digital Humanities*, edited by Jentery Sayers, 1–17. Minneapolis: University of Minnesota Press, 2017.

———. "Minimal Definitions." *Minimal Computing* (blog), October 2, 2016. http://go-dh.github.io/mincomp/.

Schmitt, Carl. *The Concept of the Political*. Translated by George Schwab. Chicago: University of Chicago Press, 2007.

———. *The Nomos of the Earth: In the International Law of the Jus Publicum Europaeum*. Translated by G. L. Ulmen. New York: Telos, 2006.

———. *The Theory of the Partisan*. Translated by G. L. Ulmen. New York: Telos, 2007.

Schnapp, Jeffrey T., and Matthew Battles. *The Library beyond the Book*. Cambridge, Mass.: Harvard University Press, 2014.

Shaviro, Steven. "The Bitter Necessity of Debt." *Steven Shaviro* (blog), May 1, 2010. http://www.shaviro.com/Othertexts/Debt.pdf.

———. *No Speed Limit: Three Essays on Accelerationism*. Minneapolis: University of Minnesota Press, 2015.

Shaw, Adrienne. "The Trouble with Communities." In *Queer Game Studies*, edited by Bonnie Ruberg and Adrienne Shaw, 153–62. Minneapolis: University of Minnesota Press, 2017.

Smithies, James. "Digital Humanities, Postfoundationalism, and Postindustrial Culture." *Digital Humanities Quarterly* 8, no. 1 (2014). http://www.digitalhumanities.org/dhq/vol/8/1/000172/000172.html.

Solanas, Fernando, and Octavio Getino. "Towards a Third Cinema." In *Documentary Is Never Neutral | Towards a Third Cinema by Fernando Solanas and Octavio Getino*. http://www.marginalutility.org/wp-content/uploads/2017/03/Towards-a-Third-Cinema-by-Fernando-Solanas-and-Octavio-Getino.pdf.

Sontag, Susan. *On Photography*. New York: Picador USA, 2001.

Spencer, Robyn C. *The Revolution Has Come: Black Power, Gender, and the Black Panther Party in Oakland*. Durham, N.C.: Duke University Press, 2016.

Stevenson, Guy. "Facebook Live Lecture." February 19, 2018. https://www.facebook.com/GoldsmithsUoL/videos/10155351834417849/?comment_id=10155351923167849&comment_tracking=%7B%22tn%22%3A%22R%22%7D.

Steyrel, Hito. "In Defense of the Poor Image." *e-flux* (blog), November 10, 2009. http://www.e-flux.com/journal/in-defense-of-the-poor-image/.

———. "Is a Museum a Factory?" *e-flux* (blog), June 7, 2009. http://www.e-flux.com/journal/07/61390/is-a-museum-a-factory/.

Stommel, Jesse. "Critical Digital Pedagogy: A Definition." *Hybrid Pedagogy* (blog), August 8, 2016. http://hybridpedagogy.org/critical-digital-pedagogy-definition/.

Tambellini, Aldo. "Biography." AldoTambellini.com. http://www.aldotambellini.com/bio4.html.

———. "Black." *artscanada* no. 113 (1967): 1–19.

Tiqqun. *To Our Friends*. Translated by Robert Hurley. Los Angeles: Semiotext(e), 2015.

#TransformDH. "About #TransformDH." http://transformdh.org/about-transformdh/.

Tzara, Tristan. "Dada Manifesto 1918." In *Modernism: An Anthology*, edited by Lawrence S. Rainey, 479–84. Malden, Mass.: Blackwell, 2005.

Ulgado, Rachel Rose, and Sarah Fox. "Critical Design in Feminist Hacker Spaces."

OpenLab. https://openlab.ncl.ac.uk/socially-engaged-art/files/2014/03/Critical
-Design-in-Feminist-Hackerspaces.pdf.

Ulmen, G. L. "Translator's Introduction." In *The Theory of the Partisan*, by Carl
Schmitt, translated by G. L. Ulmen. New York: Telos, 2007.

Virilio, Paul. *Art and Fear*. New York: Bloomsbury Academic, 2006.

———. *War and Cinema: The Logistics of Perception*. London: Verso, 1989.

Virno, Paolo. "On Armed Struggle." In *Autonomia: Post-Political Politics*, edited
by Sylvere Lotringer and Christian Marazzi, 238–39. Los Angeles: Semiotext(e),
2007.

Wark, McKenzie. "A Hacker Manifesto [version 4.0]." subsol. http://subsol.c3.hu
/subsol_2/contributors0/warktext.html.

———. "The RetroDada Manifesto." *Public Seminar* (blog), February 8, 2016.
http://www.publicseminar.org/2016/02/retrodada-manifesto/.

———. "To only see friends versus enemies is to misunderstand the whole art of
politics." June 22, 2015, 11:25 p.m. https://twitter.com/mckenziewark/status
/613186203823775744.

Weeks, Kathi. *The Problem with Work: Feminism, Marxism, Antiwork Politics,
and Postwork Imaginaries*. Durham, N.C.: Duke University Press, 2011.

Weheliye, Alexander G. *Habeas Viscus: Racializing Assemblages, Biopolitics, and
Black Feminist Theories of the Human*. Durham, N.C.: Duke University Press,
2014.

Weigel, Moira. "Silicon Valley's Sixty-Year Love Affair with the Word 'Tool.'" *The
New Yorker*, April 12, 2018. http://www.newyorker.com/tech/elements/silicon
-valleys-sixty-year-love-affair-with-the-word-tool.

Wernimont, Jacqueline. "Remediation, Activation, and Entanglement in Performative (Digital) Archives." Archive Journal, October 2017. http://
www.archivejournal.net/notes/remediation-activation-entanglement-in
-performative-digital-archives/.

———. "Remediation, Activation, and Entanglement in Performative (Digital)
Archives—MLA2017." *Jacqueline Wernimont* (blog), January 7, 2017. https://
jwernimont.com/remediation-activation-and-entanglement-in-performative
-digital-archives-mla2017/.

———. "Whence Feminism? Assessing Feminist Interventions in Digital Literary Archives." *Digital Humanities Quarterly* 7, no. 1 (2007). http://www
.digitalhumanities.org/dhq/vol/7/1/000156/000156.html.

Wernimont, Jacqueline, and Julia Flanders. "Feminism in the Age of Digital
Archives: The Women Writers Project." *Tulsa Studies in Women's Literature*
29, no. 2 (fall 2010): 425–35.

Whitson, Roger. "Does DH Really Need to Be Transformed? My Reflections on
#mla12." *Roger Whitson* (blog), January 8, 2012. http://www.rogerwhitson
.net/?p=1358.

———. "Genealogies of the Digital Humanities: The Avant-Garde and the University of Florida." *RogerWhitson* (blog), March 5, 2016. http://www.rogerwhitson
.net/?p=3439.

———. "Mea Culpa for #transformdh, and a Selection from Steampunk and
19thC Digital Humanities." *Roger Whitson* (blog), January 9, 2016. http://www
.rogerwhitson.net/?p=3365.

———. "Steampunk Anachronisms: Queer Histories of the Digital Humanities."

Rhizomes: Cultural Studies in Emerging Knowledge, no. 28 (2015). http://
rhizomes.net/issue28/whitson/.

Williams, Jeffrey J. "The Need for Critical University Studies." In *A New Deal
for the Humanities: Liberal Arts and the Future of Public Higher Education*,
edited by Gordon Hunter and Feisal G. Mohamed, 145–49. New Brunswick,
N.J.: Rutgers University Press, 2015.

Willis, Holly. "Writing Images and the Cinematic Humanities." *Visible Language*
49, no. 3 (2015). http://visiblelanguagejournal.com/issue/172.

Wright, Michelle M. *Physics of Blackness: Beyond the Middle Passage Epistemology*. Minneapolis: University of Minnesota Press, 2015.

INDEX

Adorno, Theodor W., 19, 87
adversarial design, 24, 67
affinity, 14, 27, 82, 88, 90, 110, 111; affinity groups, 17, 109; affinity-making, 15, 17, 61, 76, 114, 126, 132
African Americans. *See* blackness; critical race theory; race issues; violence: racial
Afrofuturism, 28, 126
agonistics, 28, 48, 50, 54–55, 62, 67, 85, 146
Ahmed, Ahmed, 114–15
Aitken, Ian, 167n39
Alkalimat, Abdul, et al., 117
alt-right politics, 26–27, 73–74, 168n56
Anderson, Steve F., 68
Antifa, 25
Antonelli, Paola, 147
Anzaldúa, Gloria, 76
Apollinaire, Guillaume, 68
Apter, Emily, 77
archives, 22, 23–24, 27, 65, 80, 88, 93, 111, 119, 123, 126–37; black, 96–97, 126–27; counter-memory and, 126–29, 130; elite, 96; feminist digital, 119; horizontal (vs. vertical), 28, 127–29, 130, 132; translation and, 119
Althusser, Louis, 12, 13
avant-garde aesthetics, 22, 26–27, 64, 68–75, 98, 110–11; camera and, 69–72, 78–79; reactionary co-optation of, 72–75, 168n56; war technology and, 70, 71–72

Bailey, Moya, 17, 53, 128–29, 152
Bailibar, Etienne, 19
Balsamo, Anne, 55–57, 58
Barnett, Fiona, 56, 99, 123
Battles, Matthew, 95, 96
Baudelaire, Charles, 74

Bay, Mia, 96
Benjamin, Walter, 70–71, 78, 111, 168n41
Berry, David M., 49, 50, 57, 160n60
Bey, Hakim, 18
Bianco, Jamie "Skye," 11
biopolitics, 12, 26, 41–42, 44, 45, 47, 55, 138
"Black Code Studies," 150
blackness (and black life), 27, 32, 33, 110, 120–26; Davis and, 133–34; Moten on, 27, 121, 123–26, 136, 175n22; online black communities, 121; Tambellini and, 102–3, 105
Black Mask, 27, 87–93, 95, 97–98, 99–101, 104–12, 126, 131, 170n13; decolonial Dada and, 27, 88–89, 101, 108–13, 170n2
Black Panther Party (BPP), 27, 34, 89, 120, 124, 129–32, 139, 140; films by, 131
BLACK PLUS X (film), 103, 173n55
Black Power movement, 102
black radical tradition, 45, 136–37
Blake, William, 74
body: failure of the, 85; figuration of the, 83–84; production and the, 55
Bogost, Ian, 64–65
Bolívar, Simón, 78
Braidotti, Rosi, 49–50, 57
Bray, Mark, 25
Breton, André, 69, 70
Brooks, Romaine, 92
bugs and viruses, 147
Butler, Judith, 19–20, 86

Caffentzis, George, 88
cameras: avant-garde uses of, 69–72; gun analogy with, 71–72, 77–78, 79, 82, 131